J.K. LASSER PRO ™

ADVISING MATURE CLIENTS

The New Science of Wealth Span Planning

Neal E. Cutler, PhD

John Wiley & Sons, Inc.

To my mother,
Mary B. Smiley,
— with respect and love

Published by John Wiley & Sons, Inc., New York.

Published simultaneously in Canada.

Library of Congress Cataloging-in-Publication Data:

Cutler, Neal E.
J.K. Lasser pro advising mature clients : the new science of wealth span planning / by Neal E. Cutler
p. cm. — (The J.K. Lasser pro series)
ISBN 0-471-41470-0 (alk. paper)
1. Aged—United States—Finance, Personal. 2. Retirement income—United States Planning. 3. Finance, Personal. I. Title: JK Lasser pro advising mature clients. II. Title. III. Series.
HG179 .C88 2002
332.024'0565—dc21 2001006064

Printed in the United States of America

10 9 8 7 6 5 4 3 2 1

Contents

Internet Resources

Acknowledgments

My work in financial gerontology reflects three decades of academic and practitioner relationships in the social sciences, in gerontology, and in financial services.

From my colleagues and students in political science and gerontology at the University of Southern California I developed a critical appreciation for multidisciplinary teaching and research. Of special value is the unique influence of Dr. James E. Birren, founding director of the Andrus Gerontology Center and my mentor and friend during the turbulent early years of financial gerontology.

My personal and intellectual debt to Dr. Davis W. Gregg and Joseph E. Boettner is substantial. Dave's ideas about the Wealth Span and Joe's enthusiastic support were the seedlings from which this book has grown. I hope it effectively communicates my affection and my respect for these two gentlemen.

Joe wanted his long-planned chair at Widener University to serve as a memorial to Dave Gregg and to their joint vision of an academic bridge between the worlds of financial services and gerontology. I acknowledge my deep gratitude to Dr. Robert J. Bruce, now president-emeritus of Widener, and to Dr. Stephen C. Wilhite, dean of the School of Human Service Professions, for their continuing support of this innovative enterprise.

Throughout the book are "data bits" from *American Perceptions of Aging in the 21st Century,* a giant-sized public attitude survey conducted by The National Council on the Aging. My thanks to Dr. James P. Firman, NCOA president and CEO, Dr. Nancy A. Whitelaw, vice president for research and demonstration, and Lynn Beattie, deputy director for R&D, for the opportunity to direct this important piece of financial and social research.

Because "financial gerontology" is not yet a household phrase, special thanks are due to my editors at John Wiley for encouraging this project: to

Debra Englander, whose enthusiasm nurtured its conceptualization and development, and to David Pugh, whose insights and patience brought it to completion.

Necessary and Sufficient Conditions. Contributions from colleagues are critical contributions—they are necessary but they're not sufficient. And so I turn to family. To my boys, Kari and Jori, now adults, and to Elizabeth, moving there all too rapidly—thanks for giving me so many reasons to see the value of good works and investment in the future.

Donna Crane, my wife, provides unending intellectual encouragement. Our enduring and endearing etymological debates, always accompanied by friendship and love, made this project doable and completable.

This book is dedicated to my mother, Mary Smiley. Her direct and indirect influences on the content and quality of this work are throughout. Due to the Depression she became a skillful professional secretary rather than a college student, and so not only did I learn to type fast almost before I could write, but she instilled in me a love for words, spelling, grammar, and nuance. Watching her cope as a young widow taught me about individual financial survival. She is a success story of financial literacy, will, and take-charge financial planning.

My research grew from our debates about her retirement, and later benefited from our discussions of health and long-term care. She typed my undergraduate political science thesis (on purple ditto masters!) and last month proofread some of these chapters (and found errors that MS-Word didn't). And so it is with respect and much love that I dedicate this book to her.

Neal Evan Cutler
Davis W. Gregg/Joseph E. Boettner Chair
in Financial Gerontology
Widener University
January 2002

CHAPTER 1

Advising the Mature Client: From Health Span to Wealth Span

Successful Aging

In May 1987, *Science* magazine published a landmark essay on the scientific study of aging titled "Human Aging: Usual and Successful." It argued that aging is not necessarily a process of decline set in motion by some unknowable combination of heredity and environment whose outcome is fixed by middle age. This negative view of usual aging, sometimes called *normal aging,* is neither normal nor inevitable, wrote Dr. John Rowe, MD, President of Mount Medical School (now President and CEO of Aetna, Inc.), and Dr. Robert Kahn, PhD, Professor of Psychology and Public Health at the University of Michigan. From a *Health Span* perspective, they argued, proactive changes (interventions) can improve older-age health even when the new or modified behaviors begin in midlife or old age.

The Health Span ideas became the framework for a decade-long series of biomedical and psychosocial studies of aging and middle aging funded by the MacArthur Foundation. The research included clinical, laboratory, and demographic studies—including the Swedish Twins Study to examine "nature versus nurture" as it applies to aging.

Across all this research, one unifying principle was demonstrated repeatedly: While what happens in earlier stages of the Health Span certainly affects what comes later, interventions can have a positive impact on health even when they come later in life. Five years after stopping cigarette smoking, your chances of a heart attack are reduced to just about the same odds as a nonsmoker.

The Wealth Span Model: Health Span and Personal Finance

Two aspects of Health Span—developmental stages and the efficacy of later-life interventions—caught the eye of Dr. Davis W. Gregg, then President-Emeritus of The American College, home of the Chartered Life Underwriter (CLU) life insurance designation. Texas born and Wharton educated, Dr. Gregg had been with the College since 1949, president from 1954 to 1982. A national leader in the education of financial planners for over three decades, including development of the Chartered Financial Consultant (ChFC) designation, he saw the parallels between financial planning and Rowe and Kahn's Health Span. Thus, the Wealth Span conceptualizes the accumulation and expenditure of wealth as stages in a lifelong developmental process but, of special importance and relevance to *older age,* financial interventions made even later in life will have a positive impact on later-life financial well-being.

Over the next few years, Dave Gregg and this writer (joining him in Bryn Mawr in 1989) developed the gerontological and financial elements of the model (see Chapter 13). Simply stated, the model says that the human Wealth Span can be conceptually divided into two stages: the Accumulation Stage and the Expenditure Stage. The goal is to accumulate enough wealth in the earlier stage to have sufficient financial well-being in the later stage—in *old age*.

Like any analytic model (as discussed in Chapters 5 and 6), the primary purpose of the Wealth Span model is not to scientifically or accurately describe the details of aging and money, but to simplify and therefore to more clearly reveal the developmental dynamics of wealth accumulation and expenditures.

The Wealth Span Model as a Financial Advisory Tool

As developed in *Advising Mature Clients,* the Wealth Span model adds to the tool kit of financial advisors in three basic ways.

1. The model focuses on the components of the wealth accumulation and expenditure processes *as they relate to aging*—which is becoming increasingly important for financial professionals these days because the very meaning of *aging, middle age,* and *old age* are changing.

2. While financial advisors have substantial education and experience with wealth creation and preservation, the Wealth Span model emphasizes that in advising mature clients, a substantial part of the "security" in *financial security* concerns the financing of health care and long-term care.

3. As a planning tool, the model can be used to illustrate to mature clients how historical Wealth Span changes over the past 70 years have directly affected both the responsibilities and the opportunities for financial planning over the life span. Conversations with your client about his or her own aging or the financial implications of elderly parents are central aspects of the changing dynamics of accumulation, expenditures and, ultimately, financial security.

Two Fundamental Historical Changes

Two basic changes in the Wealth Span have taken place over the past several decades: balance and complexity. The model can be used to show clients directly how these two sets of changes affect them personally. Chapter 5 discusses changes in *balance,* the number of years in the Accumulation Stage compared to the number of years in the Expenditure Stage. We talk about "back then" compared to "nowadays" because it is the broad historical *trend* that is important, not any specific date or year.

Back then, the Accumulation Stage started earlier. Many people started to work in their teens, and people accumulated until they retired, often in their sixties. The traditional Social Security full-benefits age of 65 is typically used to mark the beginning of the Expenditure Stage, which was comparatively shorter back then than it is now.

The relative balance in the number of years in the two stages has shifted. Nowadays, the Accumulation Stage is shorter: It starts later (college, graduate and professional school) and ends earlier due to early retirement. But the Expenditure Stage is longer than it used to be due to earlier retirement and greater longevity. In 1940, there was a 7% probability that a 65 year old would live to age 90 or older; by 2000, this had tripled to a 26% chance (Chapter 2).

The bottom line of these historical changes in balance between the two stages is that we now have fewer years to accumulate the resources that must last for a longer period of time.

The story gets murkier. Chapter 6 describes the second historical change: The Wealth Span has gotten a lot more complex. The stereotypical "Ozzie and Harriet family"—he works, she cooks and manages the home, and he retires at 65 with a guaranteed monthly defined benefit pension—is not around very much nowadays. Chapter 6 considers two general sets of complexities: financial and family.

New Financial Complexities

Nowadays, saving and investing are much more complex than before. Mutual funds and online stock brokers make investing more available but also more complex than ever before. The biggest new complexity, however, is the transformation of the American pension system from defined benefit to defined contribution pensions. In essence, this change is seen in the answer to the simple question: Who is responsible for the future value of the pension that I'm now accumulating? Back then, the predominant answer was: *They are*. Nowadays, the answer increasingly is: *I am*.

Even the defining event of the move from the Accumulation Stage to the Expenditure Stage—retirement—is no longer an event but can be a complex, multiyear process. The Wealth Span model uses the terms *accumulation* and *expenditure* because the meaning of and the distinction between *work* and *retirement* have changed substantially over the years. A recent (2000) national survey conducted by the National Council on the Aging found that only 54% of people aged 65 to 75 were completely retired, 25% said they are both retired *and* working full-time or part-time, and another 21% said they are not retired.

New Family Complexities

Complexities of a financial nature include the fact that nowadays both spouses are likely to be working. Chapter 6 refers to these families as *DIPPIES*—Double Income, Plural Pensions. They are earning two incomes and simultaneously earning plural pensions (i.e., two Social Securities, two employer pensions, and maybe two supplementary Individual Retirement Accounts [IRAs]). It is very important to recognize that this does not mean that DIPPIES are rich. They might be, but the essence of their situation is the *complexity of their wealth profile,* not the size of their accounts.

A second new family complexity is the complexity of elderly parents. Middle-agers nowadays are much more likely to have elderly parents. As recently as 1940, only half (52%) of 50 year olds had a living parent, increasing to 80% in 2000 (27% had both parents alive in 2000). It gets more interesting: In 1940, 13% of 60 year-old children had at least one parent alive. This number more than tripled to 44% by 2000 (Chapter 4).

The Perspective of Financial Gerontology

Much of the background of the Wealth Span model and its development as a tool in advising mature clients comes from the emerging academic field of financial gerontology. The essence of the research and education that would become *financial gerontology* started with the vision of Dr. Davis Gregg and his lifelong friend Joseph Boettner. With a diploma and varsity football letter from West Philadelphia High School and a CLU designation, Joe Boettner worked his way up from life insurance salesman to corporate CEO. Over the years he shared his wealth to educate others through endowments in the area of life insurance education to Penn State University, Temple University, and the American College.

In his eighties, Joe Boettner saw the need for something different, something broader that would serve the financial needs of older people who were not as fortunate as he. And so, together with his "little brother" Dave Gregg, they envisioned a program that would bring aging and financial issues together. In 1989–1990, the generically named Boettner Research Institute was renamed the *Boettner Institute of Financial Gerontology* to identify the intent of its activities.

Beyond the specifics of research and education projects, our larger goal was that the new field of financial gerontology would serve as an intellectual *bridge*—to bring gerontological concepts, issues, and facts more fully into financial services education and practice, and to demonstrate empirically the importance of financial services to gerontologists. Financial Gerontology would be useful to financial professionals by focusing on gerontological topics (such as the dynamics of aging families and increasing longevity) that would be of special value to Wealth Span planning. Thus, the noun is *gerontology,* identifying the source of the concepts and data, but the adjective is *financial,* identifying the broader context in which the research and education would be applied. In these terms, we would serve both financial and gerontological practitioners. (See a brief description of the *Encyclopedia of Financial Gerontology* in the Chapter 13 Resource Guide.)

Four Principles of Financial Gerontology

The Wealth Span model provides the organizing framework of this book. In addition, over the past 15 years of this writer's research and teaching, four principles of Financial Gerontology have emerged that serve as the fundamental principles of *Advising Mature Clients* and that are revisited in various ways throughout these chapters:

1. Gerontology is not the study of "old people."
2. Financial decisions are family decisions.
3. Wealth Span interventions are better when made earlier but can work at any age.
4. The Wealth Span advisor, as a trusted family advisor, will be called on to provide nonfinancial guidance.

Every gerontology class I teach, in political science, clinical psychology, business administration, or social work, opens with the statement: "Gerontology is not the study of old people. Rather, it is the study of *the multiple processes of aging* and includes middle aging as well as older aging." It comes as no surprise to financial professionals that while Wealth Span planning is generally aimed at the future and at older age, it is largely an activity of middle age. But even if gerontology is defined as concerned only with old age, we would still have a broad and variable focus of study because the very definitions of old age are also different nowadays compared to back then.

The traditional American definition of the beginning of old age is given by the Social Security full-benefits age of 65. The financial aspects of aging also provide other markers of old age that characterize the contemporary Wealth Span, from Social Security's age 62 early retirement option, to age 55 retirement in some professions, to ages 59½ and 70½ that define withdrawals from many defined contribution pension accounts.

The following box illustrates two additional features of this book. First, in addition to formal tables and figures, here and there throughout the chapters we offer "Another Story" to amplify various Wealth Span concepts. These may be special bits of demographic or financial data, mini-case studies or controversies to ponder, an especially valuable resource or web site, and even a personal reflection or two.

Second, also throughout the book (as in the "Story" following) are reports of the current perceptions and attitudes, fears and hopes of the American public on issues of aging, finance, and health. Most of these are taken from the comprehensive *American Perceptions of Aging in the 21st Century* (APA21) developed by the National Council on the Aging, a nonprofit, nonpartisan organization of aging services professionals. The APA21 telephone survey of a nationally representative sample of over 3,000 adults (age 18 and older) was fielded in January–February 2000 by Harris Interactive (formerly The Harris Poll). It is unique in its focus on issues of aging and middle aging and the breadth of its questionnaire, as described in more detail in Chapter 13. (Note: All of the APA21 tables herein are analyses done by the author. Their presen-

Another Story

But How Does the American Public Define "Old Age"?

The National Council on the Aging's *American Perceptions of Aging in the 21st Century* (APA21) asked the public directly when they think old age begins. The question was asked separately about men and women: "At what age do you think the average man becomes old?" And separately: "At what age do you think the average woman becomes old?" We were not surprised to learn that younger people think old age starts at 50 while older respondents think old age starts around 70. What was a bit surprising was that, within the different age groups, male old aging and female old aging are generally (with some exceptions) perceived to start about the same age. The exceptions: Boomers (age 35 to 53 in the survey) and those age 75+ see men as becoming old five years earlier than women become old.

Age of Respondent	Average Man Becomes Old at Age*	Average Woman Becomes Old at Age*
18–34	50	50
35–53	60	65
54–64	70	70
65–74	70	70
75+	70	75
All ages	60	65

* Median response for each age group.

tation and interpretation are the author's and are not meant to represent the views of the NCOA or its partners in the survey research project.)

Interestingly, the question of when old age begins is not completely answered in terms of chronological age. The APA21 questionnaire also asked: "In general, which one of the following five things would you say best defines the beginning of old age in America today—retirement, becoming a grandparent, a decline in physical ability, a decline in mental functioning, or reaching a specific age?"

As it turns out, health and not chronological age is the most frequently identified indicator of the beginning of old age: 41% said "a decline in physical ability," 32% said "a decline in mental functioning," and "reaching a specific age" came in a distant third at 14%. Given this public view of the importance of health in old age, magnified by longer life expectancy and the unpredictability of the costs of health care, health planning emerges as a critical financial–gerontological component of Wealth Span activity. Consequently, much of the second half of this book focuses on health finance.

Aging Viewed Through "Three Lenses"

In the discipline of financial gerontology, there are three lenses through which the processes of aging (including middle aging) are viewed: Individual Aging, Population Aging, and Family Aging. Each of these three ways of conceptualizing the *multiple processes of aging* provides a unique way of understanding the dynamics that contribute to what we now refer to as *an aging society.*

Individual Aging

Discussed in Chapter 2, individual aging is what most people think of when we use the word *aging.* It refers to the processes by which individual men and women develop, mature, and age—although it's not quite as quick as Billy Crystal's midlife crisis view of the human life span, summarized in a two-minute monologue to his son's third grade class in the 1991 movie *City Slickers:* "You're born, you get a job, you get married, you have kids, you get divorced, you retire, you pass a kidney stone, you go to a nursing home, you die."

In the last century, the story of individual aging is the story of dramatically improved longevity. Chapter 2 offers a whirlwind tour of human longevity from paleontology to Plato, from the Middle Ages to Colonial America. But the real story of individual aging is the "democratization of longevity," a phrase coined by Pulitzer Prize–winning geriatrician Dr. Robert N. Butler. Of special Wealth Span significance, old age is no longer the province of just the rich and the royal.

But every silver cloud has a dark lining. One consequence of living longer is that functional limitations in our ability to handle the tasks of everyday life begin to creep in, such as difficulties in safely taking a bath, getting dressed, or just moving around. In the extreme case, increasing longevity is the cause of Alzheimer's disease (AD): When life expectancy was 50 years, there were few cases of AD.

But, as we said, every dark cloud has a silver lining. New research (2001) concludes that people in their eighties and nineties nowadays exhibit improving rather than declining health. Even better, Harvard's Centenarian Study documents several ways of adding years to life as well as life to those years. After taking the test yourself, you can introduce your clients to the Harvard Centenarian Internet longevity test described at the end of Chapter 2. It's free, it's open 24/7, and the web site name tells it all: `www.livingto100.com`.

Population Aging

The second lens, population aging, is the subject of Chapter 3. Population aging refers to the number or percentage of older (including middle-aged) people in the population, and trends in these numbers. What is especially interesting is that a society can experience substantial population aging even if there are no improvements in longevity (individual aging).

In a way, the key to population aging is found in patterns of *fertility.* The connection between fertility and population aging is perhaps the dominant demographic fact of our time. During the years 1946 to 1964, so many babies were born that we now refer to all those births as the *Baby Boom.* It is the aging of millions of Boomers that is the primary cause of population aging. Even if every Boomer has exactly the same life expectancy as his or her grandparents, there still will be population aging simply because there are so many Boomers who will be getting older.

The environment of Wealth Span planning is clearly affected by the interaction of individual aging and population aging: As the total number of older persons in society increases, and as they live a larger number of years in old age, the demand for health care and long-term care will also increase. The Expenditure Stage of the Wealth Span should be planned with substantial resources targeted to these health needs and costs.

Family Aging

The third lens, family aging, is discussed in Chapter 4. Population aging and individual aging have a profound impact on the age and generational structure of American families. One of the biggest changes in the Wealth Span is the increased complexity of the Accumulation Stage. In turn, one of the biggest of these new complexities is the fact that middle-agers are much more likely nowadays to have surviving elderly parents than was the case just a couple of decades ago. It is even possible, as described in Chapter 4, that an older daughter and her elderly mother might be living in the same nursing home.

Wealth Span planning is clearly affected by family aging. A basic principle is that *financial decisions are family decisions,* but nowhere is this seen more emphatically than in the increasing involvement of middle-agers with elderly parents. Middle-age Wealth Span planning for health care and long-term care now involves both oneself and one's parents. And in a poignant and reflective way, watching your mother or father begin to accumulate mild and then more severe functional limitations can serve as a strong object lesson for planning and living the rest of your life.

Middle Age

Demographically, millions of men and women are moving into and through middle age over the next 10 to 20 years. To better understand the linkages between the Wealth Span and this unprecedented demographic phenomenon, Chapter 7 focuses on the financial psychology of middle age and the multiple meanings of *middle.* We start with the notion that middle age is a relatively modern invention. In the past, most people moved fairly directly from work to old age. Chapter 7 documents three "causes" of this recently invented stage of life:

1. *Longevity.* As the individual life span has gotten longer, there is now the time between full-time career and older age in which a variety of different interests can be pursued while you are still in reasonably good health.

2. *Empty nest.* With smaller families and longer life expectancy, parents are now more likely to have a number of years after the youngest child leaves home and before old age begins to limit activities.

3. *Pensions.* As discussed in Chapter 7, this stage we call *middle age* is in part "caused by" the establishment of a fairly predictable period of time during which a person receives income without current work (pension-based deferred compensation), and has the health and resources to enjoy life.

Following from Chapter 4 (Family Aging), middle age nowadays has an additional meaning—being the middle generation in a family. In this sense, the longer the parents live, the longer middle age lasts.

Health and the Wealth Span

Chapter 8 examines the primary connections between health and the Wealth Span, introducing several chapters on health care and long-term care. The discussion begins with Rowe and Kahn's debunking of the "six myths of normal aging" as presented in their 1998 book *Successful Aging.* Such myths include "To Be Old Is to be Sick" or "The Horse Is Out of the Barn" (i.e., that early-life bad health habits can't be fixed by new good habits). As I recommend in the Resource Guide, there is a very real chance that the information in *Successful Aging* will extend your and your client's healthy life span.

Another central element of Chapter 8 is the *compression of morbidity*. Longer life expectancy does not guarantee that these additional years are necessarily robust, healthy years. An idealized goal would be to live those extra 10 years on the tennis court, at the nineteenth hole, or climbing mountains—with all illness and morbidity compressed into the last year or even the last days of life. But for many older people the reality will be that illness and decline occur throughout that final decade, with accumulating disabilities, and a chronic need for both personal care and medical care. Understanding this dark side to longer life expectancy is, alas, an important conversation to have with your clients.

Health Insurance

Wealth Span advisors need not be health insurance experts, although many are. Rather, the working assumption of Chapters 9, 10, and 11 is that you should have sufficient health and long-term care information to guide the conversation with your client. These chapters offer basic concepts and facts and provide resources and directions to further information for both you and your client.

Because Medicare, the entitlement program for all persons age 65 and over, requires substantial out-of-pocket payments for deductibles and co-payments, medigap insurance is an important aspect of Wealth Span planning. Chapter 9 introduces medigap's standard features as a basis for price comparison.

From a Wealth Span perspective, health insurance can bring old-age surprises. Eligibility for Medicare does not come until age 65 even if your client chooses Social Security retirement at age 62 or 63. Yet only 52% of respondents in a 1996 *Financial Literacy* survey correctly identified the following as a myth: "Fact or Myth: If you begin receiving Social Security benefits at age 62, you are eligible for Medicare benefits at the same time."

Note: As of this writing, even as the Social Security full-benefits age rises from age 65 to age 67 over the next 20 years, Medicare eligibility age remains at 65. By the way, if you are not sure about exactly when you or your client will be eligible for full Social Security benefits under the new rules, the answer can be found in Chapter 9.

Long-Term Care

Chapter 10 introduces the continuum of long-term care. Not too long ago, *long-term care* was virtually synonymous with "that dreadful nursing home"—a dread that often acted as an obstacle to planning for later-life care. Nowadays, the continuum of long-term care ranges from home care to assisted living to the nursing home if and when needed.

These days, middle-aged as well as older people worry more about the future cost of long-term care than about outliving their pension. The APA21 national survey found that among people aged 54 to 64, 46% said they are worried about outliving their pension and other retirement income resources, but 58% are worried about spending all their retirement resources on long-term care. Chapter 10 describes such resources for selecting a nursing home as "Nursing Home Compare," a free Internet service created by the federal Medicare agency (formerly HCFA, now known as the Centers for Medicare and Medicaid Services [CMS]).

Options for the financing of long-term care (Chapter 11) include Medicaid, long-term care insurance, and reverse mortgages. A first conversation should make sure that your client understands the differences between Medicare, which does not pay for chronic residential long-term care, and Medicaid, which can. Although Medicaid is a welfare-oriented health insurance program for poor or medically needy people, in several states a middle-class family can legally qualify for Medicaid nursing home benefits. From an ethical or psychological perspective, however, not all middle-income families want to become beneficiaries of a welfare program. In these matters the Wealth Span advisor will be called on to offer both financial and nonfinancial personal advice.

All middle-income families should understand the benefits and costs of long-term care insurance. Recent data show that the *average* monthly cost of a Medicare-certified nursing home is $3,800. Questions of risk tolerance, current disposable income, estate planning, and current or anticipated health problems combine to make the long-term care insurance issue a complex one but critical for Wealth Span planning.

Finally, a unique kind of self-insured long-term care is the home equity conversion mortgage, more simply known as the *reverse mortgage.* For most older middle-income couples, the home with its paid-off mortgage is the single biggest family financial asset. For many families who are "equity rich but cash poor," a reverse mortgage may be a valuable part of the overall solution.

The Wealth Span Professional as Trusted Family Advisor

The discussion of health and long-term care raises an important set of issues about the role of the financial professional in overall Wealth Span planning. Most financial advisors have some experience with health and long-term care insurance; many are insurance specialists. Yet as health care becomes more complex, the financial, gerontological, insurance, legal, and bureaucratic issues expand, become more multidisciplinary, and require an even broader base of professional expertise.

Thus, the first reason for emphasizing health care in a book on Wealth Span planning is that the future costs of health care and long-term care are an essential part of lifelong planning. Second, however, is the issue of the Wealth Span professional as a trusted family advisor.

Aging Clients: From Young Adults to Middle Age

You may begin your relationship with a client when he or she or they are in their thirties or forties, when their children are young and they first start thinking about larger homes, future tuition payments, more life insurance, and additional future-oriented investments. Over the years you will become a trusted financial advisor and your conversations will focus on the changing circumstances that young families encounter: Financial decisions are family decisions—a basic principle of financial gerontology.

As your clients inevitably move into middle age, the children are spending those tuition dollars and the conversations include more references to retirement, gray hair, and aging. As described by pundits and advertisers, Boomers may resist aging but they certainly talk about it a lot and spend many dollars dealing with it: Gerontology is not the study of old people but of the *process of aging,* including middle aging—another basic principle.

Eventually your middle-aged client will mention something about an elderly parent. It may be about cancer or a heart attack, or something less definable but ominous: "My dad seems increasingly forgetful and I'm starting to worry." If there was a substantial medical crisis, the physicians and the surgeons are already part of the picture and your role is secondary. But if it's a matter of those ambiguous but worrisome issues, you may be the first professional involved.

After all, you have become a trusted family advisor. Your middle-aged client may be concerned specifically about the financial implications of these looming long-term care issues, or may have undefined worries (often the worst kind). As noted earlier, nowadays most 50 year olds and half of 60 year old children are likely to have living parents—and the mother of a 60-year-old child is not 74.

The Wealth Span Advisor as a Gerontology Team Member

It should not be surprising that at some point your middle-aged client will turn to you with questions about the *nonfinancial* as well as the financial aspects of health care and long-term care. In support of this additional nonfinancial role, Chapters 9, 10, and 11 identify a number of places to which you and your client can turn for more information and additional expertise (e.g., the choice of a nursing home or help in deciding between assisted living and nursing home residence).

These resources are a good place to start, but Chapter 12 directs you to a network of other professionals and resources in your community. The chapter starts with a description of the national *aging network* of federal, state, and local city–county aging agencies created by the Older Americans Act of 1965.

Two Older Americans Act programs are of special value to Wealth Span professionals. First, all Area Agencies on Aging provide a local information and referral service. If your client wants to know about neighborhood senior centers, geriatric assessment clinics, Alzheimer's disease support groups, home-delivered meals, companion and transportation services, or just how to find the local Medicare and Social Security offices, the local Area Agency is a good place to start.

Second, every state is mandated to operate a Long-Term Care Ombudsman program. This program receives, investigates, and provides information on nursing homes throughout the state. If you want to submit a formal complaint about a specific nursing home or to learn about the formal complaints other consumers have made, start here.

The second part of Chapter 12 describes local professional alliances or, more simply stated, *teamwork.* In times of medical crisis, the first professional involved will be the physician. But in noncrisis situations, the Wealth Span advisor may be the first source of information and guidance, including the task of recommending other members of the financial gerontology team.

How does your client develop a plan of in-home care for an elderly mother who needs some help but certainly isn't ready to move into a nursing home? Initially, you may be asked about the financial details, but then where do you turn for the more fundamental gerontological information and advice? Chapter 12 describes the relatively new profession of geriatric care managers (GCMs), what they do, and where you and your client can find a local GCM. Often trained as a nurse or social worker, the GCM has specific local knowledge of, for example, how to obtain medical transportation services, how to arrange for a geriatric assessment of Activities of Daily Living capacity, how to locate and evaluate in-home services or assisted living facilities, or just how to navigate the local health bureaucracies. If your client's mother lives halfway across the country, it is even more important to find a GCM in that other community. As to legal matters, you may already work with a family law attorney, but there are some issues for which it is advisable to work with an elder-law specialist. Chapter 12 describes these kinds of issues and illustrates how you can locate a local elder-law attorney.

Alzheimer's Disease

Notwithstanding all your training and years of experience (plus the knowledge you'll gain from this book), you probably don't think of yourself as a geriatric medical consultant. Yet you may well be called on to provide initial guidance or information about geriatric health. So, your worried client describes dad as showing increasing forgetfulness. Although Americans are generally optimistic about living to age 75, our single largest fear in living to age 75 and beyond (as summarized in Chapter 12) is not outliving your pension or being denied access to health care, but losing your memory.

As dreaded as the phrase *nursing home* may be, *Alzheimer's disease* is a hundred times more frightening. Consequently, the final section of Chapter 12 is about "The Wealth Span Advisor as Medical Consultant," with an emphasis on Alzheimer's disease. One of the first things you should tell your worried middle-aged client is that a certain amount of what geriatricians call *benign forgetfulness* is fairly normal in older age, and forgetfulness in old age is not necessarily a symptom of dementia or of Alzheimer's disease.

Chapter 12 provides a simple introduction to what Alzheimer's disease is and is not. More importantly, your client should know that there are several causes of forgetfulness that are fixable and reversible. For example, certain medicines, interactions between medicines and alcohol, bereavement and depression, thyroid conditions, and concussions can all produce symptoms that look like Alzheimer's disease, symptoms that are treatable and reversible. The sooner your client understands these facts, the sooner diagnosis and treatment can begin. If a geriatric assessment does point to Alzheimer's disease, there are new pharmaceuticals that can slow down the pace of the disease when diagnosed and treated in the early stages.

In addition to a brief layman's primer on Alzheimer's disease, Chapter 12 supports your Wealth Span role as medical consultant by identifying resources for locating a geriatric physician. The American Medical Association, the American Geriatrics Society, and the American Association of Geriatric Psychiatrists each offer a physician locator service.

The Search for Better Information

Throughout this book we list organizations and web sites of special value to Wealth Span advisors. Chapter 13 is a *Resource Guide* and starts out with the simple statement: "This book has no appendices." The early plan was to have several appendices listing national and state organizations where you could find additional information; the plan was zapped for two reasons: (1) A few other books already include such appendix lists, but (2) Internet lists of the same information are both more accessible and continually updated. This book also does not have a traditional bibliography that lists dozens and dozens of articles and books; such lists also can be found in other published volumes and on the Internet.

So, instead of appendices that would be outdated before the book is typeset or bibliographic titles that give little information as to their content, Chapter 13 offers a Resource Guide. The first part is a selection of 21 highly recommended books, authors, and organizations. In college this might be called an annotated bibliography, but Chapter 13 is more than this. The Reference Guide is, as a reviewer of an early draft commented, Cutler's opinionated but chatty views on resources you might want to acquire for your professional Wealth Span bookshelf.

The second section of the Resource Guide, also opinionated and highly selective, reviews a half dozen specialized web sites from which Wealth Span advisors can find a wealth of information about all aspects of aging. There are, conservatively estimated, three zillion web sites relevant to issues of money, health, and aging. They are *not* all listed in Chapter 13.

Rather, my aim is to identify the best *mega*-web sites—sites that are purposely designed and organized to guide you to specialized sites that can answer specific questions and provide relevant information. Many of the sites included in the megasites are themselves *mega*-web sites, and so the "seamless web" of Internet lore becomes a reality. A couple of these, such as the sites created by Medicare and by the Administration on Aging, include giant collections of both consumer-oriented and specialist-useful information, including the "official" rules, dollar amounts, and directions for obtaining stuff of substantial value to your clients.

The spiritual and intellectual origins of this book are rooted in the concepts and issues of financial gerontology, stimulated by Davis Gregg's and Joseph Boettner's vision to bring gerontology to financial services and to bring financial issues to gerontology. The concept of the human Wealth Span and the new science of Wealth Span planning bring these professionals and these bodies of knowledge together, and I think Dave and Joe would be pleased.

CHAPTER 2

Individual Aging: Democracy and Longevity

When most people think of aging, it's usually about how individuals get older—or how we or they get to be "old people." Developmental psychologists take a much broader view. *Development, maturation,* and *aging* are more or less synonymous terms. Aging is characteristic of babies, but it's typically labeled as development, or as maturation when talking about a 14-year-old daughter. Biologists take an even broader view of the process: Aging begins at the moment of conception and continues until death. When the person sitting next to me on a long plane trip learns that I am a gerontologist the inevitable question is: "Isn't there some way to stop aging?" "There is a way," I reply, "but you probably don't want to do it."

In this book, we'll take the more limited, more traditional view and discuss individual aging in terms of experiences, behavior, and attitudes from middle age to older age. Middle age is usually identified as starting somewhere in the forties, although as Chapter 1 demonstrated "How old is old?" or "How old is middle age?" is itself a research question. From the perspective of Wealth Span planning as well as demography, individual aging is not the only way to look at the subject. How populations as a whole age is the focus of the following chapter, and family aging is discussed in Chapter 4.

A central element of individual aging is life expectancy, also known as *longevity*. Longevity has changed dramatically over the course of human history, with much of that change taking place quite recently, within the past 100 years. Obviously, increasing longevity has dramatic consequences for the human Wealth Span. In this chapter, we first take a brief look at aging in the past, in ancient times and then in newly independent America. This is certainly not intended to be a history of aging. Rather, it is an introduction to how the modern phenomena of longevity and "old aging" lead directly to the utility of a model of the human Wealth Span. In turn, it is a model that explicitly focuses on how recent historical changes affect the Accumulation Stage and the Expenditure Stage of the Wealth Span. Consequently, we then look at how life expectancy has improved over the past several decades—not life expectancy at birth, which is the usual story, but life expectancy in old age, which has more direct relevance to Wealth Span planning.

Finally, the chapter concludes by considering health versus the inevitability of decline in older age. The likelihood of *reductions* in chronic disability in contrast to prevailing stereotypes of poor health has received new evidence in the past several years. The goal of adding life to years, and not just adding years to life in old age, appears to be responding to a combination of health education, new medical technology, and access by older people to the health system.

And finally, as a basis for planning for extended Wealth Span financial resources, is a question that should be asked of all clients: How likely is it that you will be a centenarian? The chapter ends with a lighthearted investigation of this question.

Individual Aging Across History

We typically think of aging and old age as biological conditions. To be sure, the fundamental processes of maturation and aging are biological and physiological in nature. How cells mature, age, spin off mutant cells, cease their healthy regeneration, and die are processes being substantially investigated today by a large number and a broad range of scientists. Such research investigates the multiple processes of aging, which is somewhat different from "old age."

It is only quite recently that old age has become a widespread phenomenon. By definition, aging takes place in all living species through the processes of development, maturation, and, eventually, aging. Humans are no exception, of course, but until very recently there haven't been very many people who lived to be old. That is, not many people reached what in contemporary society we now refer to as an *old person*—living into your seventies, eighties, or nineties.

In this context, Dr. Robert N. Butler, Pulitzer Prize–winning author of *Why Survive: Being Old in America* and the first director of the U.S. National Institute on Aging, coined the phrase *democratization of old age*. By this he means that aging into your eighties and nineties is now available to most citizens, and is not limited to economic and royal elites as it was throughout most of human history. The recency and acceleration of this democratization of old age is also notable: Professor Peter Uhlenberg, a sociologist at the University of North Carolina who studies historical demographic trends, concludes that "over half of this century's gain in average years lived past age 60 has occurred *since 1960.*"

Ancient History

Biologists suggest that the maximum human life span is, biologically speaking, about 110 to 120 years. Of course, relatively few early humans achieved that biological maximum. In his almost poetically written but simply titled *History of Old Age,* the French historian Georges Minois sums it up nicely: "[Old age was] a problem which had not often arisen during the three or four million years of our long prehistory; hunting, war, famine, malnutrition and illness left Paleolithic man with few opportunities to watch his hair turn white." Minois offers a few other very early pieces of the demography of old age:

- The oldest fragments of skeletons yet found all belong to individuals under age 30.
- Lucy, the paleontologists' "Eve," discovered in Ethiopia in 1974, died between age 20 and 30.
- An examination of 187 prehistoric skulls showed that only three belonged to people over 50.

To be sure, there have always been some old people around, often in positions of power and deference. In Old Testament times, elders held a place of leadership and expertise, with a fairly good starting point for their sociopolitical authority and legitimacy:

> . . . the Lord said unto Moses: Gather unto me seventy men of the elders of Israel, whom thou knowest to be the elders of the people, and officers over them . . . and I will come down and talk with thee there. [Numbers 11:16–17]

As in contemporary times, though, the status of old people has always been ambiguous. To a large extent, the sources of this ambiguity are the same now as then, with direct consequences for the Wealth Span: On a societal, impersonal level we may respect and even glorify many old people, but on a personal level we are concerned, anxious, and fearful about the trajectory of our own old aging.

Ancient Greece certainly exemplified the ambiguity of old age and old aging. Councils of Elders are often described as places where the advice of old men was solicited and debated. Old men were often the first invited to speak in general assemblies. Yet here, too, as in other historical comparisons, ancient Greece and modern America intriguingly share some ambiguity about old people: Is it social standing (socioeconomic status, or SES in sociological parlance), or is it old age per se? Old leaders were accorded their honorific statuses on account of their being elderly *heroes,* not being old men! More generally, the Councils of Elders were *advisory* to monarchic or oligarchic governments, rather than a central part of the decision-making process. Thus, Minois notes that in those days of rural society "where land was acquired and defended by force of arms, the old were necessarily relegated to an honorific role."

There is yet another illustration of what today we would characterize as the *continuing complexity* with which old age has been socially defined over much of human history. Plato is generally thought to have had a very favorable view of old age. Writing in *The Republic,* he attempts to distinguish among Old Age, Personality, and Wealth—clearly, as illustrated throughout our current discussion of the Wealth Span, a trio of very contemporary variables. Plato invents a man named Cephalus who has a conversation with Socrates about aging and old age. Cephalus argues that with aging comes a freedom from many family and social pressures, and the arrival of a certain level of peace with the world. In true Socratic fashion, Socrates challenges Cephalus in saying that many people attribute the light way he carries his old age to his wealth—"the rich have many consolations." Cephalus continues his argument that accommodation to old age is a matter of one's character and not wealth: "a good man may not find old age easy to bear if he is poor, but a bad man won't be at peace with himself even if he is rich" [*The Republic,* I: 328–330].

On balance the ancient Greek view of aging and old age, like our own, was ambiguous. The Greek gods of Olympus, not unlike contemporary drama and teenage music, are full of intergenerational conflict in which the elders lose. As Minois points out, "the story of Uranus, castrated by his son Kronos, himself the victim of his son Zeus, goes back to the oldest myths."

The Early Census Data

By the late Middle Ages the value of knowing something about old people had become established. With the importance of the enumeration of old people came a more general acceptance of the purposes and value of systematic national and local collections of human census data. The earliest pre-census data collections had both religious and financial origins. Birth, marriage, and death registries were important in establishing the number of adherents or members of religious denominations. The size and growth (or decline) of congregations could affect the church's allocation of resources for clergy and buildings. Similarly, the design and collection of taxes was also dependent on the count of persons. The metabolism of births and deaths was a part of the count. To the degree that old people (whatever their chronological age) were a growing group, more accurate information was needed.

Aiding the move toward better census data was an increase in the quantification of time. In the 1300s and 1400s, clocks became more widespread and accurate, which emphasized the importance of chronology. People became more aware of time markers. In turn, this increased the precision with which *date and time of birth* were recorded. And since this carried over to *date and time of death* as well, society began to paint a more complete and accurate picture of age and aging.

Minois reports that the first population censuses were city and county compilations collected in England, Italy, and Germany in the middle of the fifteenth century. Concern with the widespread deaths from the black plague in the middle 1300s, as well as some concern with the English peerage and associated rules of inheritance, all meant that age was becoming fully recognized as an important component of any census effort—with developing implications for the human Wealth Span.

The Newly Independent United States

The next stop on this whirlwind time-machine journey is the newly independent America. The Founding Fathers' ideology of representative government became institutionalized in a population-based Congress. In turn, the continued representativeness of the government would be assured by counting the people every 10 years and reallocating political power in response to population changes. As a consequence of this political ideology, unlike in ancient Greece, we have more than anecdotal tidbits to describe aging and the age structure of the United States.

Figure 2.1 portrays the average (median) age of the U.S. population over the country's 200-year history. The young American nation had a demographi-

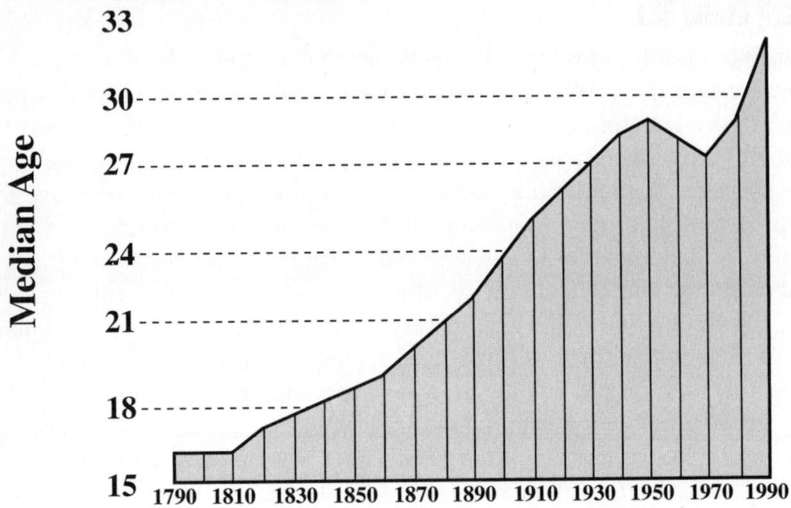

FIGURE 2.1 Two Hundred Years of Aging in America, 1790–1990

cally young population: The median age in 1790 was about 16 years old. Despite the white-hair (wig) image that survives on our dollar bills, George Washington was a fairly young father of his country. He was 44 when he commanded the troops at Valley Forge; he died at age 66. Thomas Jefferson was 35 when he drafted the Declaration of Independence. Ben Franklin was the grand old man of the events of 1776: He was born in 1706, and died at age 84.

As Figure 2.1 indicates, the first U.S. Census was collected in 1790, just a year after the Constitution was ratified. This was neither a historical coincidence nor a research strategy developed by early American sociologists. The national Census is called for in the first Article of the new Constitution: Article I, Paragraph 2, Clause 3.

In keeping with the Founding Fathers' representative republican values, the design of the legislature was placed in the *first* Article of the Constitution. The executive authority of the new presidency (which everyone knew would be held by General Washington) was written as Article II, with Article III defining the judicial branch of government. This "1-2-3" mandate called for a national census every 10 years for the purpose of reestablishing the boundaries of congressional districts as the population grew and changed, so that the House of Representatives would continue to be representative.

Since that first census in 1790 the United States has experienced a steady increase in average age. Old age as we currently define it was not populated

Another Story

Population Growth and the Giant American House of Representatives

The relationship between the U.S. Constitution, the National Census, the growing size of the American population, and the size of the U.S. House of Representatives is an intriguing story of demographics and political adaptation. In Article I, Section 2, Clause 3, the Constitution established both a "permanent algorithm" for setting the size of congressional districts using census data, and also a temporary formula to be used until the first census enumeration could be carried out. The first (pre-census) Congress, in 1789, had 65 representatives, with the number per state explicitly listed in Clause 3. Historical comparison: In the 107th Congress, 2001–2002, the House Appropriations Committee has 105 members.

Clause 3 then said that there shall be one representative for every 30,000 enumerated persons. In response to the first U.S. Census of 1790, the size of the 1792 Congress was 105. The size of both the U.S. population and the U.S. House of Representatives continued to grow; by 1852 the House had 234 members. Anticipating a substantial growth in its physical size, Congress began to amend the constitutional directive of 30,000 persons per district. Nonetheless, congressional size continued to grow; the 1890 Census produced an 1892 House with 356 members. A few selected years:

	Members	Ratio		Members	Ratio
1789	65	30,000	1892	356	173,901
1792	105	33,000	1912	433	211,877
1852	234	93,423	1932	435	282,241

Thus, in its first full century, from the 1790 Census to the 1890 Census, the House of Representatives grew by 239%. Finally, in 1910, the number of representatives was set permanently at 433, but was raised to 435 three years later when New Mexico and Arizona were admitted to the Union. When Alaska and Hawaii became States no further changes were made, and the House of Representatives now has a permanent size of 435 members.

(continued)

> But WHAT IF the 30,000 ratio was in effect today?
>
> | | | | |
> |---|---|---|---|
> | 1992 | 8,290 | 2002 | 9,381 |
>
> Compared to 1992, the 2002 Congress would have increased by 1,091 new politicians. One can only imagine what fund raising would be like, how long roll call votes would take, the cacophony of election-year campaigning, the size of the *Congressional Record,* and difficulty of finding a place to park in Washington: 435 seems like a reasonably small number after all.

by large numbers of people. In his book *Social Forces and Aging,* Professor Robert Atchley notes that the percentage of persons age 65+ was only about 2% in 1790. He comments that these few older people were largely an advantaged elite. The advantages of diet, hygiene, and health care were a province of the upper-middle class and wealthy, which accelerated the correlation between advanced age and social class. In addition, religious values suggested that to live long was to be called to carry out the will of God, with both Old Testament and New Testament support for the veneration of old age. Further, since wealth in rural society is measured by ownership and control of the land, elder heads of the family occupied positions of authority and prestige.

Atchley also notes that this societal respect for old age led to one of America's most enduring and visible symbols. It is the story of the bravery of Deacon Josiah Haynes during the Revolutionary War. At the age of 80, Haynes outraced a younger officer to lead his troops in pursuit of British soldiers in Boston. He got so close to the British that he was killed while reloading his musket, and the "gray champion" entered New England folklore. In turn, the gray champion became "Uncle Sam," who along with the flag and the eagle evolved as the most public symbols of the nation.

Longevity and Health

Over the course of the last century, life expectancy in the United States has increased substantially. Discussions in politics, advertising, and the mass media about "the graying of America" typically focus on the fact that in 1900 a person could expect to live only about 48 years, but a baby born in 1990 or 2000 could expect to live to be 75 years old or more. This pattern of twentieth century life expectancy is portrayed in Table 2.1. While the change from 47.7

TABLE 12.1 Life Expectancy in the United States at Birth and at Age 65				
	1900	**1930**	**1960**	**1990**
At birth	47.7	59.7	50.0	75.2
At age 65	11.7	12.4	14.4	16.9

years to 75.2 years is certainly substantial, it is not the dramatic cause of a rapidly aging population that the media usual imply.

Old Age Life Expectancy

The dilemma in the table is simply that these first numbers refer to *life expectancy at birth.* To be sure, compared to 1900 a baby born nowadays does have a dramatically longer life expectancy. In general, however, this is only indirectly relevant to the older aging of society. Improvements in life expectancy at birth, and therefore trends in this number, are largely a function of improvements in prenatal and neonatal health care. Prenatal nutrition, maternal access to doctors and clinics, and overall improvement of obstetrics, as well as neonatal care, have all contributed to a dramatic decrease in infant mortality in the United States.

The reduction in infant mortality, and the consequent improvement in life expectancy at birth, does have an *indirect* impact on the older aging of the population. The more babies who survive the crucial first six months of their life, the more people there are to develop and mature through adolescence, young adulthood, middle age, and eventually old age.

Of more direct concern to Wealth Span planning, however, is the twentieth century improvement in *life expectancy at age 65,* also shown in Table 2.1. In 1900, a 65 year old could expect to live another 11.7 years, to age 77. By 1990, the average 65 year old could expect to live another 16.9 years, to age 82. A difference of five years may not appear as dramatic as the 25-year jump in life expectancy at birth, but in fact it represents substantial improvement in the likelihood that a person will survive into old age.

Table 2.1 indicates that from 1900 to 1990, while the life expectancy at birth has improved by 58%, life expectancy at age 65 has improved by 44%. From the Wealth Span perspective, additional years of life at the older end of the life span signal the need for additional financial (as well as other) resources and financial planning. Other sections of this book consider issues of health care and long-term care, both of which are direct consequences of greater longevity. Whether we are truly adding life to years or just adding years to life (also an issue to which we return throughout this book) may well be a function of successful Wealth Span planning.

Figure 2.2 provides a more Wealth Span–focused way of viewing recent improvements in longevity. Here, the question may be stated as follows: What is the likelihood that a person who is 65 years old will survive to age 90? A person who celebrated his or her 65th birthday in 1940 had about a 7% chance of living to at least age 90. By 2000, the likelihood of surviving from 65 to at least age 90 had more than tripled, to 26%.

These probabilities of living to 90 are, of course, averages and estimates. Wealth Span planning should start with two broad assumptions or guesses about the applicability of Figure 2.2 to an individual client: To what extent will those years from 65 to 90 likely be healthy or not? What about the height of the right-hand bar—what is the probability that it will get higher over the next 10 to 30 years? The next few pages consider both of these questions.

Aging and the Five Activities of Daily Living

The most widely used summary indicator of an older person's functional capacity is a measure of the help she or he needs in performing a standardized set of Activities of Daily Living (ADLs). Over the course of three decades of medical, behavioral, and social research, this set of five activities has been

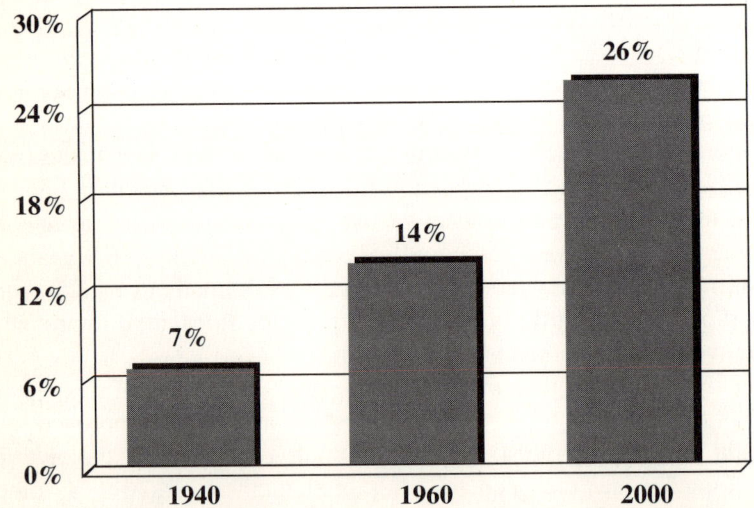

FIGURE 2.2 Individual Aging: Survival from Age 65 to 90 Has Tripled

identified as a valid measure of an older person's level of functional capacity and limitations. While some researchers use variations, the standard ADL scale includes the following five activities: bathing, dressing, transference (i.e., getting into or out of a bed or chair), using the toilet, and eating.

A person's ADL score can range from zero to five ADL needs. The assessment could be made in a hospital as part of a discharge plan, by a geriatric care manager (usually a social worker or nurse) hired by the family or by a care facility, or as part of an overall medical geriatric health assessment. A score of 2 simply means that the person needs the help of someone else on a regular basis to successfully perform two of the five activities. Whether the other person is a relative, friend, or paid helper is not relevant to the measure. A score of 2 could be any combination of 2 of the 5 ADLs. Research over the years has shown, however, that the limitations have a usual or typical time order of appearance. That is, needing help in taking a bath usually develops before requiring help in eating or getting dressed.

This set of ADLs certainly does not include all functional limitations or disabilities for which an older person is likely to need help. This set of five focuses on everyday physical tasks of personal maintenance. Cognitive decline may cause or exacerbate these limitations, and should be assessed separately. Nonetheless, the standard ADL scale, based on the five activities noted here, is used in a number of ways regarding older people and their health care. For example, some long-term insurance policies require ADL triggers before the insurance benefits can be paid. In such a case, a doctor or other qualified health professional would have to certify that the policyholder does indeed have the number of ADLs the policy requires as the benefits trigger.

In reviewing different long-term care policies for their clients, financial planners should take special care in examining these ADL triggers. Sometimes the trigger is simply a specific number of certified ADLs. Some may require both a number of ADLs and a separately assessed cognitive or chronic illness. Other policies require both a minimum number and a *specific ADL pattern,* for example, two ADLs, one of which must be eating. Since needing help with eating is typically (but not always) not needed until a person is more severely disabled, such an ADL benefits trigger is much more restrictive than it may first appear.

ADLs are also often used by assisted living facilities to calculate the cost of living there. New residents are typically assessed by the facility's nursing, social, and medical staff. A person may need meals and housekeeping services only, or might also require regular assistance in taking a bath or getting dressed. Levels of care, from independent to substantial functional limitations, then become the basis for the daily or monthly fees and rent. The kinds of long-term care and their costs are discussed in Chapter 10.

Using the ADL rates for people aged 75 to 84 for purposes of illustration, the following is the typical order or pattern of ADLs:

Based on a U.S. Bureau of the Census study completed in 1991, these numbers say that among all noninstitutionalized persons in the United States age 75 to 84, 7.0% of them needed daily assistance in taking a bath, 4.8% of them needed help in moving from or to a chair or bed, and 1.9% needed everyday help in eating.

	Percentage Needing Daily Assistance
Bathing	7.0%
Dressing	5.0%
Transferring	4.8%
Toiletting	3.9%
Eating	1.9%

In considering aging and functional limitations, it is important to keep the magnitude of these numbers in perspective. The good news is that they are very low. At their worst, so to speak, only 7% of this older age group (age 75 to 84) needs daily help. Some of these men and women may need help with more than one ADL, but it's likely that those who need help with one of the activities lower on the list also need assistance with an ADL higher on the list. That is, if a person needs help to eat, he or she is likely to also need assistance in taking a bath. Although further analysis of the national ADL data could identify all the different patterns and combinations more precisely, the 7% level is a reasonably good estimate of the higher-range overall magnitude of functional limitation in this age group. (As noted above, however, specific patterns and combinations do become important when ADLs are used to trigger benefits from long-term care insurance policies.) Overall, from the perspective of Wealth Span planning, these ADL rates don't look so bad.

The not-so-good news, however, is suggested by the more detailed ADL distributions in Table 2.2. The table shows the national ADL rates for three age groups: 65 to 74, 75 to 84 (the numbers above), and 85 and older. Since the Wealth Span focuses on the future, which includes planning for the client's capacity to pay for health care and long-term care in old age, the ADL rates for the oldest group are of special importance.

TABLE 2.2 Activities of Daily Living

		Age Rates	Change from 75–84 to 85+
Bathing	65–74	3%	
	75–84	7%	
	85+	21%	200%
Dressing	65–74	2%	
	75–84	5%	
	85+	11%	120%
Transferring	65–74	3%	
	75–84	5%	
	85+	11%	120%
Toileting	65–74	1%	
	75–84	4%	
	85+	8%	100%
Eating	65–74	1%	
	75–84	2%	
	85+	3%	50%

Source: U.S. Bureau of the Census, 1991.

The ADL range for the 85+ age group is from 21% to 3%: a fifth of these older people need daily assistance in taking a bath, while only 3% need help in eating. While even these rates seem low, it is the age-related change that signals the need for anticipatory Wealth Span planning.

The right-hand column of Table 2.2 calculates the percent change in each ADL rate from age 75 to 84 to age 85+. Some of the ADL increases are rather substantial. The ADL rate for bathing increases by 200%, and for dressing and transferring the increases are over 100%. When we add the right-hand bar in the Figure 2.1 bar chart, which shows the increasing probability of living to age 90, to the right-hand column of Table 2.2, the results suggest an increasing number of people living into their eighties and nineties who will need personal care.

After seeing these numbers, your client may still argue that, after all, the numbers in Table 2.2 are really quite low. At their highest, only 21% of the oldest group needs daily assistance. As optimistic a view as this may be, the problem is in not having a truly accurate crystal ball. For most of us, it's hard to know if we will be one of the fortunate 79% or one of the 21% who is likely to develop one or more of these functional limitations. From the perspective of Wealth Span planning, it's prudent to hope for the best but plan for the worst.

Surprising Improvements in Chronic Disabilities

We began this discussion of individual aging with reference to Robert Butler's phrase, the "democratization of old age." In a very real sense, the improvements in human longevity plus their *democratic availability* throughout the population are the fundamental reasons for our financial concern with the Wealth Span. Equally relevant to Wealth Span planning, however, improved life expectancy has its own dark side. Chapter 8 considers more directly the several connections between Health and the Wealth Span. One of these is the fact that modern medical science can keep people alive who a generation ago, or even 10 years ago, would likely have died. Given the age patterns of ADL functional limitation, is increased likelihood of individual aging from age 65 to age 90 (the right-hand bar in Figure 2.1) a gift of life or a life sentence?

In early 2001, Dr. Kenneth Manton, Director of the Center for Demographic Studies at Duke University, published a paper in the *Proceedings of the National Academy of Sciences* with dramatic findings about continuing improvements in the health of older Americans. Manton and his team are responsible for an ongoing series of studies called the National Long Term Care Surveys (NLTCS). These are very large longitudinal studies of approximately 20,000 persons age 65 and over, which were completed in 1982, 1984, 1989, 1994, and most recently in 1999. Chronic disability is measured in several ways, including the use of ADL questions. The studies are longitudinal in that the same older individuals are studied over several years.

For background it should be noted that Manton's analytic statistical techniques are extraordinarily sophisticated. In order to establish valid national rates of chronic disability, the analysis must take into account the constantly changing mix of the older population in terms of age, gender, race, ethnicity, education, and disease and health characteristics. Statistically adjusting for the age composition of the surveys is especially exacting in a gerontological study, since death rates differ by age, gender, and race, and those rates also change over time. The statistical and mathematical sophistication of the analytic models are important to mention because the results themselves appear to be so straightforward—and quite dramatic.

The initial analysis published in 1993 examined changes in chronic disability among the same older individuals over the period 1982 to 1989, and showed a *decline* in the prevalence of disability. The medical–historical context should be kept in mind. Aging, and especially advanced aging, has been typically associated with *increases* in disability, not a decline in disability. The analyses were so surprising that a special panel of the National Academy of Sciences was convened to scrutinize the data, the mathematical research design, and the statistical procedures. The NAS Panel concluded that the observed 1982 to 1989 changes were indeed real, but that continued analysis over time was needed to see if the results were unique to a specific time period, or if a continuing pattern and trend were emerging.

Results from the 1994 National Long Term Care Survey were used to extend the analysis. Manton and his colleagues presented the results to the National Academy of Sciences in 1997, and the National Institute on Aging issued a press release that opened with the following statement:

> America's elderly continue to defy negative stereotypes that aging is synonymous with increasing decline and disability. According to new findings from the National Long Term Care Surveys, disability rates among older people in the U.S. are falling dramatically, and the reduction in disability is gaining momentum.

Note the dual results of the new analysis: (1) The previously documented decline continued; and (2) the rate of decline is accelerating.

The 1999 survey was added to the analysis and the results published in 2001. The new analysis responded to lingering doubts that the previously documented declines would continue. Manton reported that not only did the declines continue in the 1994 to 1999 period, but that the decline in chronic disabilities was greater in the 1990s than in the 1980s.

- In 1982, 26.2% of the older population was classified as having chronic disability. In 1999, this had dropped to 19.7%, an overall relative decline of 25%.
- While this 25% represents an average annual decline of 1.5% over the 17-year period, in fact the rate of decline is increasing over this period; the decline was:
  - 1.0% in 1982–1989
  - 1.6% in 1989–1994
  - 2.6% in 1994–1999
- These reductions are not only different across time, they are different across levels of ADL functional limitation. From 1982 to 1999 the number of older persons with one or two ADLs declined by 13% but the number of five or six ADLs declined by 22%.

Manton and his colleagues suggest that a number of factors may contribute to these continuing optimistic results: medical advances, widespread availability of health care due to the Medicare system, improvement in lifestyle health habits such as cessation of smoking, and exercise, and generally improved education of the elderly. To the degree that education is a contributing factor, there is again cause for optimism; a related analysis noted that the number of persons aged 85 to 89 with only a grade school education will decline from 65% in 1980 to 15% in 2015.

Population aging, the focus of the following chapter, is concerned with the overall number of older (and middle-aged) people in the country and the impact that these large numbers have on societal institutions and programs, such as Social Security, private pensions, and Medicare. Manton's comments on the implications of his research provides an optimistic connection between individual aging and population aging in the future. In his earlier research, he estimated that an annual reduction of 1.5% in chronic disability could ensure the long-term fiscal solvency of Medicare. The fact that these reductions are not only continuing to take place but are doing so at an accelerating pace—2.6% in the 1994 to 1997 period—provides an especially positive future context in which Wealth Span planning will develop.

Another Story

Living to 100: Willard Scott versus Dental Floss

The continuing positive results of the Manton research are a welcome antidote to the menacing implications of the ADL patterns. Our own research found that 85% of people age 75 and older say they would be very happy if they knew they would live another 10 years. So what do you think really motivates people to work at living to an older old age?

Well, there is an intriguing hypothesis across the land that Willard Scott is responsible for much of the aging of America. It is said that elderly men and women all over the country keep themselves going just so they can be eligible to receive the NBC-TV weatherman's video birthday cards.

It appears to be working. Centenarians are reported to be the fastest-growing segment of the American population. (The second fastest is the 85+ age group, which grew by 37% from the 1990 Census to the 2000 Census.) The New England Centenarian Study (NECS) reports that there are currently about 50,000 centenarians in the United States and that 90% are women.

In recognition of the changing demographics and improving health opportunities that characterize contemporary society, the Harvard Medical School–based NECS was established to investigate the biomedical, health, and social–behavioral factors that lead to advanced old age. The study is directed by Thomas Perls, a geriatrician, and Margery H. Silver, a neuropsychologist.

Their web site, `www.med.harvard.edu/programs/necs`, notes the distinction between life expectancy and life span. *Life expectancy,* the number of years the average person can expect to live, has been growing over the course of the last 100 years. *Life span* is the maximum age that is likely to be attainable by a member of the species. Even when average life expectancy was low, there were individuals who attained those maximum ages of over 100 years old. Hence, studying centenarians provides insight into how successful aging might bring average life expectancy closer to maximum life span. The first results of their study of over 100 centenarians are reported in their 1999 book *Living to 100: Lessons in Living to Your Maximum Potential at Any Age.*

Given what the researchers have already learned, how well are you and your clients doing in this regard? Perls and Silver have developed a 23-item yes/no test that allows you to estimate your own life expectancy. After asking for your gender and age, the test asks about your eating, drinking, smoking, and exercise habits. It then asks about environmental and social–behavioral factors, such as pollution in your community, visiting with family members, and sex behavior. When finished, your grade arrives in the form of your estimated personal life expectancy. Each of the 23 test items (i.e., risk factors) is then explained in terms of how it affects your overall longevity.

Some of the factors are fairly well known, such as excessive sun exposure, eating too many French fries, risky sex, obesity, stress, and radon under the house. There are some surprising factors that just might change your behavior, including the relationship between coffee, tea, and heart attacks, and the positive effects of moderate alcohol consumption on risk of heart disease. But perhaps the most unique test item and explanation is this: "*Do you floss your teeth every day?*" Recent scientific evidence reveals that chronic gum disease leads to the release of inflammatory, toxic substances and certain bacteria into the bloodstream which potentiate plaque formation in arteries and ultimately lead to heart disease.

The greatest thing about this test is that is available on the web at

(continued)

www.livingto100.com, so you and your clients can take it free of charge, 24/7. And you can also take it as many times as you want, comparing your current estimated longevity with how your longevity might be improved by changing your current behavior in various, different ways. Just by changing my coffee, wine, and dental floss habits, I increased my life expectancy by 4.6 years! I hope Willard is around long enough to send me my birthday card.

CHAPTER 3

Population Aging

The second lens for looking at the processes of aging is known as population aging. How is this different from individual aging? Population aging refers to the number (or percentage) of people of different ages in the population as a whole. This is separate from how long these people might live. Over time a nation's whole population could get older, that is, a larger number or percentage of older persons, even if the average life expectancy of people in the population does not change at all.

Birth Rates and Population Aging

Consider a scenario in which suddenly and for a brief six-year period a country's birth rate increases dramatically. There would be an atypically large number of babies, adolescents, and adults aging through that country's social, economic, and political system. When this unusually large birth cohort matured into its seventies and eighties, the country would experience a brief time of population aging. Even though the overall life expectancy had not changed at all and the members of each generation live about as long as members of prior generations in that country, 70 years after the rise in the birth rate there would be a parallel rise in the number of old people.

This hypothetical country is the story of what is happening in the United States today. The unusual rise in birth rates over a not-so-brief period of

19 years, 1946 to 1964, produced so many babies that it became known as the *Baby Boom.* Seventy to eighty years later, these babies will become an "Elder Boom" or a "Gerontology Boom" (the official word hasn't been anointed yet). The point is that the country as a whole (population aging) will get substantially older in 2020 to 2040 because of the number of births in 1946 to 1964 and not because of any changes in life expectancy (individual aging).

This is an especially important aspect of the Wealth Span. Because of the huge numbers involved, population aging—and its maturational antecedent, population middle aging—has a direct impact on all social, health, and economic programs, both public and private, that affect (and are affected by) aging. This is not quite a dramatic revelation. From a Wealth Span planning perspective, however, it emphasizes the point that individual-level (or family or business) financial planning should anticipate the impacts of population aging. Having a lot of money at age 75 is certainly an appropriate goal. But the degree to which that wealth is sufficient to provide financial security is in part dependent on the future financial context in which that wealth will be spent. Population aging will have a major impact on how that financial context develops and is well illustrated by the national debate over Medicare and Social Security.

An Alternative Kind of Population Aging

A baby boom is not the only avenue to population aging. Imagine a country in which the birth rate *drops* from its previous pattern and stays low. Even if the life expectancy of the current adults and the newly born citizens is no different from what it has always been, in the future the country as a whole will experience population aging. As the new smaller birth cohorts with fewer babies mature into adolescence and young adulthood, the bulk of the population continues to age. Within a comparatively short period of 10 to 30 years there will be many more older than younger people. Again, all of this is taking place totally independent of the processes of individual aging, that is, independent of any improvements in old-age longevity.

This alternative path to population aging is not just hypothetical. A number of countries are experiencing precisely this kind of demographic change. Like the United States, most economically developed countries are anticipating future population aging. In some of these countries, however, the process is accelerated because of more rapid changes in the balance of children to older persons. Contrary to the U.S. Baby Boom, in this situation it is *decline* in the birth rate that is a cause of future population aging. In a most unique piece of research, James Schulz, Allan Borowski, and William Crown analyzed the interaction of demography and economics in an ambitious cross-national and cross-cultural study.

Their research and writing is unique in that cross-national comparative studies are usually either highly quantitative reports whose value depends mainly on the volume and quality of the statistics or highly descriptive reports whose value depends on understanding and communicating the texture and nuance of other countries and cultures. In *Economics of Population Aging: The "Graying" of Australia, Japan, and the United States,* these authors manage to accomplish both with great success. Anyone interested in how demographics and economics can affect aging, retirement policy, pension finance, and family caregiving in different cultures should take a look at this very readable book. Although some of the national policies have no doubt changed since the book was published in 1991, the overall description, analysis, and insights remain valuable.

Schulz and colleagues note that while most developed countries are starting to experience substantial population aging, some countries have more of it than others. Sweden and France are notable examples because of a greater relative decline in their birth rates. But the clearest example of this acceleration is Japan, "which is unique in the speed with which its population is aging." Consider the comparisons in Table 3.1.

In 1980, the age distribution showed less population aging in Japan than in the United States: 13% of Japanese were age 60 and older compared to 16% of Americans. Japan also had a slightly larger percentage of children and young teenagers. The projections for 2025, however, show that population aging in Japan is taking place more rapidly than in the United States. The percentage of children in Japan has declined by almost a third, and the disparity in population aging is quite clear. Where the percent of people age 60+ is estimated to increase by a third in the United States, the percentage of Japanese older persons will have doubled, from 13 percent to 26 percent.

A more dramatic illustration of the impact of a *Birth Dearth,* rather than a Baby Boom, on population aging is the situation in China. After decades of

TABLE 3.1 United States and Japan: 1980 to 2025

	1980			2025		
	0–14	**15–59**	**60+**	**0–14**	**15–59**	**60+**
United States	22%	62	16	20%	56	24
Japan	24%	64	13	17%	56	26

explosive population growth, the Chinese government now has a national policy and campaign to stabilize or lower population growth by limiting the size of families to one child. The consequence is that as the large population already born ages, there will soon be a relatively smaller number of young adults. With fewer younger people in the population, the relative proportion of older Chinese will rise dramatically. Consequently, it is only in recent years that China is coming to grips with such financial and social policy issues as pensions and nursing homes.

Overall, then, population aging is a measure of both the number of older persons in a society and the relative proportion of older persons. Sometimes the subject of population aging is used to imply that older people are a "burden" imposed on the rest of society. Indeed, an increasing ratio of old to young will logically (and arithmetically) mirror other indicators of population aging. (How such ratios have been used and misused in public policy debates is controversial, as discussed at the end of this chapter.)

In Table 3.1, for example, the ratio of 60+ to the 15 to 59 working-age population increases in the United States from .25 in 1980 to .42 in 2025, and from .20 to .47 in Japan. That these demographic dependency ratios describe an actual burden on the working-age population is not proven or even demonstrated by the numbers alone. For a country as a whole, *dependency* or *burden* is a matter of social policy. At the individual and family level, dependency is a matter for Wealth Span planning. In this context, we will conclude this chapter with further assessment of the meaning of dependency ratios in the context of demographic patterns. At this point, however, it should not be assumed that population aging necessarily defines a pattern of gerontological dependency.

Population Younging

Interestingly, populations can do something that people cannot. Populations can "young" rather than age. In Chapter 2, Figure 2.1 showed the average age of the American population from 1790 to 1990. There was a steady pattern of population aging (largely caused by increasing longevity) over the course of these 200 years.

Within this trend, there was a brief period that displayed a dip in the upward slope of American aging. From 1950 to 1970 the United States was experiencing *population younging*. There's no mystery, of course: It is the Baby Boom. When the Boomer babies started entering the population in 1946, the average age began to drop. Millions of age-zero humans entering the population continued to bring down the average age. After the last Boomer was born in 1964, and relatively fewer age-zero people entered the population, the country stopped younging and began its historical pattern of aging again. Now as the millions of Boomers move into their sixties, seventies, and beyond, the age of the average American will continue to rise.

Individual Aging Versus Population Aging?

So, which is it? Is the graying of America caused by the dramatic increases in human life expectancy discussed in Chapter 2, including the widespread democratization of old age? Is it the availability of good health and the desire of Boomers to be nationally greeted on their 100th birthday by Willard Scott on NBC that is pushing the country into a Gerontology Boom? The modern Wealth Span, as discussed in Chapters 5 and 6, describes how changes in individual aging are shaping the relative number of years involved in the accumulation and expenditure of personal wealth.

Or is population aging the driving force? After all, a country can experience population aging even in the absence of any improvement in life expectancy whatsoever. People in China today may not live longer than their ancestors, but there will still be massive population aging in that country over the next two to four decades.

Of course, the answer is both. The facts of the matter indicate that the aging of America over the next 30 to 50 years is a reflection of both kinds of aging. Perhaps the best way to answer the question is to say that individual aging is the *magnifier* or the *multiplier* of the effects of population aging. Even without improvements in life expectancy, the United States will experience substantial population aging as a consequence of the inevitable maturation and aging of millions and millions of Boomers. Individual aging, however, will magnify and extend the impact of the aging of millions of Boomers. Boomers will live longer than their grandparents and parents. Millions will live longer and healthier than their parents, although other millions will live longer and more frail. (The question of adding years to live without adding life to years is explored in Chapter 8.)

And so Conclusion 1 is that, from a large-scale societal perspective, population aging is the more critical process. But from the perspective of Wealth Span planning, Conclusion 2 is that it's individual aging that is of primary concern. That is, absent other information about illness and mortality, a client should prepare for a long life. The several implications of increasing longevity for Wealth Span strategies (such as balancing personal risk tolerance with alternative ways of financing long-term care) should be integrated into the planning process. In this regard, population aging is secondary because it defines the environment for the individual's Wealth Span planning. The abundance or scarcity and therefore the price of health care, housing, and long-term care, are all affected by the economic (and political) context of population aging. To this degree, population aging acts as an influence on the individual aging concerns of the Wealth Span.

The Context of the Modern Wealth Span: Old Aging and Middle Aging in the United States

Middle Age versus Old Age: The Broader View

Figure 3.1 sets the stage for both seeing in broad perspective the changing nature of America and examining the impact of population aging on the Wealth Span. The figure shows both older age and middle age over the 75-year period from 1950 through 2025. As noted throughout this book, we know full well that old age does not magically start at age 65 or at any other arbitrary age. There are variations in legal and regulatory definitions of old age regarding program eligibility and tax benefits, as well as personal, subjective differences in the way that people identify themselves as middle-aged or old (as documented in Chapter 7). Gerontologists used to make a similar kind of point in the context of retirement. A person is not young on Friday of the week of his retirement, and old on Monday morning. Even this illustration has lost its ef-

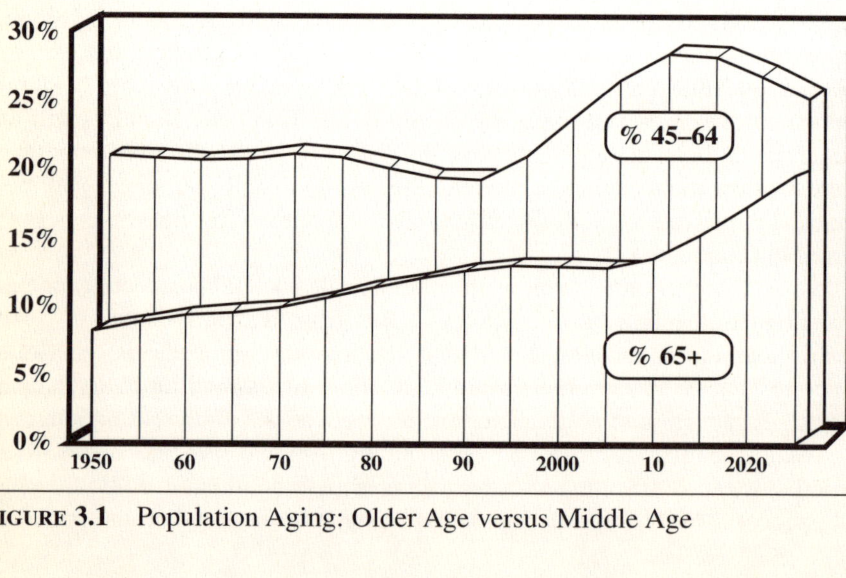

FIGURE 3.1 Population Aging: Older Age versus Middle Age

fect, since retirement itself nowadays is more a process than an event. As shown in Chapter 5 (Another Story: "Retirement: The Wealth Span's "Fuzzy Fulcrum"), many middle-aged and older people consider themselves simultaneously to be "retired" and working.

From a variety of perspectives, consequently, we know that there is no single all-purpose definition of *old age.* But because the U.S. Department of Labor, Bureau of the Census, and the Social Security Administration have been using age 65 as a traditional definition for many years, it remains a useful way to examine trends over time. As we will see in this Chapter and elsewhere, age 65+ is also a useful "foil" against which we can challenge interpretations and incorrect or out-of-date views about how the United States is aging.

Figure 3.1 shows the pattern of both older aging and middle aging in America from 1950 to 2025. The bottom curve shows that the percentage of people age 65 and older grew from 8% of the total population in 1950 to 12% in 2000. This 50-year continuing upward march of the size of the 65+ population clearly symbolizes the country's growing public and private awareness of an aging society. The early years in this period of emerging national age consciousness saw the enactment of the early retirement option in Social Security, Medicare, the Older Americans Act, automatic Social Security cost of living allowances (COLAs), the outlawing of age-based mandatory retirement, and the Employee Retirement Income Security Act (ERISA), just to name a few. Both the U.S. Senate and the House of Representatives established their own Special and Select Committees on Aging.

In 1974, the National Institutes of Health established a separate National Institute on Aging. Retirement courses, seminars, and specializations in financial planning became expanding fields of professional activity. All over the country, colleges and universities began to add aging-related courses to their curricula, from biology and psychology to political science and business to architecture and social work. The first university-based School of Gerontology opened in the early 1970s, at the University of Southern California, offering liberal arts undergraduate majors as well as professionally oriented master's degrees, and a few years later the first Ph.D's in gerontology.

Overall, business, government, science, and education all reflected the graying of America, as illustrated by the increasing proportion of men and women age 65 and older. But as emphasized in Chapter 1, gerontology is not the study of *old people,* but is the study of the *aging process,* and therefore includes middle aging as well as older aging. Thus, the other trend-curve in Figure 3.1 shows growth in the percentage of middle-aged Americans over the period 1950 to 2025. Middle-agers represented a fairly constant 20% of the country from 1950 to 1990. Starting in 1995 there is a substantial and rapid rise in the number and percentage of people age 45 to 64, with some tapering off in 2015. There is no mystery here to readers of this book, of course: It is middle aging of the Boom.

While the basic message of the impact of the Boom on American aging is certainly no secret, the two curves in Figure 3.1 illustrate in graphical terms an important comparison. Even as the country has and continues to be concerned with older aging, the current "demographic action" is in middle aging. Given the many connections between middle aging and the changes and complexities of the Accumulation Stage (described in Chapters 5 and 6), the first decade of the twenty-first century promises to be a very important period of Wealth Span activity.

The Older Age Groups

Although middle aging clearly represents the "demographic action" of the next decade, Boomers will become elderly soon enough, and the fundamental demographics of old age should not be ignored. Indeed, even as Boomers swell the ranks of middle age, from 2000 to 2020 the number of older (65+) persons will continue to increase by an additional 53% (as the upward slope of the 65+ curve in Figure 3.1 illustrates). If individual aging sets in motion the financial dynamics of the Wealth Span for individuals and families, then population aging establishes the larger societal and economic context. The word *aging* implies process and change, and so population aging also implies that the country is changing—in the direction of becoming older.

The profile of these older-age changes in the United States, from 1900 through 2000 and estimated through 2050, is shown in Table 3.2.

The numbers (N's) using the traditional definition of old age, 65+, are shown at the bottom of the table. There were only about 3 million older people in 1900, comprising 4% of the total population. The table is arranged in 30-year periods because 30 years is often used as the chronological measure of a new generation. (2000 is substituted for 1990, however, to make this discussion more timely, and because the 2000 U.S. Census data are just being released as this is being written.)

With this in mind, notice that the rate of population aging in the twentieth century was rather dramatic. The number of people 65 and older doubled from 1900 to 1930, from 3.1 million to 6.6 million. The number doubled again "a generation" (i.e., 30 years) later, and doubled yet again by 2000, to 35 million. The percentage increase isn't as dramatic since the total U.S. population has also expanded during the twentieth century. Nonetheless, the growth from 4.1% to 12.4% of an expanding national population is substantial.

TABLE 3.2 Older Aging in the United States, 1900–2050

		1900	1930	1960	2000	2020	2050
65–74	N*	2.2	4.7	11.0	18.4	31.0	31.6
	%**	2.9%	3.8%	6.1%	6.5%	10.5%	10.5%
75–84	N*	0.8	1.6	4.6	12.4	14.4	21.7
	%**	1.0%	1.3%	2.6%	4.4%	5.0%	7.2%
85+	N*	0.1	0.3	0.9	4.2	6.7	15.3
	%**	0.2%	0.2%	0.7%	1.5%	2.3%	5.1%
65+	N*	3.1	6.6	16.6	35.0	52.1	68.5
	%**	4.1%	5.4%	9.2%	12.4%	17.7%	22.9%

*N's in millions
**% of the total U.S. population

If all Americans age 65 and older lived in just one state, it would be the country's largest state, with 35.0 million people compared to California's 33.9 million. Interestingly, this new state of *Gerontonia* would have twice the population of Florida, identified as our oldest state, which has only 16.0 million older residents. Being the size of California, Gerontonia would have had 54 electoral votes in the 2000 election, noticeably more than Florida's decisive 25 electoral votes.

Now, as to this hypothetical electoral importance of Gerontonia: No one seriously argues that older Americans are homogeneous with respect to income, gender, ethnicity, political ideology, or party affiliation. On the other hand, neither are California and Florida. (With apologies; the writer's pregerontology years as a professor of political science sometimes returns without warning.)

As retirement patterns and cultural definitions of aging change, we become more interested in the older-old population, and not simply in age 65+. Table 3.2 also shows the growth of the 75 to 84 and 85+ age groups. These days, 75 to 84 year olds are the surviving elderly parents of the 1946 to 1964 Boomers. People of this age were fewer than 1 million in 1900 but are 4.4% of the population in 2000. A third kind of aging discussed in this book, family aging, is introduced in Chapter 4. And so the 12.4 million persons age 75 to 84 in Table 3.2 begin to suggest something of the new Wealth Span complexity facing

Boomers. That there are now so many middle-aged children who have surviving elderly parents is a trend that describes an age pattern of family interaction that is very different from a generation ago. If this age group of parents-of-Boomers all lived in one state, it would be (according to the 2000 Census) larger than Maine, New Hampshire, Hawaii, Rhode Island, Montana, Delaware, South Dakota, North Dakota, Alaska, Vermont, Wyoming, and the District of Columbia *combined.* (In the 2000 election, these eleven states accounted for 39 electoral votes.)

As a final observation, in 1900 the 100,000 persons aged 85+ did not represent much of a high-profile society-wide issue. The dramatic rate of this older-age population increase is indicated by the fact that in 1960 the country still had fewer than 1 million people aged 85 and older. By 2000, however, there were 4.2 million people in this age group, an increase in 40 years of over 350%.

The size of the 85+ age group in the year 2000 *is not affected by the number of Boomers.* The future, however, is a different story. The first Boomer will be 85 in 2031, and the last Boomer will celebrate her 85th birthday in 2049. The numbers in Table 3.2 for 2050, then, fully reflect Boomer aging. It is estimated that there will be 15.3 million elderly survivors of the Boomer generation; they will be 86 to 104 years old.

Much of current older-old aging reflects the recent improvements in longevity discussed in Chapter 2. These connections between population aging and individual aging have important implications for the Wealth Span, and for Family Aging discussed in Chapter 4. They clearly imply that the Boomer children of these surviving elderly parents will have substantial responsibilities for individuals who may require more medical, financial, and personal care than had been anticipated. Consequently, Wealth Span planning should now involve not only the future of the middle-agers themselves but the future of their parents.

Fifty Years of Middle-Agers

These days, it is sometimes difficult to separate middle-agers from Baby Boomers. In 2000, the Boom was 36 to 54 years old. While only the first half of Boomers are officially middle-aged (although there is no official definition), nonetheless our culture and our economy is gearing up for millions and millions of Boomer middle-agers. In large part this concern reflects an increasing appreciation of the dynamics of the Wealth Span. *Middle-aged* Boomers aren't the problem; *old-age* Boomers are. To be sure, we are not positing old age as "the problem." To the contrary, in looking at the these issues in terms of the Wealth Span, it is in middle age that we anticipate problems but design and implement solutions, which is why financial planning and financial professionals are such a critical part of the solution.

As detailed throughout this book, the Accumulation Stage of the Wealth Span is a time of crucial financial activity on the part of people in their forties and fifties. A major part of the challenge for financial planners is that the Accumulation Stage nowadays has become substantially more complex compared to back then and puts greater responsibilities on middle-agers and their financial advisors. In the past, middle age was not a prominent part of the life span. Over the past half century, however, both demographically—as we have seen here—and psychologically (Chapter 7), middle age has become a more clearly defined stage of life.

The message communicated by Figure 3.2 is that starting in 2000 and continuing for another two decades, middle age is occupying a preeminent place in American society and economy. There was substantial middle-age growth from 1990 to 2000 as the first half of the Boom moved into their mid-forties and fifties. But over the next 10 years, from 2000 to 2010, there will be an additional 27% growth in this age group as *all* Boomers will have matured into middle age. (By a quirk of calendar arithmetic that offers a useful memory device, the 1946 to 1964 Boomers will be 46 to 64 years old in 2010.) The increasing height of the bars in Figure 3.2 indicates an increasing overall size of the American population; and from 2000 to 2020,

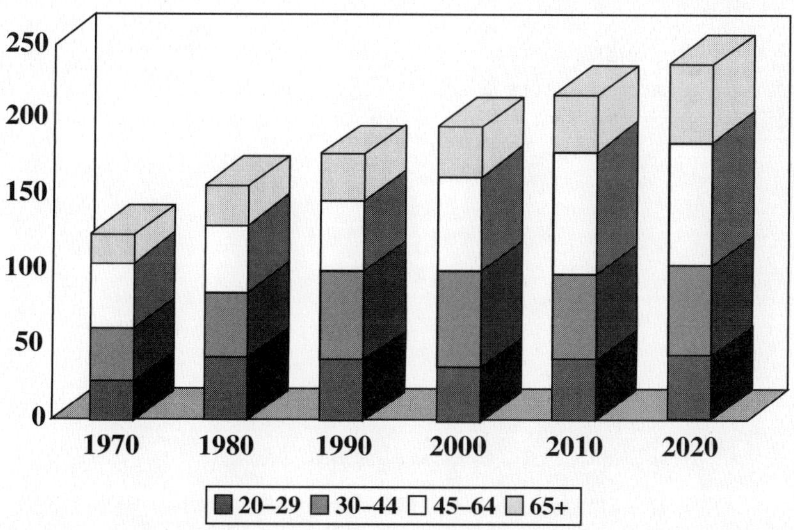

FIGURE 3.2 50 Years of Middle-Agers

middle-agers are a growing segment of this expanding population. The bottom line is simply that because of the important connections between the Wealth Span and middle age, the next two decades are of special importance for financial professionals.

Another Story

How Japanese Middle-Agers Helped Create the Roth IRA

Earlier, we compared American and Japanese age structures to illustrate the rapid older aging that is taking place in Japan. There's another U.S.–Japan age comparison that might have played a small role in the creation of the Roth Individual Retirement Account (IRA). In 1991, the Senate Finance Committee was holding hearings on proposals for a new kind of IRA. With the Democrats in control of the Senate, the hearings were about what was then called the "Bentsen–Roth" IRA; Lloyd Bentsen of Texas was Chairman of the Finance Committee. I was invited to testify and decided to use my 15 minutes in the national spotlight to make just one point: Because middle age creates an opportunity for increased saving, Congress should capitalize on the middle aging of the Baby Boom and create programs that would encourage retirement savings. Since the high Japanese savings rate was always being compared to the low American savings rate, I decided to illustrate that when a population with a high percentage of middle-agers is offered tax incentives to save, as was the case in Japan, the result is likely to be increased retirement savings, as had been happening in Japan.

BENTSEN–ROTH IRA

HEARING

BEFORE THE

COMMITTEE ON FINANCE

UNITED STATES SENATE

ONE HUNDRED SECOND CONGRESS, FIRST SESSION

ON S.162—MAY 16, 1991

Statement of Neal E. Cutler, PhD, President and Scientific Director

Boettner Institute of Financial Gerontology Bryn Mawr, PA

DR. CUTLER: Good morning, Mr. Chairman and members of the committee. My name is Neal Cutler. I am the director of the Boettner Institute of Financial Gerontology, a research group in Bryn Mawr, Pennsylvania. We focus on the connections between the social and the financial aspects of aging. We are located on the campus of the American College in Bryn Mawr. I am also a professor in the Gerontology Graduate Program at the University of Pennsylvania.

This hearing represents the well-known "Graying of America." But I would like to this morning, at least slightly, modify the terms of the discussion away from aging, and focus on "The Middle Aging of America."

Mr. Chairman, our Institute is not here this morning to take a partisan or political view on the issue of IRAs. But I am happy to summarize some of our work, in the hope that it will focus discussion on the individual responsibility for financial and retirement planning.

May I make just two brief points and then add an international footnote? The two points have to do with the two kinds of aging which gerontologists study. We distinguish between individual aging and population aging.

First, about individual aging. It was not too long ago that we would not be talking about middle age.

But in the past 50 to 75 years, circumstances have changed so dramatically that we now recognize middle age as a separate stage in the life cycle. Life expectancy has steadily gotten longer during this century, at the same time Americans are retiring earlier and earlier.

So, our financial resources for old age must be accumulated during a shorter work life, but must be adequate for a longer period of old age. And at the same time, somewhere between our late forties and our earliy sixties, we begin to see and feel our age. Our children grow up and leave home; our parents grow old and leave us. We begin to sense our own mortality, and we feel the need to plan for the future.

I realize, Mr. Chairman, that this is a short summary of a complex stage of life, but middle age is a time when family earnings are expanding, and when most major household purchases are complete. As a consequence of these separate but interconnected elements of financial and

(continued)

gerontological dynamics, discretionary income may be growing, and the family pattern of savings versus spending begins to change in the direction of savings.

Let me briefly turn to the second of the two kinds of aging: population aging. Here we refer to the overall number of people of different ages in the nation. It is not shocking to say that the Baby Boom will be middle-aged before it is older; 1991 begins a period when 80 million Baby Boomers become 80 million middle-agers. The specific numbers are in my written testimony, but the conclusion is that for the quarter century that begins in 1990, middle-agers will grow by 70 percent, as indicated by the top line in our graph. [*See Figure 3.1.*] The dramatic growth is in the middle aging of the population.

In conclusion, Mr. Chairman, when we combine the dynamics of individual aging with the demography of population aging, the importance of the legislation you are considering today is ever more apparent.

The United States is facing a gerontological and financial opportunity that is literally unprecedented in human history. The number of individuals who would be affected by incentives to save and to plan is simply staggering.

And to emphasize the connection between saving and middle-age our research offers a final, international footnote. Perhaps we should look at the next graph (Figure 3.3).

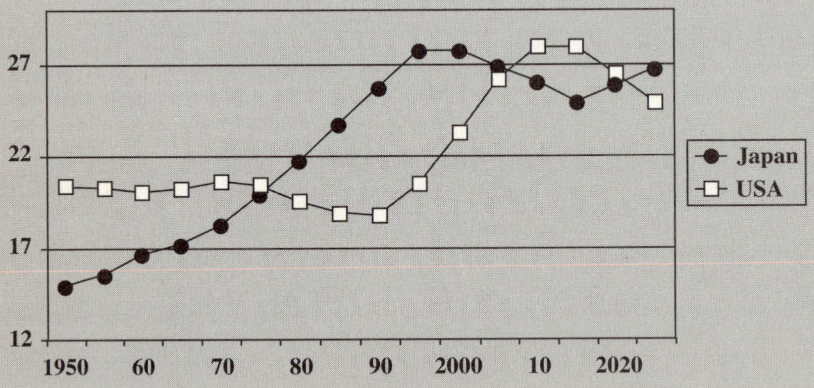

FIGURE 3.3 Japan and the United States, 75 Years of Middle Aging

DR. CUTLER: Over the past few years, as we all know, there have been many comparisons as there were this morning between Japan and the-United States on the issue of our national savings rate. We recognize, of course, that many factors contribute to a high or low national savings rate. But to the degree that middle age plays a role, then a comparison of American and Japanese demography is quite revealing.

And so I conclude by directing your attention to this graph, which is also included with my written testimony. It compares the percentage of the population that is middle-aged in these two countries over a 75-year period. The top line is the Japanese line. The bottom line, the one to the right, is the United States.

It is clear that substantial Japanese middle aging began back in the 1950s. In other words, Japan has had a substantial proportion of its population in the high savings rate of their life cycle for a long time. But by comparison, from the 1960s to the 1980s, the 80 million American Baby Boomers were teenagers and young adults. But now, the United States is beginning a period of very high middle aging. But it is obviously not simply demographics alone. During the previous three or four decades, Japan has had a large middle-aged population, but it has also had a national policy that encouraged private savings.

And so this research suggests that now just might be the right time for the United States to evaluate its own national policy in this regard. Because, Mr. Chairman, whatever financial and gerontological benefit Japan got from its middle aging, the United States is about to get a lot of it over the next 25 years. Thank you.

Relationships Among Age Groups

An important aspect of population aging is the differential pattern of growth of various age groups over time. In turn, these patterns describe different *relationships* among the age groups. The planning for such key Wealth Span issues as pension income and the costs of health care are influenced by the population aging context that includes the relative size of the working age population in contrast to the retired or dependent population. Certainly, public perceptions and political debates are influenced by the presumed relationships among these older and younger age groups.

The Fifty-Year Pattern of Young, Working, and Old

Table 3.3 arrays the 1970 to 2020 trend for three basic age groups: children and teenagers (age 0 to 19); the working age population traditionally defined (age 20 to 64); and the 65+ population. The top half of the table lists the size of each age group in millions. The bottom section of the table indicates the percentage change on a decade-to-decade basis.

These are the three age groups that are traditionally referred to in public policy debates. The population aging demographics, such as the numbers in Table 3.3, are then typically used to document the societal burden of the *dependent population* on the working population. Yet more often than not it is the *implied* dependency rather than the demographic numbers themselves which are highlighted in the debates. The policy debates and the public policies that emanate from them are critical parts of the context in which Wealth Span planning takes place.

The relative change in the growth of the three age groups should be seen alongside the growth in the total U.S. population. The 80.4 million children and teenagers in 2000 (mainly children of the Boomers, and hence sometimes

TABLE 3.3 Growth and Change in Three Basic Age Groups

A. Age Group Size (in millions)

	1970	1980	1990	2000	2010	2020
0–19	77.2	72.4	71.8	80.4	81.5	86.2
20–64	106.8	130.1	146.3	166.0	176.8	183.4
65+	20.1	25.8	31.2	35.0	39.5	53.2
Total	204.1	228.3	249.3	281.4	297.8	322.8

B. Percentage Change by Decade

	1970–1980	1980–1990	1990–2000	2000–2010	2010–2020	2000–2020
0–19	–6%	–1%	12%	1%	6%	7%
20–64	22%	12%	13%	7%	4%	10%
65+	28%	21%	12%	13%	35%	52%
Total	11%	9%	13%	6%	8%	15%

known as the "Echo Boom") represents a 12% increase over 1990. Although this 80-million level is estimated to continue through 2020, their percentage of the total U.S. population remains low. The number of people of traditional working age increases over these years, but their decade to decade increase is about the same as for the total population. The most notable change is with the 65+ age group. The numbers show slow and steady increase through 2010, but then a substantial increase from 2010 to 2020.

It is due to the juxtaposition of the change in 65+ versus 20 to 64 that public policy sirens begin to sound. The change is even more dramatic if we look at the change in the first 20 years of the new century. The youngster and working-age groups show an increase of 7% and 10%, but the 65+ group increases by more than half, from 35 million to 53.2 million men and women.

Dependency and Dependency Ratios

The numbers in Table 3.3 are often presented using a demographic calculation that has for many years simply been called the *dependency ratio.* The intent of the dependency ratio is to track over time the relationship between the older population and the working-age population. The ratio is arithmetically defined by an easy-to-calculate fraction: 65+/20–64. Sometimes this ratio is more correctly labeled as the *old age dependency ratio* because children are also a dependent population group. A total dependency ratio would then be calculated as (0–19 + 65+)/20–64. However, most of the public policy use of these calculations is with the old-age dependency ratio because of its assumed relevance to the financial support of retired old people. And since this discussion, too, is concerned with working, retirement, and their relationship to the Wealth Span, our interest is in the dependency ratio as usually defined, with only 65+ in the numerator.

The dependency ratios in Table 3.4 were computed directly from Section A of Table 3.3. The top row of Table 3.4 shows that the dependency ratio steadily increases across the 50-year period, from .188 to .290, a 54% increase. Unfortunately, this decimal way of presenting the ratio does not have much intuitive meaning. Technically, it means that there is around a fifth of an older person (0.198) for every one working-age person. To give the numbers

TABLE 3.4 Old-Age Dependency Ratios

1970	1980	1990	2000	2010	2020
0.188	0.198	0.213	0.211	0.223	0.290
5.3	5.0	4.7	4.7	5.5	3.4

more human meaning we simply swap the age groups in the numerator and the denominator, producing the ratios in the second row of the table.

This ratio is more directly interpretable in seeing the *implied dependency* charted by the numbers. In 1970, there were approximately 5.3 "working-age persons" for every one older person. This ratio shows a continuing decline, to only 3.4 working-age persons per older person in 2020. Over the course of the twentieth century, these current declines appear to be even more dramatic: In 1900 there were 14.2 working-age persons per one person, and in 1930, 11.1.

Quite often, these dependency ratios and the demographic facts behind them are used as swords in public policy battles over such issues as the financial viability of Social Security and Medicare. The problem is that the dependency ratio does not really define *dependency.* In fact, the ratios measure only changes in the size of age groups, with any dependency implied by the user of the numbers. It is an example of the danger of a partial truth: The concept does not match the data, which renders the inferences invalid, but the demographic numbers are accurate, which lends scientific legitimacy to the inferences.

As a measure of financial dependency, the dependency ratio is misleading for the following three reasons:

1. Certainly not everyone who is age 65 or older is financially dependent on working-age people. The underlying assumption of the dependency ratio is that age 65 is synonymous with retired, clearly a false assumption. Chapter 5 includes the results of our research, which recently found that only 54 percent of persons age 65 to 75 are completely retired. The others are either retired and working or not retired at all.

2. What if age 65 is replaced with the actual number of fully retired persons, independent of whether they are older or younger than 65. This hardly solves the problem either since retirement is certainly not synonymous with financial dependence. Although pension coverage is not universal, most research shows that it is a small percentage of older people who are totally dependent on Social Security or welfare payments.

3. The increasing number of working retired persons further reduces the value of the ratio as a valid measure of financial dependency. Our research found that 25% of persons age 65 to 75 and 14% of those age 54 to 64 said "I am retired" and also said "I am working" (full time or part time). Some continue to work because they have to, others because they want to. Whatever the reason, it is inappropriate to label these retired people as dependent.

For many older people, some increasing dependency does come with aging, but it is more often a matter of declining health than it is financial dependency. The Wealth Span model provides a framework for understanding and planning for both financial and health dependency. It focuses on the increasing complexity of the Accumulation Stage that has developed in the past several decades, as well as the changes in the Expenditure Stage brought about by increasing longevity. It also recognizes that with extended longevity, both health and financial resources may become strained. Wealth Span planning during the Accumulation Stage should anticipate this longevity by assessing how the client can pay for health care and long-term care.

At the same time, substantial research (as well as everyday observation) documents that much of the personal, health, and financial assistance provided to elderly persons comes from members of their own family, and not from public programs and agencies. In this context, Wealth Span planning also focuses on how the responsibilities that middle-aged children may have for their elderly parents can complicate their own Accumulation Stage planning. It is to this third view of aging, family aging, that we now turn.

CHAPTER 4

Family Aging

As the previous chapters demonstrate, there should be little doubt that the *graying of America* is one of the major domestic political stories of the past quarter century, politically and economically as well as demographically. Yet, until recently, the focus has more or less concentrated on population aging and individual aging and the various crises that (according to some) these two kinds of aging are causing. Population aging measures changes in the number and percentage of older persons in the country. Some financial prognosticators see population aging and middle aging as a primary engine of future economic growth. More often, the graying of America is seen as responsible for escalating Social Security and pensions costs and the crisis in health care and Medicare budgets.

Individual aging is similarly given a lot of negative attention. Despite the research findings of Dr. Kenneth Manton described in Chapter 2, the public attention on individual aging often focuses on the increasing number of older persons who will be needing health care and supportive services in their advanced age. The image of older-old age is often one of Alzheimer's disease and its personal as well as medical, social, and financial consequences.

What is often overlooked in these public discussions, however, is a third kind of aging, a third lens through which the connections between aging and the human Wealth Span can be examined and understood: family aging. As noted in Chapter 3, population aging is *multiplied* by individual aging. That is, not only will there be more older people in the next four decades due to the inevitable aging of 76 million babies born between 1946 and 1964, but most of these Boomers will live longer than their parents and grandparents did. The additional consequence of these dynamics is a substantial change in the age structure of a primary social institution, the family.

Family aging refers to the fact that compared to the past, even the fairly recent past, families are more likely to have surviving old parents and grandparents around. This simple fact has profound implications for Wealth Span planning. Perhaps the first thing that comes to mind, at least from the older person's perspective, is that estate planning becomes more complex when surviving family members include great-grandchildren as well as grandchildren, children, and spouse. As mentioned at the beginning of this book, however, aging and financial gerontology are concerned not just with the elderly but with middle aging as well.

When discussed in general terms, longevity (individual aging) means that people are on average living longer than in the past. On balance, middle-aging Boomers should feel good about their forthcoming greater life expectancy. These demographic trends also mean that one's own parents are entering into a longer older-old age than was the case in the past. This is especially salient for Boomers who are entering middle age at a time when parents are likely to live much longer lives than was the case a century ago.

Professor Peter Uhlenberg at the University of North Carolina is a demographer who has examined historical trends in American population dynamics over the past 100 years. His research findings are directly relevant to the issue of family aging. He assesses the impact of improvements in longevity on several kinds of family relationships, for example, the likelihood (then versus now) that a young child will become an orphan, that teenagers will have living grandparents, or that divorce is more likely than widowhood.

Looking at historical census data and other vital statistics, Uhlenberg combined trends in such factors as differences in age of mother and father when their first child is born, overall fertility rates, infant mortality, age at marriage, and, of course, life expectancy. The analysis allowed Uhlenberg to answer the question: What is the probability that X will happen in 1974 compared to 1900? (His later work extends the analysis to 2000.)

	1900	1974
■ That a child would experience the death of at least one parent by age 15?	24%	5%
■ That marriage would end in widowhood before the 40th anniversary?	67%	36%
■ That a 15-year old would have three or four living grandparents?	10%	47%

From the perspective of the human Wealth Span, however, the most dramatic results of Uhlenberg's research focus on trends in the probability that middle-agers will have living parents. These results are summarized in Table 4.1. In 1900, there was a 39% probability that a 50 year old would have at least one parent still alive. As recently as 1940, there was still only a 50% chance that one parent would still be alive. By 2000, however, 80% of 50 year olds are likely to have at least one parent alive. The likelihood that a 50 year old would have both parents alive has similarly accelerated from 8% in 1940 to 27% in 2000.

In the context of these numbers, an important connection between individual aging and family aging should be emphasized. Recall (Figure 2.2) that from 1940 to 2000 the probability that a 60 year old would live to age 90 more than tripled from 7% to 26%. Given even modest reductions in deaths due to heart disease, stroke, and cancer over the next few years, the number of men and women who will survive to (and beyond) age 90 will increase dra-

TABLE 4.1 Family Aging:
The Impact of Longevity on Family Structure

	1900	1940	1960	2000
AT AGE 50				
At least one parent alive	39%	52%	67%	80%
Both alive	4%	8%	14%	27%
AT AGE 60				
At least one parent alive	7%	13%	24%	44%

matically. Kenneth Manton's findings suggest that this is a realistic scenario. In turn, this means that the number of middle-agers with surviving elderly parents will also increase substantially.

The Dual Meaning of Middle in Middle Age

As the Wealth Span model suggests, middle age is a time when serious retirement and financial planning for the rest of one's life should take place in earnest. The numbers in the bottom row of Table 4.1 highlight the increasing complexity of Wealth Span planning in the context of how family aging has become affected by individual aging. These numbers answer the question: What is the likelihood that a 60-year-old child will have one or more surviving parents?

Sixty-year-old child may not be a phrase that we hear every day, and even less so in the past. In 1900, there was only a 7% chance that a "60-year-old child" would have at least one parent still alive, and only a 13% chance as recently as 1940. By 2000, there is a 44% likelihood that the 60 year old will

Another Story

Two Generations, One Nursing Home

Consider a gerontological extension of the trend in the bottom row of Table 4.1. As longevity increases, what about the possibility of a 70 or 75 year old with surviving elderly parents? It was just this possibility that intrigued *Wall Street Journal* writer Ellen Graham a few years ago after she saw an earlier version of Table 4.1. Graham decided to see if this possibility was really happening. The result is her article "Two Generations, One Nursing Home," published in the *Journal* on May 13, 1998.

Graham found a nursing home in Mobridge, South Dakota, that is home to not one but *three* parent–child families. Of course, each is a unique story but together they sketch a picture of things to come. Ninety-two-year-old Mary lives in the same nursing home as her 69-year-old son, Leroy. He had polio as a teenager but lived independently and ran his own small insurance agency. But after 35 years his crippling paralysis returned, just about the time his widowed mother was becoming frail. His younger brother, age 67, couldn't take care of both the family farm and his mother and brother, so when Mary moved into the nursing home, Leroy did too. They live in separate wings of the home but see each other every day.

Ramona, age 66, has severe arthritis and occasionally has been wheelchair bound. Emma, her mother had lived alone for 11 years, but as her health declined she recognized the need to be with people her own age. After her own illness became worse, Ramona too realized that living alone, even with the assistance of visiting social workers to help with household chores, was too difficult and lonely, and so joined Emma in the nursing home. As the youngest resident in the home she is also an informal caregiver, fussing over the other old people as well as her mother.

John, age 49, represents a special role that nursing homes and assisted living will have to play in the years ahead. John has Down syndrome, has lived at home, but now lives in the same nursing home as his 86-year-old mother, Christie. Currently, John is worried because his mother's health is declining and she is confined to her bed. The patterns in Table 4.1 take on special meaning when we consider the middle aging of children with Down syndrome as their parents survive into advanced old age. The situation represents both a special challenge of Wealth Span planning for these families and a unique view into how nursing homes and assisted living residences can respond to the more general phenomenon of elderly parents who have disabled aging children. The physical, architectural resources may be there, but the financial and caregiving characteristics and systems need to be developed.

Ms. Graham correctly observes that the fact that mother and child live together in a nursing home might seem to be "an affront to the natural order of things." Usually by the time parents become frail, their children are still in "vigorous middle age." But with increasing longevity, people living into their nineties may experience aging children who may need care themselves. The image (and here the reality) of "Two Generations, One Nursing Home" may not describe a typical pattern of aging, but it certainly dramatizes and appropriately illuminates the more general realities of how individual aging and population aging are changing the nature of family aging—and therefore changing the requirements of Wealth Span planning.

have at least one parent alive, nearly double the likelihood in 1960. At a time in life when the middle-ager is (or should be) involved in serious Wealth Span planning and is personally moving toward and into old age, there is now a substantial and increasing likelihood that mother or father is still around. These probabilities are likely to be higher given the increasing likelihood of survival from age 60 to age 90 and older. In addition to all its other implications, the Manton research suggests (1) the likelihood of an even greater number of surviving older parents, but also (2) that while their health may improve somewhat, many will still suffer chronic disabilities and everyday functional limitations.

As mentioned, until recently the words *60-year-old* and *child* were not typically part of the same sentence. By the same token you don't have to be the proverbial rocket scientist or even an actuary to recognize that the mother of a 60 year old is not 70! In just a few years, in 2006, the first Boomers will turn 60. The patterns in Table 4.1 suggest that for at least half of them (it was 44% in 2000) their current Wealth Span activities should include planning for parents who are 85 years old or older.

Do these data and personal experiences mean that all middle-aging children have to be ready, able, and willing to provide care to aging parents? Of course not. Does it mean that all octogenarians need daily assistance? Again, the answer is no. As documented by the age patterns of increasing need for ADL assistance (Table 2.2), however, substantial changes in health, mobility, frailty, and general need for assistance do take place as people age from their 70s to their 90s. It may be true that only 21.9% of people age 85+ need daily assistance in taking a bath. But from the perspective of planning for that care, including the prudent financial and insurance aspects of Wealth Span planning, few of us can know if our father or mother will be part of the larger healthy, independent group of 85 year olds or part of the other group.

Another Story

Mine

A few years ago, a book on the *New York Times* best-seller list was titled *Everything I Need to Know I Learned in Kindergarten.* As a gerontologist, researcher, and teacher, my version of that book would be titled something like *Everything Important I Know about Gerontology I Learned from My Mother* (which is why this book is lovingly dedicated to her). My mother is almost exactly 30 years older than I. I was almost her 30th birthday present, she reminds me periodically. But that 30-year gap turns out to be an instructive and a very human embodiment of the older parent data in Table 4.1.

About six years ago, it became increasingly difficult for Mother to walk up and down the stairs to her second floor apartment. Southern Californians are a very healthy race, so few two-story buildings in the San Fernando Valley deign to have elevators. We jointly decided that since she was still in reasonably good health except for her back and hip problems, she should now evaluate her options and make a choice about moving into assisted living. (The financial and other aspects of the assisted living decision process are discussed in Chapter 10.) She made her decision, and after the moving van transferred the big pieces of furniture to her new place or to storage, it fell to me to go through the accumulated folders and files to decide which to keep, store, or discard.

My personal connection to Table 4.1 soon became abundantly clear in a way that motivated me to later congratulate Mother on the wisdom of her and my late father's family planning. As a young 50-something I was able to survive dozens of trips up and down the two flights of stairs, none of them empty-handed, removing dozens of boxes full of old receipts, recipes, newspaper and magazine clippings, and hundreds of canceled checks from the 1950s. If Mother been 20 instead of 30 when I was born, I would now be the 60-year old child of an 80-something parent. Helping her adjust to her own aging-related changes would have been considerably more difficult than it has been. The sons and daughters in the bottom row of Table 4.1, as well as those of us in the top row, face a comprehensive range of personal as well as financial challenges. Demography may not be destiny, but it sure can be demanding.

Family Aging and the Sandwich Generation

Family aging, this third lens through which we view the aging process, adds substantial complexity to the middle-age Wealth Span. What might have been anticipated as a period of *empty nest* reduced family responsibilities, including reduced financial responsibilities for others, might now become a period of renewed and intense caregiving oriented toward aging parents.

The alternative to a relatively quiet empty nest is the picture of the highly burdened *sandwich generation* that provides care simultaneously to two family generations: parents and children. While both of these views of middle aging have their financial implications, the sandwich generation metaphor provides a valuable way to assess the impact of family aging on the Wealth Span. Our research suggests that the reality for many middle-agers is neither the empty nest nor the two-sided sandwich, but a more demanding relationship with aging parents.

The One-Generation Caregiver Sandwich

The origins of the sandwich generation metaphor are usually traced back to the work of Elaine Brody, a long-time senior researcher at the renowned Philadelphia Geriatric Center. Professor Brody documented the competing demands on midlife women of simultaneously caring for elderly parents and teenage children. Her 1981 article was titled "Women in the Middle" and gave rise to the sandwich metaphor.

The traditional image is that of a middle-aged daughter sandwiched between two generations, her parent(s) and her children. Recent evidence suggests, however, that the impact of caregiving on the Accumulation Stage is more complex than a traditional sandwich implies. This is due to the fact that in the modern family, elder care is itself becoming more diversified. To continue the metaphor; the evidence (presented in Figure 4.1) suggests that American society is moving toward an open-faced sandwich profile. In many if not most families, the caregiving burden on middle-agers concentrates on taking care of one generation, their elderly parents.

In a 1996 article published in *Generations* (the journal of the American Society on Aging), we examined empirically the sandwich nature of middle-age family responsibilities through an analysis of trends over the period 1970 to 2025. Using national census data, we calculated an *older parent support ratio* and a *teenage support ratio.* The numerator of the two ratios is the number of persons in the care-receiving age, 60 to 74 and 10 to 19. For both ratios, the denominator is the number of middle-agers age 40 to 49. We purposely put middle-agers into the denominator to emphasize that the burden of responsibility is on their shoulders. The ratio thus represents the number of care recipients (teens or older parents) per one middle-ager.

As Figure 4.1 indicates, in 1970 there were about 1.7 teenagers per each middle-ager. The teenage support ratio then rapidly declines as the Baby Boomers mature out of their teenage years. The ratio declines until about 2000 to 2005, after which it remains fairly flat—at less than one teenager per

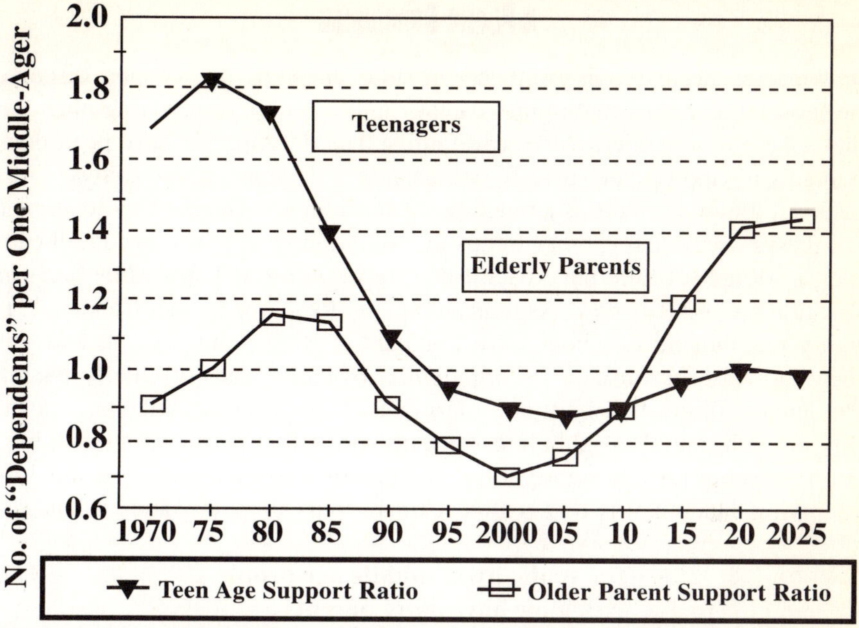

FIGURE 4.1 Middle Age Support Ratios: Teenagers and Their Parents

middle-ager. About this same time, in 2000 to 2005, the slope of the older parent support ratio begins to increase substantially and is calculated to continue to increase over the next quarter century. It is estimated that in 2025 there will be about 1.4 elder parents per each middle-ager.

We recognize that the true story of intergenerational caregiving and responsibilities is only hinted at by the census-based patterns shown here. For example, the people represented in Figure 4.1 are not actual parent–child families, but rather census aggregates of age groups representing middle-agers, their parents, and their teenage children. Different age definitions of middle-aged parents of elderly parents would change the specific values of the two support ratios, but the picture would look just about the same. Further, not all of the parental-aged persons in the numerator will need help over the next quarter century. And not all of the denominator's middle-agers actually have living parents. Rather, the message is that for society as a whole, the impact of family aging on the Wealth Span requires a stronger focus on middle-age responsibility for elder parents than is suggested by the traditional sandwich metaphor.

A Poetic Conclusion

Drawing on the materials from the previous chapters, this chapter discusses the substantial impact that improvements in longevity and surviving older parents have on the modern American family. The descriptions have been documented with appropriate surveys, census data, and demographic analysis. As it turns out, however, there is a much more succinct and elegant way to summarize these twenty-first century trends in family aging. A few years ago, I came upon a wonderful little paperback titled *Aging Parents: When Mom and Dad Can't Live Alone Anymore.* As indicated in the Resource Guide (Chapter 13), I highly recommend this book as a poignant starting point for you and your clients to read and discuss *in anticipation of* taking care of elderly parents. The author, Eldon Weisheit, is a clergyman from Tucson, Arizona, who not only has substantial insights into working with aging families, but also has a gift for turning just the right phrase. His comment summarizes a mountain of caregiving data in a way that is almost *Haiku* in its simplicity and elegance:

The majority of middle age people
now have more parents
than they have children.

CHAPTER 5

Wealth Span Changes I: The Changing Balance of the Wealth Span

In developing their broad conceptualization of *successful aging,* geriatrician John Rowe and psychologist Robert Kahn invented the phrase and the construct *Health Span.* They argued that the Human Life Span can be seen in terms of identifiable stages as a way of first understanding individual health, and then changing and improving it.

Our model of the human *Wealth Span* builds on Rowe and Kahn's Health Span. It's not at all surprising to suggest that successful aging includes a wealth dimension as well as a health dimension. And from the perspective of financial advisors, as our own research has recently documented, the connections among wealth, health, and planning for a vital old age are more complex than one might imagine.

In particular, two fundamental aspects of Rowe and Kahn's Health Span are directly transferable to the Wealth Span:

Another Story

The Wealth–Health Connection to a Happy Old Age

The National Council on the Aging's (NCOA's) *American Perceptions of Aging in the 21st Century* survey asked people of all ages a set of questions about living to age 75 and beyond and the likelihood that medical science will help to get there. Americans are an optimistic people, but as the results of the study also reveal, we are also pessimistic, or maybe it is realistic, about getting there. Interviewers asked the following age-happiness question: If you knew you would live to be 75 years old, would that make you very happy, somewhat happy, or not at all happy?

Later in the 35-minute interview, respondents were asked: In your lifetime, do you think there will be dramatic new treatments or cures that will improve your chances of living past age 75 or not? A financial follow-up question asked: How worried are you that you will not be able to afford dramatic new treatments that may appear—very worried, somewhat worried, or not worried at all?

Looking at people who are in their prime Accumulation Stage ages, most would be quite happy to know that they might live to age 75 or older. And a substantial majority are also optimistic that medical science will bring forth dramatic new cures to make old age possible. But the realism is revealed on the financial front. More than half of all respondents are worried that they will not be able to afford those treatments and cures. This clearly argues the case for strong Accumulation Stage strategies to plan for health-focused expenditures in later life.

AGE	Happy-75? % Happy	New Cures? % Yes	Afford Cures? % Worried
35–43	93%	87%	56%
44–53	95%	89%	58%
54–64	92%	86%	58%

1. *Like the Health Span, there are identifiable stages in the Wealth Span.* Since it is virtually a truism that what you do earlier in life has measurable impact on what happens later, it's important to understand the nature and dynamics of the stages. This chapter and the next focus on the two stages of the Wealth Span.

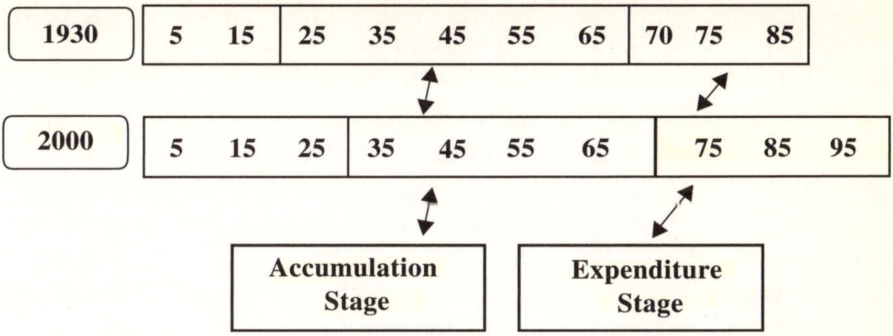

FIGURE 5.1 The Wealth Span in the Twenty-First Century: Different *Balance* and *Greater Complexity*

2. *For wealth as well as for health, it's better to start good habits early in life.* Nonetheless, as both financial advisors and health counselors admonish us, it's never too late to start. It's best to start exercising, have a healthy diet, start a retirement account, and put as much as you can into tax-deferred investments early in your health/wealth span. But starting late is better than doing nothing at all.

Figure 5.1 portrays the Wealth Span model in terms of two basic stages: the Accumulation Stage and the Expenditure Stage. Like any analytic model, it is not intended to accurately portray reality but is purposely designed to simplify reality in order to more clearly understand the component parts. An especially important reason for this simplification is so we can focus on the changes in the Wealth Span that have taken place over the past 50 years or so—changes that can have a direct influence on how consumers and clients should evaluate such things as their portfolio diversification and estate planning strategies.

The Unrealistic and the Realistic Nature of the Wealth Span Model

Of course, people spend during the Accumulation Stage and accumulate during the Expenditure Stage. For example, substantial amounts of what might be called *family capital expenditures* take place during the Accumulation Stage of the Wealth Span, along with lots of other spending. In the other half of the model, the degree to which older people these days spend or continue to save and invest is an important researchable question. Indeed, using the phrase *dissaving,* there is substantial theoretical and empirical disagreement among economists concerning the degree to which today's older or retired persons are really dissaving in their retirement years, or continuing to save, invest, and accumulate.

Due to improving life expectancy and because more Americans are retiring at earlier ages, and because retirement itself has a greater number of meanings than it had 100 or even 50 years ago, the linkages among age, retirement, earning, and spending are very different and more complex than in the past. Nowadays, there is a substantial number of postretirement years during which retirement funds and other savings and investment accounts will continue to accumulate. As a result of these well-documented trends, the simplified categorization of the Wealth Span into the Accumulation Stage and the Expenditure Stage is certainly not meant to be a scientifically accurate description of the real world of work, saving, and retirement.

"Good grief", you may well exclaim, "then why offer such an unrealistic portrait of such important real-world processes?" Figure 5.1 portrays the Wealth Span in 1930 and in 2000. In keeping with the premise that the model is not intended to be factually or scientifically accurate, 1930 and 2000 are simply place-holders. The real concern is about fundamental contrasts between *then* and *now.* There have been substantial changes in the Wealth Span when we compare *back then* and *nowadays.* The analytic structure of dividing the Wealth Span into an Accumulation Stage and an Expenditure Stage focuses our attention on how these changes directly affect retirement and financial planning.

The Wealth Span Model as an Advisory Tool

How can we use the Wealth Span model, its vocabulary, and its underlying structure in the analysis and practice of financial planning? On an analytic level, the model can help to conceptualize and assess the several elements of financial and retirement planning in a historical, social, and gerontological perspective. For example, a comparison of demographic trends and changes in retirement policy for the country as a whole allows us to see more directly how an individual's personal life expectancy interacts with a variety of older-age retirement, income, and health planning choices.

Similarly, the model offers a valuable client tool for education and persuasion. On the one hand, the model doesn't tell us much that is dramatically new: Nowadays people retire earlier and live longer. On the other hand, looking at the Wealth Span and its stages in historical perspective allows the client to see more directly the importance of starting now. Both the Accumulation Stage and the Expenditure Stage are different nowadays than they were back then, and the model graphically portrays the difference.

When seen in the broader context of the Wealth Span, the financial differences between then and now become more apparent. Consider the educational and motivational value of demonstrating the importance of starting to plan and invest early, or at least starting now, because the Accumulation Stage is much shorter than it used to be. More to the point of future later-life financial well-being, the Expenditure Stage is now longer than it used to be. The combination of both these changes is *simply* that what is accumulated in a shorter period of time has to support a larger number of older or retirement years of expenditure.

These historical changes in the balance of years between the two stages are only the first half of the Wealth Span story (and the focus of this chapter). The second half concerns the substantially greater *complexity* of the Accumulation Stage nowadays compared to back then. These dynamics are discussed in Chapter 6.

In sum, the Wealth Span is by definition a simplified portrait of the human life span in financial terms. Its value is in providing a structure and a vocabulary for discussing and analyzing (for both academics and practitioners) the two basic stages. Following Rowe and Kahn's Health Span lead, the Wealth Span first and foremost represents human development, in which actions taken earlier in life will affect later outcomes. But the model also emphasizes interventions, suggesting that actions taken even somewhat later in life can have a positive, affirmative impact.

To this discussion we add the dimension of historical change in order to emphasize how several financial, demographic, gerontological, and cultural trends combine to change the nature of Wealth Span planning. As my colleague the late Dr. Davis Gregg characterized the interaction of these dynamics: "As continuing efforts [in research and practice] proceed, and new and higher goals in life-span and health-span are achieved, so will efforts be initiated to achieve a revolutionary increase in wealth-span—*the maintenance of full financial function as nearly as possible to the end of life.*"

Historical Change in Balance

In the Wealth Span model, *balance* simply refers to the relative number of years in the Accumulation Stage as compared to the Expenditure Stage. This is not intended to mean that the two stages are or necessarily should be equally balanced like a teeter-totter on a fulcrum. Rather, the point is that from a historical perspective there has been a significant change in the number of years in each stage. If there is a fulcrum that separates the two stages, it would be named *retirement.*

As noted, two fundamental changes characterize the Accumulation Stage and Expenditure Stage: the change in the relative number of years between the two stages (balance), and the change in the complexity of the two stages, especially in the Accumulation Stage. To use the word *retirement* in reference to a fulcrum that divides the two stages, however, draws attention to a third historical change: the very meaning of the concept of retirement. As the final section of this chapter will show, recent research clearly documents that age, work, and retirement are no longer linked together as closely as they used to be.

Thus, in the context of the changes identified by the Wealth Span model, even the fulcrum is becoming less distinct; the line between work and retirement is becoming more and more fuzzy. Even more so than in the past, *retirement is a process rather than an event.* In fact, it is because of these several changes and trends that we use the terms *Accumulation Stage* and *Expenditure Stage* rather than the more traditional *work* and *retirement.*

As noted earlier, although Figure 5.1 refers to 1930 and 2000, the specific dates are of little consequence. It is really back then versus nowadays that is of interest. Back then, for example, most people started their work careers fairly early in life. Few states had mandatory age 18 high school attendance laws until the 1930s and 1940s. Certainly, post–high school education was not a widespread experience. And so, the Accumulation Stage started relatively early in life.

Back then, compared to nowadays, the Accumulation Stage lasted for quite a few years. Although some historians suggest that the early-retirement trend in the United States started in the first decades of the twentieth century, for most workers the Accumulation Stage lasted until their mid-sixties. For historical analysis, most demographers and economists use the labor experience of men age 60 and older to historically trace national retirement patterns. Figure 5.2 shows the labor force participation pattern of this group from 1900 to 1990.

As recently as 1950, more than half of men age 60 and older were still in the labor force. Because of changing patterns of work and retirement, however, fewer than a third of this age group are still in the labor force in the last decades of the twentieth century.

So, back then, the Accumulation Stage was relatively long. At the same time, as the Wealth Span model indicates, the Expenditure Stage was relatively short. Life expectancy was shorter than it is now. As documented in Chapter 2 (Figure 2.2), in 1940 the probability that a 65 year old would live to age 90 was only about 7%, a probability that has since tripled. The 1900 U.S. Census found that only 4.1% of the population was 65 and older; in 2000, it was 12.8 percent.

Nowadays, however, the situation is fairly different. The Accumulation

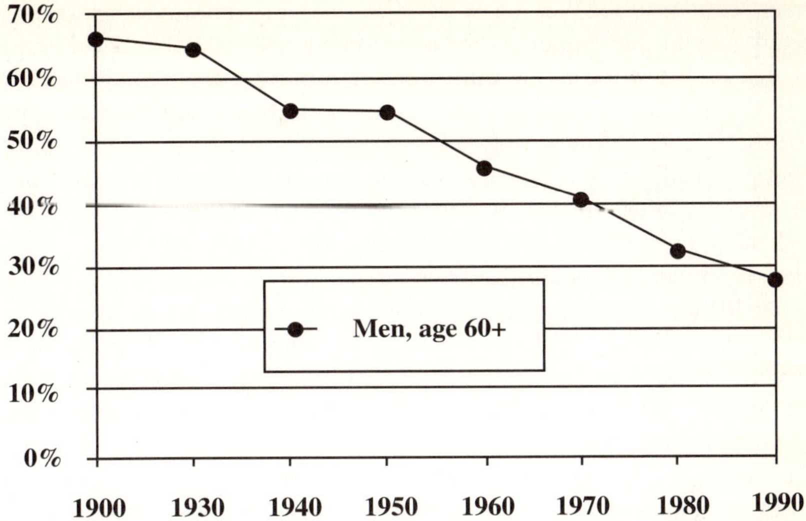

FIGURE 5.2 Labor Force Participation, 1900–1990

Stage typically starts later in life. High school until age 18 is largely mandatory throughout the country. Although many young adults work their way through college, the college experience delays the formal start of the Accumulation Stage for at least four years. Professional school and graduate school add a few more years of delay for many. In discussing this point in class last year, my graduate students animatedly reminded me that the costs of graduate education, in the form of continuing loan repayments, delay the start of the Accumulation State beyond the four or five years of their bachelor degree program! In many occupations, a kind of educational inflation has made a bachelor's degree as widespread as a high school diploma used to be, so that in many professions an advanced certificate, designation, or master's degree is required or preferred—all of which can delay the start or slow down the pace of accumulation.

Not only does the Accumulation Stage start later, it ends earlier. As the labor force participation trend in Figure 5.2 illustrates, American workers are increasingly leaving the work force earlier than age 60. Some historians suggest that Social Security caused the trend in early retirement. The age-62 early retirement option was offered to women in 1955 and to men in 1961. The data certainly show that nowadays it is a minority of workers who wait until age 65 to leave the workforce.

Other scholars argue that the Social Security early retirement option simply reflected a trend that began earlier in the century as social and cultural attitudes that define work as the ultimate definition of a man began to change. The 1935 enactment of Social Security itself, in this historical view, simply served to institutionalize a postwork retirement stage of life in which a minimal but personally earned pension was guaranteed by the federal government. More recently, other financial–cultural trends, such as the age 59½ IRA withdrawal rules, have helped to further change American images and definitions of when retirement can legitimately begin.

Alongside the shortening of the Accumulation Stage, and affected by many of the same dynamics, the Expenditure Stage is now longer. Because of early retirement, it starts earlier in life. And due to the well-documented trends in increasing life expectancy, the Expenditure Stage is destined to last longer than in previous years.

The longer Expenditure Stage has its own new and emerging set of complexities. Although these are discussed throughout the book, they can be highlighted as follows:

- In its most fundamental Wealth Span meaning, a longer Expenditure Stage simply means that the wealth that is accumulated in the Accumulation Stage has to provide for financial well-being for a longer period of time. The logical investment extension of this concern, of course, is that while wealth accumulation will have to continue in the Expenditure Stage, the foundation of this continuing wealth accumulation should be established in the Accumulation Stage. Some clients may need to be reminded that 15 years of compound interest or investment growth is 15 years of compound interest or investment growth whether the owner of the money is 30 years old or 60 years old. In this sense, the financial version of Rowe and Kahn's "better late than never" late-life intervention principle is a valuable piece of Wealth Span education.

- Unfortunately, a longer life does not necessarily mean a healthy long life. Several of the processes that describe such a situation are discussed in Chapter 8. The consequence of "living longer but not necessarily living better" is that the Expenditure Stage will need more resources to pay for health care and long-term care than when the Expenditure Stage was relatively shorter. These financial and health issues are discussed in Chapters 9, 10, and 11.

- As described in Chapter 4, because of the impact of greater life expectancy on family aging many more middle-agers and young-old people than in the past are likely to have surviving elderly parents. The personal, health, and financial assistance that the older child provides is typically provided during the child's own Expenditure Stage. Again, the financial groundwork for more complex expenditures should be established in the Accumulation Stage.

- A final issue is that of inflation. In the past few years of almost invisible inflation, it may be easy to lose sight of the double-digit inflation of the 1970s, which pushed many fixed-income retirees into dire straits. A consequence of the longer Expenditure Stage is that there is a greater number of years in which even low inflation rates can erode the value of accumulated wealth. To be sure, any decent retirement financial plan will include an inflation factor. Our basic message is simply that, nowadays compared to back then, a longer Expenditure Stage also means that the eroding effects of inflation will have more time to interact with the other new characteristics of the Expenditure Stage (such as health care and caring for elderly parents).

Another Story

Retirement: The Wealth Span's Fuzzy Fulcrum

In describing the change in the balance of years between the Accumulation Stage and the Expenditure Stage, we also noted that the two stages do not necessarily have to be in balance. Still, the notion of some kind of balance between the traditional notion of *working* versus *retirement* is so well established that the fulcrum of this balance, retirement, deserves special comment. The basic plotline of this story is that the connections among age, work, and retirement are becoming increasingly fuzzy. Consider the following:

- In contrast to the traditionally defined (Social Security–based) retirement age of 65, there are a number of official early retirement laws, rules, and options. The official Social Security early retirement age is 62 and is slated to remain such even as the full-benefits age rises to age 67. In the case of IRA withdrawal rules, tax law defines or at least strongly suggests that age 59½ is a reasonable and legitimate retirement age. AARP lowered its membership age to 50, but also changed its name from American Association of Retired Persons to simply AARP. (And, by the way, it's pronounced as "A-A-R-P," 4 distinct letters, and not as a single-syllable word that rhymes with *carp*.)

(continued)

- On the other hand, the 1978 Amendments to the Age Discrimination in Employment Act (ADEA), made age-based mandatory retirement illegal. Although all legislation and policy changes have multiple and mixed motives, the campaign to outlaw mandatory retirement was as much a concern over discrimination and civil rights for older people as it was concerned with work. Indeed, as we have seen, the trend toward retirement earlier than at age 65 had been going on for many years, and it did not change noticeably after mandatory retirement was outlawed.

- All of this moved a graduate student of mine to ask, almost angrily: What's wrong with American retirement policy anyhow? It allows people to work 'til they drop and simultaneously encourages them to retire early. Is American public policy in this regard schizophrenic? No. The answer, of course, is that there is a simple common denominator to these seemingly conflicting policies, and that denominator is the option of *choice*. American law gives people the choice to retire early if they want to and have the financial means to facilitate not working. And people have the legal right to not be forcibly retired due to their age, to work as long as their energy, desire, skills, and productivity allow. Of course, the execution of either of these choices, early retirement or later-life retirement, is dependent on many factors that may be outside the control of the individual worker. The basic idea is that as a starting point for the Wealth Span planning, it's a matter of choice and planning, and not a matter of age.

- The consequences of all this choice are seen in an interesting pattern of age, work, and retirement at the beginning of the twenty-first century. In recognition of the fact that work versus retirement is a false dichotomy these days, NCOA's *American Perceptions of Aging in the 21st Century* departed from usual polling practice and asked respondents of all ages *a pair of questions* rather than the usual "Are you working full-time, part-time, or retired?" Early in the questionnaire, we asked "Do you consider yourself to be retired or not? (yes/no)?" A later question asked respondents if they worked, full-time or part-time. Combining responses to the two questions (no rocket science here) yields a three subgroup classification: (1) not retired at all, (2) retired *and* working, and (3) completely retired. Cross-tabulation of the three subgroups by age shows the pattern of how Americans are currently implementing a retirement policy characterized by choice.

Age	Not Retired	Retired and Working	Completely Retired
25–34	100%	0	0
35–53	95%	4	1
54–64	66%	14	20
65–75	21%	25	54

- Hardly any Boomers (35–53) or younger Gen-X'ers are retired, of course. The more notable numbers are that barely half (54%) of the traditionally defined retiree age group (65 to 75) are completely retired, with 21% not retired at all. Equally fascinating are the middle-agers, usually-labeled *pre-retiree.* Only two-thirds of us are not retired, with a fifth already completely retired. Choice. And informed Wealth Span planning!

CHAPTER 6

Wealth Span Changes II: The Increased Complexity of the Accumulation Stage

As Chapter 5 demonstrated, over the past century there has been a significant reduction in the number of years in the Accumulation Stage at the same time that the Expenditure Stage has gotten longer. Collectively, these changes signal the need for an accelerated pace of Wealth Span planning and financial activity. The bottom line of the Changing Balance story is clear: Individuals and families have a shorter period of time to accumulate wealth. Financial resources now have to last for a longer Expenditure Stage.

Thus, the Wealth Span activities that are planned and carried out in the Accumulation Stage loom more critical and more demanding. In this regard, therefore, an even more significant Wealth Span change is the increasing *complexity* of the Accumulation Stage. That is, even if the Accumulation Stage were not getting shorter, the greater financial and family complexities of this stage suggest the critical importance of carefully designed and carried out Wealth Span strategies. As the following discussion also indicates, this increasing complexity is especially challenging for middle-agers—those clients who are or should be involved in their most active Wealth Span accumulation activities.

Of course, hundreds of bits of modern society have arisen over the last few decades to make everyday life ever more complicated. The concern here, however, is with two sets of life-orienting financial and social factors that together greatly add to the complexity of the Accumulation Stage. The first set of factors is directly financial. Larger numbers of middle-aged and older Americans have a more diverse profile of retirement income sources and opportunities than in the past. Managing the portfolio at the present time plus planning for growth, conservation, and expenditure in the future represents substantially more complexity than in the past.

Added to this diversity of retirement income sources is an even bigger complexity: the fundamental transformation of the American pension system from traditional gold watch defined benefit pensions to defined contribution plans for which the employee is personally responsible.

The second set of factors focuses on the family. Throughout this book is a subtheme that *financial decisions are family decisions.* A significant component of the greater complexity of the Accumulation Stage has already been discussed: the increasingly likelihood that middle-agers at the peak of their Accumulation Stage will have responsibility for aged parents.

There is, however, a different area of emerging family-based financial complexity that directly affects the Accumulation Stage of the Wealth Span: the DIPPIES. There's a good chance (as Table 6.3 documents) that many of your clients are DIPPIES: two-earner households with **D**ouble **I**ncome (now) and **P**lural **P**ensions (in the future). We conclude this chapter with their story.

Complexity 1: The Trend Toward Multiple Sources of Income

Preparation for retirement was much simpler when there was only one or two likely sources of retirement income. Even today, Social Security remains the largest single source for most people in the bottom 60% (poorest three quintiles) of the American income distribution. The point is not that some people have a large primary source of retirement income, but that so many people have *multiple sources.*

A key proposition of this chapter, and throughout the book, is that complexity of income does not necessarily mean a lot of income. When we show that the income profiles of American middle-agers and elderly are becoming more complex, in no way is this meant to say that these people are rich! Rather, it is meant to indicate the increasing complexity of the Accumulation Stage, which adds new and more demanding personal and professional responsibilities to the processes of Wealth Span planning.

Income Diversity of Older People

Table 6.1 documents a 20-year increase in the diversity of income sources of people 65 and older. These U.S. Census Bureau data, arrayed by income quintiles from low to high, show the percentage of each group that gets at least some of their income from pensions, from assets, and income from wages or salary. From 1974 to 1994, each income group had an increase in the percentage of people who receive at least some pension income and at least some income from assets.

Not surprisingly, comparatively few of the least wealthy older people receive much pension income. Only 33% of the middle quintile receives some

TABLE 6.1 The Increasing Income Diversity of Persons Age 65+ 1974 to 1994*

		1974	**1994**
Pension income	1	2	5
	2	5	12
	3	15	33
	4	40	59
	5	51	66
Asset income	1	17	49
	2	23	52
	3	42	68
	4	63	83
	5	82	92
Income from wages/salary	1	9	5
	2	9	5
	3	14	10
	4	26	21
	5	48	36

* Arranged from low (1) to high (5) income level. Numbers are the percentages of each income group that had at least some income from the source indicated. Numbers not intended to add to 100%.

Source: U.S. Census Bureau Current Population Survey data tabulated and reported by the Employee Benefit Research Institute, *EBRI Databook,* 4th ed., Table 7.5.

pension income in 1994. Since pension participation and coverage in general for this generation of older people is fairly low, the overall pattern appears to reflect a combination of generational–historical pension dynamics, magnified by socioeconomic differences. Tomorrow's 65 year olds (i.e., today's middle-agers) will have greater pension coverage.

The more important point, however, is the *increase* in the number of people who receive pension income regardless of income level. In each of the five income levels, the percentage of people receiving pension income increased from 1974 to 1994. For example, the percentage of middle-income older persons (the third quintile) receiving at least some of their income from pensions more than doubled from 1974 to 1994 (from 15% to 33%). The amount of pension income received is not shown in Table 6.1. Rather, the dominant pattern is that of an increasing number of people at all income levels who are adding at least some pension income to their profile of retirement income resources.

If the pension income distribution is interesting, then the increasingly widespread distribution of asset income is dramatic. For 1974, each income group shows that a substantial number of older persons received some of their income from assets. It is the change from 1974 to 1994, however, that documents the increasing financial complexity of the Accumulation Stage. All five of the income groups show a substantial increase in the number of older persons receiving some income from assets. For the lower two income groups the increase is more than double. The other income groups show equally substantial changes. More than two-thirds (68%) of middle-income older persons receive at least some of their income from assets in 1994.

A significant component of the change from 1974 to 1994 is generational. Over the 20-year period, a new cohort of consumers has aged into the 65+ age group. This newer generation of older persons is less dependent on income from wages and salary, as Table 6.1 also shows, and is more likely to have income from assets. This reflects both the changes in public policy that encourage retirement savings and the advice these people received and the planning they did in response to these new opportunities during their younger Accumulation Stage years.

Again, the bottom line is one of complexity, not riches. The numbers in the table say only that these people received some of their income from the various sources, not that they received a lot of money. Yet even among the less wealthy income groups, substantial numbers of people receive income from pensions and income from assets—and these numbers are increasing substantially.

The Retirement Income Diversity of Nonold People

Table 6.1 offers one view of the increasing complexity of the Accumulation Stage: the perspective of people already 65 years old, across a 20-year period. An additional view of the future is to compare the current versus the anticipated future retirement income sources of younger, middle-aged, and older people. The National Council on the Aging's (NCOA's) *American Perceptions of Aging in the 21st Century* study (APA21) did just that, and the results are shown in Table 6.2. People who were not retired were asked to identify what they anticipate will be the biggest source of their future retirement income; retired persons were asked to name their biggest income source. The categories were: (1) employer-provided pension, (2) personal 401(k)-type pension, (3) Social Security, and (4) other personal savings and investments.

Table 6.2 shows how four age groups answered the question: younger adults in the very early years of their Accumulation Stage, Boomers, traditionally defined middle-aged pre-retirees, and people of traditional retirement age. The first two columns represent defined benefit versus defined contribution pensions (the national trends for which are shown in the next section). The results show a clear pattern of generational change in the kind of future retirement income that is anticipated. Consider first the age 54 to 64 pre-retirees. They are *split evenly* between defined benefit and defined contribution pensions. Forty-one percent of the 65 to 75 age group named Social Security as their biggest source; among others in this age group, twice as many identified a defined benefit employer pension (27%) as their biggest income source compared to defined contribution pensions (13%). This generational trend is further confirmed by the Boomers, who named defined contribution pensions

TABLE 6.2 Biggest Source of Retirement Income

Age	Employer-Provided Pension %	Personal 401(k)-Type Pension %	Social Security %	Other Personal Savings %
25–34	16	49	9	26
35–53	21	47	13	19
54–64	30	31	21	19
65–74	27	13	41	18

Source: APA21 national survey (2000).

(47%) as their anticipated biggest source by a two-to-one margin over defined benefit pensions (21%).

The pattern is further verified by adding employer pensions and Social Security together (both defined benefit programs) and adding personal pensions and other personal savings (both defined contribution type investments). Again, the 54 to 64 age group shows a 50-50 split, the older age group has a 2:1 ratio of defined benefit pensions, and the Boomers show a 2:1 ratio of defined contribution pensions.

Overall, the trend is clear. As retirement income sources change in the direction of defined contribution pensions, the Accumulation Stage of the Wealth Span becomes much more complex. While the data in Table 6.2 are taken from a single point in time (the year 2000), the age patterns are consistent with a generational view of the trend toward defined contribution pensions. These patterns illustrate the most important factor in the increasing complexity of the Accumulation Stage: the transformation of the American pension system.

Complexity 2: From Defined Benefit to Defined Contribution Pensions

There is probably no greater impact on the changing nature of the Wealth Span than the transformation of the American pension system from defined benefit to defined contribution pensions. The reasons for the transformation are many, including corporate preferences, federal tax complexities, changes in the age and educational level of the workforce, and changing preferences on the part of employees in the kind of compensation they prefer. While the history and economics of these developments are beyond the scope of this book, the implications of the transformation are directly relevant to the Wealth Span in general, and to the increasing complexity of the Accumulation Stage in particular.

Investment Responsibility for Future Pension Value

When all is said and done, from the perspective of the employee whose compensation includes a future retirement income benefit, the primary distinction boils down to a simple answer to a simple question: *Who is responsible for the future value of my pension?*

- Defined benefit pension: → They are responsible.
- Defined contribution plan: → I am responsible.

Aside from questions of the dollar level and financial adequacy of traditional defined benefit pensions, a worker could be reasonably assured that the union, the company, or the pension plan would have enough money to pay the promised defined-in-advance monthly pension. Although nothing in financial contracts is ever guaranteed absolutely, the political system saw the implied and contractual guarantees of traditional pensions to be so important that the Employee Retirement Income Security Act (ERISA) of 1974 established a federally administered insurance company to pay retired workers at least some of their guaranteed pension benefits in case the employer or the pension plan failed financially. During the Accumulation Stage the employee's pension-related responsibilities are minimal. Who is responsible for the future value of my pension? They are.

The number of American workers for whom "they are" responsible is declining, and the number for whom "I am responsible" is growing, as Figure 6.1 makes clear. During the period 1975 to 1990, the distribution of pension participants changed from a 75%–25% split in favor of traditional pensions to just about even. Since the majority of defined contribution plan recipients are relatively younger employees, one of the primary implications of the trend portrayed in Figure 6.1 is the increased complexity of middle-aged Accumulation Stage responsibilities for these maturing men and women.

Another way of describing the increased Accumulation Stage complexity is to note, as many retirement specialists do, that the shift in pension type is also

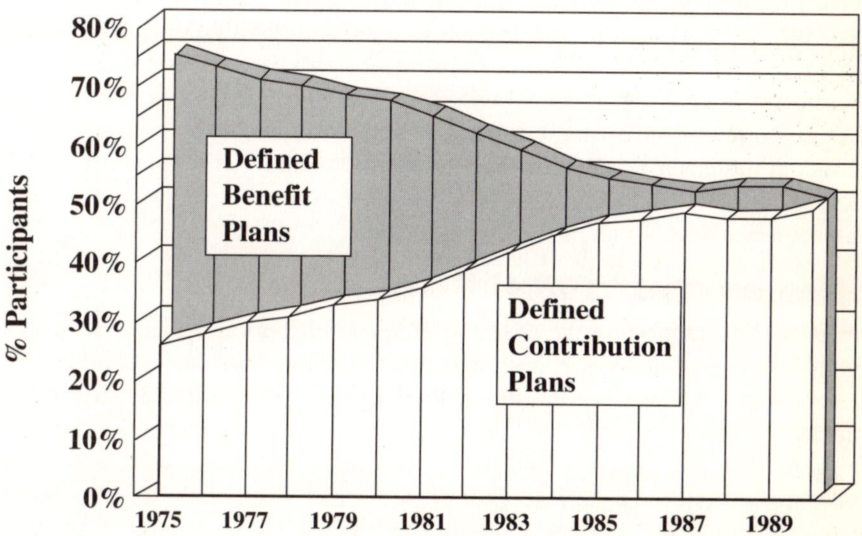

FIGURE 6.1 Participation in Defined Benefit versus Defined Contribution Plans, 1975–1990

a shift of financial risk, from the employer to the employee. In the defined contribution plan, the only element that is defined is the input to the pension account. One economist criticized these pensions as nothing more than savings accounts with some tax-deferral benefits. Of course, defined contribution plans could be just savings accounts, but in fact for virtually all participating workers they are much more—and much more complex.

Over the past dozen years or so, there has been a figurative explosion in the number and kind of mutual funds and other investment vehicles for investing defined contribution account funds. Consequently, the future output is dependent on a number of choices and decisions that the employee makes. To be sure, in many such plans the employer establishes or outsources a specified set of investment choices with a range of risk and return profiles. Ultimately, however, the employee makes the choices of where and how to allocate his or her defined input. The output many years later is then a function of knowledge, skill, advice, risk-taking propensity, and luck.

The federal Pension Benefit Guaranty Corporation, which insures most defined benefit pensions, provides no such insurance for defined contribution plans. If by way of good professional advice, skill, intuition, or luck an employee had invested her 1991 \$2,000 and 1992 \$2,000 defined contribution individual retirement account (IRA) limit in shares of Microsoft, she has relatively few retirement income worries. If instead she put most of those dollars into KayPro Computers, her financial security is on less solid ground. Being personally responsible for the future value of defined contribution pension dollars adds a substantial complexity to Accumulation Stage responsibilities. Even investors who rely heavily on the services and advice of a professional investment counselor need to monitor the investments, returns, and alternative allocations. For most consumers the question and the answer remains: Who is responsible for the future value of my defined contribution pension? I am.

Additional, Noninvestment Complexities

Most of the attention on the shift to defined contribution pensions focuses on input investment decisions, and how they are monitored and calibrated over the account holder's working life. From the perspective of the increasing complexity of the Accumulation Stage, however, defined contribution pensions bring with them a series of additional responsibilities, many of which are not present for traditional defined benefit pensions. Most of these decisions involve technical tax and legal issues, which add to the responsibilities and complexities of middle-age financial life in the Accumulation Stage. And, because of their technical nature, we offer the following as a checklist with little additional commentary.

- Because defined contribution accounts typically offer immediate ownership and vesting, the account holder usually has the right and sometimes the obligation of moving—rolling over—the account when he changes employers. The decision to roll over funds to a new employer's system versus into a personally directed IRA, as well as the amount of time between withdrawal and redeposit, involve both tax and investment understanding.
- In many situations the job-changing employee has the option of not rolling over the money, but taking it as a lump-sum withdrawal, with consequent tax penalties. There may be a need and good use for such withdrawal, but employees, especially younger heads of families who are choosing between an important current expenditure and future retirement security, need to be able to calculate the social and the financial costs of the transaction. In terms of opportunity costs, the 30 year old who withdraws and doesn't reinvest a lump sum of even a few thousand dollars is giving up 30 to 40 years of the compounded growth of those dollars.
- Part of all good Wealth Span activity is estate planning, which involves, both federal and state tax laws which are, it seems, in a constant state of flux. In this regard, defined benefit and defined contribution assets can be treated differently with respect to both estate tax and income tax obligations of the beneficiary.
- The bottom line: financial literacy. When the consumer takes on the risk to be responsible for the future value of his pension, the focus is on financial literacy. Whether the investor decides on which stocks and funds to purchase or only selects from among a relatively small number of packages and funds organized by the employer, at base is the worker's financial literacy. Financial literacy is not just information, but information combined with understanding of process that makes an individual confident in making financial decisions. For example, in our national Financial Literacy survey done in conjunction with the University of Pennsylvania's Boettner Institute of Financial Gerontology, we found that while 67% correctly know what a mutual fund is, only 32.1% said they felt confident that they knew enough to make a good decision about purchasing shares of a mutual fund. Interestingly, this distinction between information and confidence held up for respondents of both high and low formal education, and higher and lower income levels.

Complexity 3: Increasing Family-Connected Complexity

Financial Decisions Are Family Decisions

As discussed in Chapter 4, the demographics of longevity have had a profound impact on the age structure of the American family. In turn, these changes are creating substantial new complexities for the Accumulation Stage of the Wealth Span. The fact that 80% of 50 year olds and 44% of 60 year olds—men and women who are in the thick of their own Accumulation Stage responsibilities—have living elderly parents adds substantial complexity to their lives. To be sure, many 80- and 90-year-old parents are social and financial assets to their children and grandchildren, and we are not suggesting that all elderly parents are a burden. But this new complexity added to an already complex Accumulation Stage is clearly in evidence.

Is Your Client a DIPPIE?

Sociologists as well as economists often refer to the family as an *economic unit.* The U.S. Census and other official collections of social and economic indicators regularly collect, analyze, and publish their numbers both for individuals and for family units. Professional advisors as well as the general public all recognize that many financial choices, rules, and procedures—from tax tables to welfare program eligibility—are officially affected by family status and family size.

Among all the connections between finance and family, one of the most dramatic changes has been the increasing number of dual-earner households. Journalists sometimes refer to the traditional "Ozzie and Harriet" family: He works while she stays home to take care of the house, two kids, the dog, and the white picket fence. Such pop imagery is never perfectly accurate, but the United States continues to experience decline in the traditional husband-only-earner family and growth of dual-income households.

Enter the *DIPPIES.* Dual-earner households these days are not just earning two current incomes. From the perspective of the Accumulation Stage of the Wealth Span, and looking ahead to the Expenditure Stage, husband and wife are earning both current income and accumulating wealth for later-life (retirement) expenditure. Thus, while they are working, these are *D*ouble *I*ncome households. Simultaneously, however, she and he are earning plural or multiple kinds of retirement-focused wealth, or more simply: *P*lural *P*ensions.

The DIPPIES acronym was coined a decade ago by my colleague Professor Richard Rose, Director of the Institute of Public Policy at the University of Strathclyde in Glasgow, Scotland. DIPPIES is a purposely offbeat phrase intended to draw attention to a quite serious financial-behavioral profile. The complexity of several current investment and tax issues affected by the spouses' dual incomes can be magnified by their several future-oriented savings, investment, tax, and retirement pension responsibilities.

It should be emphasized that the DIPPIES concept is intended to focus on a situation of *financial complexity* and not a situation of great riches simply because the household has two earners. The first time I presented the DIPPIES idea in a public lecture was in a large, dimly lit hall to an audience of 50-somethings as part of a community pre-retirement program. My introductory comments about the increasing number of dual-earner families were intended only to set the stage for the central issue: the increasingly complex financial situation facing many middle-aging families.

Midway through my colorful introductory slides, the easy going professorial tranquility of the evening was shattered by a loud, anonymous shout from the back of the dark room: "Yeah, big deal! That's because it takes two incomes these days just to make ends meet!"

Very true. And so it is important to emphasize that the point of the DIPPIES concept is financial complexity—a complexity that does not automatically produce great wealth. Some, perhaps many, DIPPIES families do accumulate substantial wealth as a result of having two incomes over a successful Accumulation Stage. But while being rich is not a necessary characteristic of DIPPIES, financial complexity is.

In addition to having two current incomes, double income plural pension couples are also likely to have a financial profile that includes:

- Two Social Securities
- Two employer pensions
- One or two additional IRAs
- Home equity

And possibly:

- General, nonretirement investments
- Cash-value life insurance
- Savings bonds
- Annuities

Any combination of these plural pension resources suggests a complexity greater than the traditional single-earner household of days gone by. Having two employer pensions itself can add substantial complexity to the range of available current choices and decision making about future tax and withdrawal strategies. Of even greater concern, if *either or both* of the employer pensions is a defined contribution pension, there are likely to be even further complexities of investment choice and financial literacy.

How many DIPPIES are there in today's population? Table 6.3 is based on the 45.1 million married couples in the United States in which at least one spouse was in the labor force in 1998. In 30.6 million of these couples (68%), both husband and wife were in the labor force, (i.e., double-income households). Given recent historical and generational trends in the economy and in female labor force participation, it is not surprising that Boomers (73%) and younger families (71%) have a higher percentage of DIPPIES than do middle-agers and today's pre-retirees in their late fifties (61%) and early sixties (47%). (*Note:* The age for a married couple in the table is the age of the *householder,* the primary earner, as reported by the family member who responded to the U.S. Census Bureau questionnaire.)

Single-Parent Households

The DIPPIES phenomenon is not the only significant trend in the American family structure that points to new profiles of Accumulation Stage complexity and the need for more attentive Wealth Span planning. Alongside the middle-aging of the Baby Boom and the increasing percentage of dual-income married couples is an increasing number of single-parent families. The 2000 U.S.

TABLE 6.3 Age Distribution of American DIPPIES

Percentage of all U.S. married couples in which husband, wife, or both work (1998)

Age	Husband Only	Wife Only	Both [DIPPIES]
20–34	27%	2	71
35–54	23%	4	73
55–59	28%	11	61
60–64	28%	25	47
TOTAL*	26%	7	68

*Based on 45 million couples in the labor force.

Source: U.S. Bureau of the Census, Current Population Survey, March 1998.

Census documents that the number of single-parent families, and especially single-mother families, has continued to rise over the past three decades.

Most of the plural pension complexity that characterizes the DIPPIES will be felt by single-parent families. Social Security, employer pension, nonretirement savings and investment, life insurance, and home equity are all part of a future that has to be planned for in the present. To these future-oriented Accumulation Stage planning complexities, many single-parent families are also working with the current issues of alimony, child support, and a multiplicity of nonfinancial aspects of divorce and remarriage.

CHAPTER 7

The Financial Psychology of Middle Age—The Multiple Meanings of Middle

Although "When does middle age start?" and "Are you middle-aged?" seem to be reasonably straightforward questions, there are few straightforward answers. There are, for example, no standard legal or cultural chronological ages that define middle age, as age 18 or 21 do for becoming an adult, or age 65 does for old age. While precise definition is difficult—for the citizen and for the professional—the importance of middle age from a financial perspective is undeniable.

It is in the middle-age years of the Wealth Span that many, if not most, people really begin to recognize the importance of preparing for their later years. Many people may have given some thought to financial planning in their younger years, maybe because of pension plan choices to make and documents to sign at a new job. But the more demanding tasks of envisioning later life in a serious personal and financial context come somewhere in the period we call *middle age.*

In their outstanding textbook *Adult Development and Aging,* eminent Pennsylvania State University psychologists Warner Schaie and Sherry Willis suggest that it's good to use fairly broad definitions. They suggest that middle age begins somewhere around 35 to 40 and ends somewhere around 60 to 65. The imprecision of "somewhere around" is given on purpose because chronological ages are only crude indicators of more complex social and psychological circumstances and conditions—all of which eventually have important Wealth Span implications.

For example, some people in their late thirties are already well into the concerns and planning that are usually associated with middle age, while others of the same chronological age are still involved in such traditional tasks of younger adulthood as graduate school and family formation. Under current pension rules, some people are moving into older age as they begin individual retirement account (IRA) withdrawals age 59½, while others are starting new jobs or careers at age 55.

When Does Middle Age Start?

Chapter 1 looked at how the general public answers the question "When Does Old Age Begin?" based on the results of the National Council on the Aging's (NCOA's) national study of *American Perceptions of Aging in the 21st Century.* In line with traditional, cultural definitions, the responses were in the range of 60 to 65. As it turns out, public perceptions of the start of old age vary according to the age and gender of the perceiver.

The same national survey asked parallel questions about middle age. "At what age do you think 'middle age' begins?" would seem an appropriate way to ask the question. As usual, the question and the issue are not as simple as they first may appear. Because of social, cultural, and biological differences between men and women, the survey asked a pair of questions:

1. At what age do you think the *average man* becomes middle-aged?
2. At what age do you think the *average woman* becomes middle-aged?

ANOTHER STORY

ALERT—STOP READING—ALERT

- Before reading any further, take out a piece of paper and quickly jot down your own answers to the preceding questions about middle age.

- Also write down how you think your spouse or significant other would answer them.
- How do you think your parents would answer them?

By and large, middle age in America these days is perceived to begin at about age 45. That is, the average of all people polled (total sample, men and women of all ages) sets the start of middle age for both men and women at 45. There are, however, some interesting patterns in these public responses, some expected and some unexpected. Table 7.1 gives the full pattern of responses. The numbers are the median starting age for each of the respondent age groups listed.

The not-so-surprising result is that the older you are, the later in life you perceive middle age to begin. Boomers (age 35 to 53 at the time of this survey) define the beginning of middle age at 45. People in their fifties and early sixties said 50, as do those in the traditionally defined old age group of age 65+. (By contrast, adults under age 25 percieve middle age as starting around age 40!)

What is perhaps more unexpected is that there is no large difference as to when men and women are perceived to begin middle age. That is, no matter what the respondent's age is, the average man and the average woman are perceived to start middle age at just about exactly the same age. The average Boomer, for example, sees both men and women entering middle age at age 45.3. We asked the two questions separately because—considering such recent cultural patterns as early retirement among men, more open discussion of menopause, and public analysis of midlife crisis—we thought public perceptions of male aging and female aging would be different. Not so.

The difference between men and women comes through loud and clear in terms of how they perceive the beginning of middle age. Simply put, no matter how old they are, female respondents define the start of male middle age and female middle age as coming later than male respondents do. The gender differences are shown in the bottom half of the table. There is no difference between the sexes regarding when male middle age begins compared to when female middle age begins. That is, reading the numbers horizontally, there is literally no difference between the beginning of male and female middle age.

Looked at vertically, however, for each of the age groups there is a consistent difference in how men and women define the beginning of middle age. For the public as a whole there is an almost five-year difference: Men see middle age as starting at age 45 and women see middle age as starting at age 50.

TABLE 7.1 At What Age Do You Think That the Average Man and the Average Woman Become Middle-Aged?

[Numbers are each group's median response]

	Average Man	Average Woman
Total Sample	45.2	45.2
18–24	39.5	39.6
35–53	45.3	45.3
54–64	50.3	50.3
65+	50.8	54.7
Total Sample M	44.8	44.8
F	49.5	49.6
	+4.7*	+4.8*
35–53 M	44.9	44.9
F	49.7	49.7
	+4.8	+4.8
54–64 M	49.6	49.5
F	50.6	50.7
	+1.0	+1.2
65+ M	50.3	50.4
F	54.8	55.5
	+4.5	+5.1

* Number of years later in life that women compared to men define as the beginning of middle age.

This male–female difference is noticeably smaller among respondents age 55 to 64, but the pattern is still there. Female Boomers and women age 65+ all see middle age as starting four to five years *later* than do men.

There are, no doubt, multiple factors that might explain why women define the onset of middle age as coming later than men do. Maybe it's helpful also to restate the conclusion from the opposite side of the data: There are multiple factors to help explain why men define the onset of middle age as coming earlier in life. As retirement has come earlier, men may have come to perceive the end of youth and the beginning of midlife as arriving earlier. On the other side of the pattern, the more public discussion nowadays of working women, later childbearing, and menopause may have established a cultural view of a later start of middle age for women.

These data describe general societal patterns of middle aging. That is, the responses describe perceptions of when the average man and the average woman enter middle age. From the perspective of Wealth Span activities, knowing a client's chronological age alongside knowing how he or she perceives the start of middle aging in modern society offers an additional tool to understanding the client's willingness to work with alternative Accumulation Stage strategies. Toward this end, the rest of this chapter reviews the several causes of middle age as well as the important idea that middle age is a very modern invention. As yet a further tool in understanding how clients perceive middle age, we conclude the chapter with public responses to the more personal age question: What about you, yourself? Do you think of yourself as young, middle-aged, or old?

Middle Age as a Modern Invention

As Schaie and Willis suggest, "The difficulty in defining and discussing middle age is partly due to the fact that middle age is a Twentieth-Century development in the human life cycle." Applying their comment to the human Wealth Span and financial planning, there are three sets of interconnected developments—biological–demographic, financial, and social–cultural—that together contribute to this invention of middle age.

Longevity as a Cause of Middle Age

By expanding life expectancy over the past 100 years, biomedical improvements have created a middle set of years between the working years and the advanced years of old age. When life expectancy at birth was about 47 years, as it was in 1900, people more or less worked until they died, or until they couldn't work for reasons of strength and health. With life expectancy in 2000 now exceeding 75 years, there is chronological room for a number of years in the middle. Sometime after the traditional years of family formation and child raising and before leaving the labor force either partially or completely is a period of time to plan for a span of older years that has become the defining characteristic of modern longevity.

The psychology of financial behavior makes a direct contribution to the invention of a middle-age stage of the life cycle. As psychologists, Schaie and Willis appropriately note the personal, human developmental aspect of the new middle age. Not only do people now live longer, but middle age provides several years during which people develop an awareness of their extended aging and mortality.

For example, nowadays most adults will live longer than their grandparents, and they know it. And as part of this awareness of aging and mortality, the new middle age also brings an awareness of the biomedical and financial dependencies that might come with advanced old age. Watching one's parents get very old is an experience that your grandparents didn't have. Seeing the age–ADL (Activities of Daily Living) patterns in Table 2.2 could encourage more middle-agers to consider the role of long-term care insurance as part of their Wealth Span strategies. Alternatively asked, where on the *squaring of the mortality curve* (see Figure 8.1) are you likely to be? Understanding the several sources of this socio-cultural invention we call middle age offers insights into how to better educate and motivate middle-agers to engage in Wealth Span planning.

Pensions as a Cause of Middle Age

In a sense, the creation of pension plans in the early years of the twentieth century helped to invent middle age as a distinct life stage. In the early years the purpose of pensions was *not* primarily to provide a comfortable old-age income for retiring workers. Indeed, nowadays, pensions usually are seen as the financial mechanism by which an employee can retire from work and still live a comfortable financial existence, but back then, pensions were developed and used by employers to keep a good worker from leaving the job.

In those early days of the traditional defined benefit pension, the worker was promised a specified or *defined* amount of income per week or per month, typically based on level of wages and the number of years served on the job. From the employer's perspective, the key element was the vesting requirement, the minimum number of years the employee was required to work for a company before any pension would be paid. Vesting could take the employee as many as 25 or 30 years. If the employee worked fewer than the required minimum number of years, then he could lose all the earned, accumulated pension benefits. Back then, quitting or being fired just a few months before the 25-year vesting requirement could cause a complete loss of the pension. (Recall all those television shows in which the corrupt cop pleads with his partner not to turn him because he has only seven months to go to get that pension.)

The fundamental workforce management principle was simple: The more attractive the pension the more power the employer held to retain the employee. Over the years, through the Employee Retirement Income Security

Act (ERISA) and other pension legislation, collective bargaining, and court decisions, the world of pensions and pension rights has changed substantially. Minimum vesting is now closer to five years, and some pension plans vest even more quickly. More to the point, the pension is perceived to be an employee benefit consisting of future wealth, rather than primarily as a management tool.

Through years of labor–management negotiations, and not a few strikes, pensions are now a major component of employee compensation. Like health insurance, pensions are no longer a fringe benefit. Early retirement options are found in many pension contracts. In some downsizing and mergers, sweetened early retirement pension incentives are sometimes offered to persuade employees to voluntarily retire earlier than they had planned. And so the pension has come full circle, from a management tool to encourage workers to stay with the company, to a management tool to encourage workers to leave early.

The more general consequence of the evolution of pensions has been the invention of middle age. We can paraphrase in financial terms the psychological insights offered by Dr. Schaie and Dr. Willis: Longer life expectancy in the context of the availability of an institutionalized pension system causes people to be concerned about, to anticipate, and to plan for their personal aging and mortality.

Empty Nest as a Cause of Middle Age

A further consequence of longevity that has clear financial implications is the empty nest phenomenon. When people lived to be about 50 or 60 years old, it was likely that in his older years the father was still working, and the youngest of the several children was still at home. The fact that parents now live long enough to see their children leave home creates a new component of the life cycle. Even as the young adults go out on their own, however, everyone fully recognizes that emotional and financial responsibilities to the children continue long after they physically leave the residential home.

From a Wealth Span perspective it is important to recognize the wide range of variation—social, psychological, and financial—in how families adjust and respond to these parent-child changes that are now called the *empty nest.* A substantial resource in this area is the prolific work of Dr. Vern Bengtson, a Professor of Sociology and Gerontology at the University of Southern California. His stature as the most knowledgeable researcher in the country in the area of aging and family intergenerational relations is rooted in a unique study that he has been guiding for three decades.

In the early 1970s, Bengtson began what was then called the "Three-

Generation Study." In order to assess directly how the social, personal, religious, financial, and political views of members of the same family affected the structure and solidarity of the family, Bengtson's team interviewed a child, a parent, and a grandparent from the same family, and did this for a representative sample of southern California families. Within the constraints of illness and death, the study has reinterviewed the *same* family members for over 30 years. Many of the children have become parents, the parents have become grandparents, and families have faced deaths and bereavement, as well as births. New three-generation family units have been added to the study, and the original sample is now a "Four-Generation Study."

In assessing the relationship of parenting to middle age, Bengtson notes that while some parents feel a sense of personal freedom when the children leave the nest, other parents may feel depressed and lonely. For some, empty nest symbolizes the closing of an important life chapter, while for others it is seen in terms of changing patterns in how parents and children negotiate the continuing relationships between them. Certainly, the circumstances of the child's leaving or not leaving affect the nature and quality of the empty next experience for the middle-aged parents. In periods of national economic downturn, for example, children may delay leaving the parental home or return to the nest after a trial flight. (In the 1960s and 1970s, this was sometimes referred as the *Baby Boomerang syndrome.*) Whatever the timing and direction of the children's residential mobility, empty nest is clearly a dynamic process that continues to redefine a new stage in the individual and family life cycle and thereby directly affects the Wealth Span.

The range of responses to the onset of empty nest also reflects the social–psychological complexity of every parent's multiple roles. To the degree a person receives substantial satisfaction from roles and activities outside the family, the feelings of loss suggested by empty nest may be muted. While the psychological evidence is incomplete, there is a more general conclusion that has direct relevance for financial planning: First, it is generally recognized that even as it changes, the parental role is a lifetime role. Second, whatever else it may become, the empty nest experience represents an emotional and substantial change—the equivalent of a *teachable moment* in the education field. In Wealth Span terms we should call this a *planning moment,* an occasion for middle-age reflection, contemplation of the rest of one's life, and the serious consideration of later life financial planning.

The Other Meaning of Middle

The old aging of one's parents is yet another cause of being in the middle. As mentioned earlier, a central Wealth Span principle is that financial decisions are family decisions. The discussion of Family Aging in Chapter 4 demonstrates how longevity is changing the age structure of the American family. In this way the historical changes seen in Table 4.1 point to yet another meaning of *middle.* We usually think of middle age in terms of being in the numerical middle of one's own life span (or thereabouts, even though the definition of the middle is illusive). In terms of family dynamics, however, middle-agers are also the generation in the middle, between their children and their parents.

As Eldon Weisheit was quoted as saying at the end of Chapter 4: "The majority of middle aged people now have more parents than they have children." The empty nest experience supports the idea that many middle-agers do not have children *at home* at the very time that responsibilities for their own elderly parents expand. Nonetheless, parenting remains a lifelong set of obligations of one kind or another, with financial responsibilities lasting longer than homework and PTA meetings. Indeed, even if they don't have children, middle-agers continue to be the generation in the middle for as long as their own parents are alive. And as Chapter 4 documents, nowadays compared to back then, this can stretch middle age into one's own seventh decade of life.

There are substantial implications for Wealth Span planning created by this additional dimension of middle age. Because we stay in the middle longer, there is a longer period of time for which Wealth Span planning must take into account the potential needs of both children and parents. That is, in these years when middle-agers are reflecting on their own aging and needs associated with that aging, the continuing needs of adult children and elderly parents are also part of the picture.

Financial Psychology and Midlife Crisis

Multiple Causes of the New Middle Age

We've mentioned four causes of this relatively new stage of the Wealth Span: (1) increased life expectancy, (2) pensions, (3) empty nest, and (4) elderly parents. It's worth emphasizing that although each of the four has some independent impact on the need for financial planning, the bigger story is that they are closely intertwined. Increasing longevity is certainly the biggest component of the story. Pensions were not invented as a response to increasing life expectancy and a longer period of old age, but their expansion since the first decades of the twentieth century certainly coincided with the financial needs of a longer life span.

The psychological impact of longevity and pensions has created middle age as a period in which people look ahead and become increasingly aware of their longevity, vitality, and mortality. The empty nest experience dramatically punctuates these feeling of middleness. One stage of their children's development is complete, and another is starting. Around the same time, the children's grandparents may show increasing need for social, medical, and financial assistance; or if not, certainly the anticipation of such geriatric needs begins to emerge. Both sets of family-based experiences become major stimuli to reflect back, look ahead, identify worries as well as confidences about the future, and to consider or reconsider a range of social, personal, and financial goals—all integral to the Accumulation Stage of the Wealth Span.

It was in 1965 that Elliot Jacques published "Death and the Midlife Crisis" in the *International Journal of Psychoanalysis,* describing how artists dealt with the recognition of their own mortality. Since then there has been debate about whether these changes are necessarily a crisis, or fairly standard characteristics of human development and transition. The more relevant lesson is that these changes and associated turmoil create what we could or should refer to as a Wealth Span planning moment—the financial analog to the teachable moment.

Middle Age as a Wealth Span Moment

Fortunately, this planning moment is measured in years, not in minutes. Because middle age represents an opportunity to start or to reenergize the process of financial planning, how can these multiple causes be brought together so that financial planners can build on middle age as a productive period of Wealth Span activity?

The key is that middle age should be seen in functional and behavioral terms, and not in terms of specific chronological ages. The public perceptions of middle age in Table 7.1 may be intriguing and offer some general guidance, but the functional dimensions or causes of middle age are more valuable. By using these multiple causes of middle age as tools, and seeing them as Wealth Span planning moments, financial planners can better identify the degree to which their clients are likely to request and use different financial services and products.

For example, the age within a couple's Wealth Span when the empty nest occurs reflects the chronological age at which they began their family formation. Thus, for some families empty nest can start as early as age 40, while in other families 60-year-old fathers are buying senior prom dresses for their daughters [Elizabeth, why does this example keep returning?]. As further illustrated in Chapter 4, how the parents of middle-agers timed the birth of their children is also important in the timing of middle-age responsibilities. The parents of a 50-year-old child could be 70 and the parents of a 60-year-old child could be 90 years old. The synchronicity of the empty nest and the needs of elderly parents will have a strong bearing not only on the psychological and sociological definition of *middle age,* but also on the shape of Wealth Span financial planning.

This flexibility in the functional, planning-oriented definition of middle age is further affected by accumulated pension assets and retirement opportunities. To the degree that middle age has traditionally been defined as the years between empty nest and retirement, then patterns of retirement and early retirement also affect when middle age arrives as a Wealth Span planning moment.

In turn, the timing of the retirement decision itself is partly influenced by the availability of retirement income. With defined contribution plans allowing withdrawals as early as age 59½ and Social Security offering de facto "normal retirement" for most workers at age 62, the planning activities inherent in middle age will arrive at an earlier age. However, as the official age of Social Security full retirement benefits rises from 65 to 67 (or older) and if the early retirement trend becomes reversed, middle age may become extended.

Are You Middle-Aged?

Given all these variations, it is not surprising that middle age has no single, clear chronological age definition. At the beginning of this chapter we saw how Americans of different chronological ages defined when the *average man* and *average woman* enter middle age. But those data described how respondents defined middle age for the average somebody else.

Given the range in the causes and meaning of *middle age,* as well as the differing financial implications of those meanings, try to understand how your clients might answer the question. Better yet, ask them—not abruptly, of course, but as part of a more general conversation that identifies how close they might be to a Wealth Span planning moment.

The NCOA's *American Perceptions of Aging in the 21st Century* survey asked, "Do you consider yourself to be young, middle age, or old?" in a national sample of all ages. Some of the results are included in Table 7.2. It is not surprising that chronological age (i.e., objective age) is strongly correlated with these subjective age responses. But since Table 7.1 displayed some interesting differences in how men and women define the beginning of middle age for the average man and average woman, Table 7.2 similarly arrays the subjec-

ANOTHER STORY

ALERT—STOP READING—ALERT

- Before reading any further, take out a piece of paper and quickly answer the following question for yourself: Do you consider yourself to be middle-aged?
- To be more empirically accurate, the full question is: DO YOU CONSIDER YOURSELF TO BE YOUNG, MIDDLE-AGED, OR OLD?
- How do you think your significant other would answer this question? What about your parents?
- Okay, continue reading.

TABLE 7.2 Do You Consider Yourself to Be. . . .

		Young	Middle-Aged	Old
18–34	Men	81%	18	1
	Women	86%	14	<1
35–44	Men	39%	59	2
	Women	48%	52	<1
45–53	Men	10%	84	6
	Women	18%	81	1
54–64	Men	3%	80	17
	Women	9%	77	14
65–74	Men	9%	38	53
	Women	9%	46	45
75+	Men	7%	26	68
	Women	6%	27	67

tive age responses for men and women within each chronological age. We end this discussion of middle age with four observations:

1. Most people who are in the 45 to 64 age range—those who most financial professionals would agree are middle-aged—do in fact identify themselves as middle-aged. The results of the survey are consistent with the long-term census trends shown in Figure 2.1.

2. The heterogeneity of the Baby Boom is once again validated. We know that 76 to 80 million Boomers, a population the size of Canada, are not all like each other. We still refer to *the* Boom, yet notice how the older first-born Boomers (age 45 to 53) differ from the latter-half Boomers (age 35 to 44) in terms of their subjective age. The older Boomers have a similar percentage of middle-agers to the 54 to 64 pre-retiree age group. The younger Boomers are truly in transition: Most say they are middle-aged, but a sizeable minority identify themselves as young. Many of these younger Boomers are just becoming involved with marriage, children, home ownership, and career start-up—all challenging Wealth Span issues.

3. The gender differences, as before, offer a fairly clear and intriguing pattern. Virtually without exception, for every age level, women are more likely to see themselves as young rather than middle-aged, or middle-aged rather than old. Among the younger Boomers (age 35 to 44), for example, 48% of the women identify themselves as young (compared to 39% of men), and only 52% say they are middle-aged (compared to 59% of men). The gender difference continues into older age: Among people age 65 to 74 years old, only 45% of women identify themselves as old (compared to 53% of men), while 46% of women themselves identify as middle-aged (compared to only 38% of the men of the same age). For Wealth Span professionals, the challenge is to use these public patterns and the clients' own response to the basic question as an educational and motivational tool in support of the planning process. For older age groups, identifying oneself as old rather than middle-aged may be a response to current or anticipated health problems or the presence or absence of grandchildren or great-grandchildren. For the older Boomers, it will be important to sort out continuing involvement with adult children versus their emerging worries about aging parents.

4. But let's not lose sight of the proverbial forest. For whatever reasons or combination of reasons, in twenty-first century America lots of people identify themselves as middle-aged. The core of personally defined

middle-agers is still a 20-year-long span, 45 to 64, in which between 77% and 84% identify themselves as middle-aged. But over half of people in their mid-thirties and over a third of men and women in their sixties to mid-seventies also consider themselves to be middle-aged. We have suggested throughout this chapter that the various causes and crises of middle age create occasions for Wealth Span planning moments. These numbers show that there are lots of them.

CHAPTER 8

Health and the Wealth Span

It goes without saying that there always have been important connections between health and wealth. Because of the twenty-first century dynamics of population aging and individual aging, however, these connections are becoming even more important for tomorrow's elderly. Consequently, before looking at the range of financial choices through which older individuals and families can finance their health care (Chapter 9) and long-term care (Chapter 11) during their Expenditure Stage, let's examine two important new connections between health and the Wealth Span:

1. The widespread distribution of old-age longevity throughout American society (i.e., the democratization of old age) is now accompanied by a parallel *democratization of good health.*

2. Greater longevity creates increasing potential for older men and women to stay healthier for a longer period of old age, often referred to as the *squaring of the mortality curve,* but the same circumstances also create the potential for a longer period of physical and mental decline and dependency.

Good Health and Longevity

As documented in Chapter 2, people are living longer nowadays than at any time in human history. Modern society is experiencing what Pulitzer Prize–winning psychiatrist and geriatrician Dr. Robert Butler calls the *democratization of old age.* Old age is no longer the unique province of royalty as it was in centuries past. The 2000 census documents that there are now 4.2 million men and women age 85 and older in the United States. This number was only 929,000 in 1960 and 2.2 million as recently as 1980, representing increases of 90% and 35%, respectively, compared to 2000. In the 2020s to 2040s, when Boomers are in their eighties, there will be 8 to 12 million octogenarians.

The story is more complex and more interesting than just the inevitable aging of the Boomer generation. People are not just living longer, they are living longer in the older stage of their lives. The probability that a young-old person would live to his or her older-old years has increased dramatically. As recently as 1940 (as detailed in Figure 2.2), the probability that a 65 year old would live to age 90 or older was only about 7%. By 2000, this had tripled to 28%. Furthermore, as the next several paragraphs will reveal, there is strong reason to expect that these older-old longevity trends will accelerate in the next few decades.

Why are these trends likely to accelerate in the coming years? Certainly, medical science has a lot to do with it. Discoveries of new cures for cancers, new pharmaceuticals, and new biochemical and genetic approaches to illness, as well as new transplant and bionic techniques, are all part of it. But a major part of the story is the social and personal context of health. Alongside medical science and the democratization of old age, there is also a *democratization of good health.* Today's younger generation, and therefore tomorrow's older men and women, have more comprehensive information and greater access to the tools and techniques of improving and maintaining health than was the case in years past.

Along with these new personal capacities—or perhaps *because* of them—there is a societal norm, an expectation, that we will be healthier and live longer than our parents and grandparents did. Nowhere are these societal changes in personal health seen more dramatically than in aging and gerontology. Where aging was once seen only in terms of decline and poor health, the societal images of aging are improving, although the public perception of old age is not improving as rapidly as is healthy old age itself.

For example, although there's only about a 25% chance that an older person will live in a nursing home, a recent national poll found that 63% of respondents of all ages agreed that more than half of all older people will spend some time in a nursing home before they die. As the data showing rates of needed Activities of Daily Living assistance (Table 2.2) indicated, it is only a minority of 13% of persons age 85 and older who need daily help in getting dressed.

Successful Aging Replaces Normal and Usual Aging

In 1987, a landmark article titled "Human Aging: Usual and Successful" was published in *Science* by Mount Sinai Hospital and Medical School President John Rowe (now the CEO of Aetna U.S. Healthcare) and gerontologist Robert Kahn, University of Michigan Professor of Psychology and Public Health. They argue that what has been typically perceived as usual aging (i.e., decline and frailty) is in fact not usual, not normal, and not necessary. The images of inevitable decline with old age, including the inability to improve one's health in old age, are all factually false perceptions and inappropriate stereotypes of old age. To the contrary, as their research persuasively demonstrates, the idea of successful aging includes some very easy-to-accomplish actions that provide effective responses to a broad range of changes, including health-related declines in later years.

The negative public perceptions and stereotypes of aging are what social scientists refer to as the *social construction of aging*. If professionals (including financial advisors), corporations, and public policy all embrace or act on a negative view of aging and old people, then middle-aged and older individuals themselves might buy into this socially constructed view of aging (rather than the scientifically more positive, optimistic view of the processes of aging). A critical message of Rowe and Kahn's article, therefore, is that older people do have the medical, the physiological, and the psychological capacity to maintain and improve health into the eighth, ninth, and even tenth decade of life. Certainly, Dr. Kenneth Manton's recently (2001) reported research summarized in Chapter 2 validates the message.

As Rowe and Kahn see it, the long-standing social construction of aging lags behind the documented science. In this sense, it is crucial for financial professionals to recognize the changing societal as well as biomedical realities of contemporary aging and old age. In the vocabulary of the Wealth Span, nowadays the Expenditure Stage is not only getting longer, but it potentially includes a larger number of healthier and more active years than in years past. At the same time, however, for some people this greater longevity can mean more older-old years in which health and capacities decline.

As a consequence, clients now moving into and through middle age need to be aware of and integrate knowledge about these changes into their forward planning. One critical implication is that where Wealth Span planning in the past may have focused primarily on pension income in old age, it must now pay more attention to issues of health and long-term care, health care costs, and appropriate health insurance.

Rowe and Kahn's concept of successful aging became the organizing framework for a decade-long series of studies conducted by a national team of scientists supported by the MacArthur Foundation. This multidisciplinary and interdisciplinary team examined the social as well as the medical aspects of transitions from middle age to older age. A revealing (and at times even startling) nontechnical introduction to and summary of the full set of MacArthur Aging Studies is presented in Rowe and Kahn's 1998 book *Successful Aging*. They introduce the book by debunking Six Myths of Aging. Collectively, the debunked Six Myths illustrate how the social construction of aging is being changed from one of inevitable frailty and decline (usual aging) to a reality of personal health knowledge, efficacy, and improved health status (successful aging).

Of more immediate value, the Six Myths offer a valuable tool to Wealth Span planners working with middle-aged and older clients. By discussing the debunked myths, the client can see (if he or she has not seen it already) that health can be maintained and improved in older age, and that frailty and dependence are not inevitable. The financial implications of this new social construction of old age include a greater concern for the capacity to pay for health care and long-term care, as discussed in Chapters 9 and 11.

ANOTHER STORY

The Six Myths of Aging, Debunked

John Rowe, MD, and Robert Kahn, PhD, organize much of *Successful Aging* around broad areas of public misinformation that they have boiled down into one-sentence myths. The following is a quick overview of the myths and the facts that debunk them.

Myth 1: To be old is to be sick. Most people over age 75 report little or no disability. Only about 5% of older people live in nursing homes, a number that has declined over the past two decades. In 1957, 55% of older people had no teeth; the number is about 20% today. There are 1.4 million fewer disabled older persons today than in 1982. As Table 2.2 notes, less than 25% of people age 85 and older need daily help bathing, the most common kind of the five primary functional disabilities affecting older-old people; only 13% need daily help getting dressed. Our research reported at the 2001 World Congress on Aging found that in 1974 26% of people age 75 and older responded that poor health was a very serious personal problem. When we asked the same question in 2000, the proportion had declined by half: 13% said it was a very serious problem.

Myth 2: You can't teach an old dog new tricks. Although the pace of learning is more restricted in old age, research clearly demonstrates that older people *can* learn new things. Research (summarized in *Successful Aging*) shows that strong mental function in old age is rooted in regular physical activity, a strong social support system, and the belief in one's ability to handle what life has to offer. As Rowe and Kahn note, "happily all three can be initiated or increased, even in late life." Since vision and hearing are part of learning, old-age deficits in these areas can look like inability to learn. Thus, controlled experiments document that older people can master learning tasks when given more time or more stimulating environments. Secretaries trained on manual typewriters make the transition to word processors. Institutions and professionals who teach older people, formally or informally, need to understand that differential learning conditions do not mean inability to learn new information and skills.

Myth 3: The horse is out of the barn. It is a myth that years of bad habits mean that change to good habits won't have a positive effect. It's simply *not* true that after many years of smoking (or drinking or lack of exercise or eating fatty foods) all the damage is done so there's no point in stopping. The risk of heart disease from smoking declines as soon as smoking stops: In 5 years an ex-smoker is not much more likely to have heart disease than a person who has never smoked. Much age-related risk of heart disease is due to overweight, not to age. High blood pressure responds to diet and exercise for many older persons; for others, blood pressure medicine is the appropriate response. Pumping iron (weight resistance exercise) can enhance bone mass, limiting the risk of osteoporosis in both men and women. Rowe and Kahn: "The horse may have been headed out of the barn, but some good rope tricks lured it back in."

Myth 4: The secret to successful aging is to choose your parents wisely. It is not true that heredity *controls* the rate of aging-related declines. A genetic predisposition is not genetic control. Genes do play a role in predisposition to certain diseases that certainly affect aging, for example, heart disease, certain cancers, high cholesterol. But the good news is that the probability that a genetic predisposition becomes a disease can be substantially influenced by lifestyle and environmental factors. According to the Twins Research done as part of the MacArthur

(continued)

Aging Research, the results are very clear: Only about 30% of physical aging and half of change in mental function can be blamed on the genes. Even better news: The impact of heredity *declines* with aging; for example, the likelihood of being fat or the rate of age-related decline in lung function are by and large not inherited. "How we live, and where we live, has the most profound impact on age-related changes in the function of many organs throughout the body."

Myth 5: The lights may be on, but the voltage is low. Advertisements and jokes in poor taste to the contrary, older men and women are not disinterested in sex. Although sexual activity can both decrease and change in older age, this is due less to lack of interest than to matters of health limitations or lack of partners. The biggest reason for lowered rates of sexual activity is widowhood. A recent National Council on the Aging study found that over 50% of men and women over age 60 who had partners were sexually active at least once a week. Attitudes toward sex and aging are in part generational in nature. Along with their better health, the sexual activity of elderly Baby Boomers will no doubt be significantly influenced by the sexual attitudes and context of their youth.

Myth 6: The elderly don't pull their own weight. This is as much a *political* myth as anything else. Not only is the line between work and retirement becoming more and more diffuse, but the assumption that all paid workers are productive and all people receiving a pension are a societal burden is clearly false. Many of the laws and rules regarding older age, pensions, and public programs come from a time when life expectancy was shorter and work was more physically demanding. Both conditions are changing faster than laws and rules. Indeed, our own analysis of this issue, recently published in the *Journal of Financial Service Professionals* (and summarized in Chapter 5), found that only half (54%) of the traditionally defined retirement age group (65 to 75) said they were completely retired; 25% said they were retired *and* working, and 21% said they were not retired at all.

Source: Parts of this summary were adapted from "Breaking Down the Myths of Aging," Chapter One in Rowe and Kahn's *Successful Aging* (1998).

Squaring the Curve

The Six Myths, and the substantial research that supports their debunking, should be reviewed in greater detail in *Successful Aging,* a book that should be at the top of the reading list for every Wealth Span professional who works with middle-aged and older clients. It is currently available in both a paperback and a large-print edition. Our main purpose in summarizing the Six Myths here is to emphasize that the expectations aging persons have for themselves should be optimistic. When the demographics of individual aging (i.e., longevity) are combined with the documented physical and psychological health facts and *interventions* described by Rowe and Kahn, the financial inference is that today's middle-agers can realistically anticipate a long and healthy older age.

Or maybe not! There is, alas, another important idea in health demography that throws a bit of cold water on the optimistic expectations of *Successful Aging.* In demography, the idea is known formally as the *compression of morbidity.* Informally, it is known more simply as the *squaring of the mortality curve.* The basic idea is that if we plot a person's health status (from good to bad) on a graph from birth to death, for most people we would expect to see a gradient from good health in the younger years to declining health in the older years (approximating a 45-degree line from the upper left to the lower right of the graph). But wouldn't it be great if we could stay very healthy throughout our life span, with all the aging-related illnesses and causes of death (i.e., morbidity) compressed into just a few years, or even a few days, at the end of life. Figure 8.1 portrays this set of age-health curves.

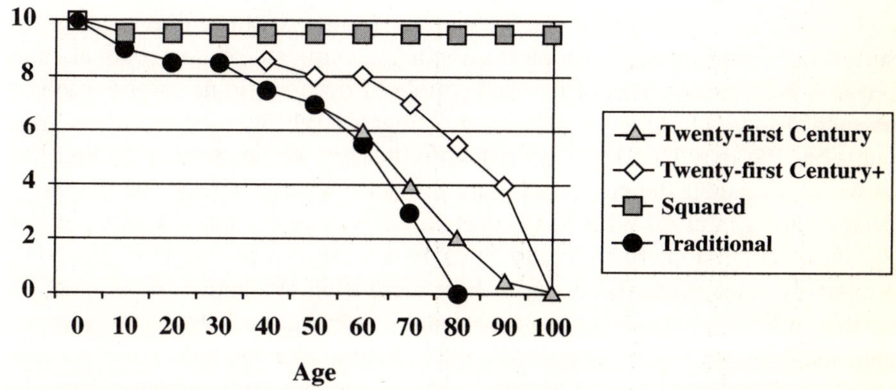

FIGURE 8.1 Compression of Morbidity, a.k.a. Squaring the Curve

Note that the curves in Figure 8.1 are hypothetical, intended only to illustrate the concept. That is, the data points in the figure are intended to be realistic, but are not drawn from any real life expectancy or morbidity data. The horizontal axis is age, from birth to death, 0 to 100. The vertical axis is health status measured on a hypothetical health scale from perfect 10 wonderful health to declining health and ultimately death (0).

Consider the traditional age–health curve. At birth and through the first decades of life health is at its peak, in the 8 to 10 range. Somewhere around age 30 to 50 some loss from perfect-peak health is seen, but health status is still around 7, and at about age 50 to 60 health begins to show some decline. From 60 to 80 health declines more rapidly, with death (in this hypothetical chart) at age 80.

Her Last Dollar, Her Last Ace

But what if health does not decline at all until the very, very end? Such a Health Span would look like the squared curve in Figure 8.1. For this hypothetical Health Span, health stays at its maximum throughout her lifetime, and then just as her 100th birthday arrives all systems fail. From a Wealth Span perspective, we could describe this person as someone who spends her last dollars to pay today's court fee, smashes her final ace, and collapses and dies immediately with no pain and a smile of victory. We all know of people whose health allows them to continue to work (and play) until late in life. The cliché is "he died with his boots on." In twenty-first century America, she dies with her Nikes on. The metaphor of the squaring of the curve is given by the fact that the health decline is not gradual, but precipitous, producing a squared corner at age 100.

The squared mortality curve is an attractive ideal and may be a reasonable goal: long life at maximum health without frailty, decline, illness, pain, or suffering. Unfortunately, all of the medical, surgical, pharmaceutical, and physiological discoveries of the past couple of decades do not assure each of us such a squared curve. A well-known slogan might well be rephrased as a question: We may be adding years to life, but are we necessarily adding life to years? Consider the curve in Figure 8.1 that we have labeled the "Twenty-First Century" curve. With life expectancy now longer than it was in earlier decades, our hypothetical Health Span is now shown to last until age 100. Unlike the squared mortality curve, here there is an elongation of the years of poor health. It is similar to the traditional curve, but stretched out over two additional decades of life beyond age 80. Decline and death do not come relatively soon at age 80 as in the traditional years, but are stretched across 20 years or so.

Finally, consider the curve labeled "Twenty-First Century+." Here health stays relatively robust until around age 60 to 70. There is some noticeable decline between 70 and 90, with a more precipitous drop from 90 to 100. This curve shows life lasting as long as in the squared and twenty-first century curves, but with a pattern of decline that falls between the two: not quite the full compression of illness into the last weeks or days of life, but not the more drawn-out two decades of declining health either.

Planning for the Squared Curve

It's important to keep in mind that Figure 8.1 is only a heuristic graph intended to illustrate the changes that could be emerging as a consequence of improvements in health care and the continued lengthening of life expectancy. Such hypothetical curves are simply a set of averages, each of which summarizes a range of evolving Health Span patterns that we can expect over the next several decades. We know people who remain healthy until the end, just as we also know individuals who live long but increasingly frail and dependent lives.

Clearly, the challenge to the health care industry—which includes both medical science on the one hand and health care providers on the other—is one of how society can pull the curve from the twenty-first century curve toward the squared curve (as illustrated by the twenty-first century+ curve). Adding years to life is certainly of diminished value if we have only added two decades of decline and dependency, frailty and pain, and expense.

Inherent in such a discussion is that this is an important challenge for the Wealth Span professional. As long as society has not reached the squared curve for most people, clients need to anticipate and plan for the costs of health care stretched over those additional years of life that may be accompanied by declining health. The adage "Hope for the best but plan for the worst" is as relevant here as in any area of planning.

Most clients have retirement income sources that are reasonably sufficient for everyday life, and sufficiency can be built into a well-calculated financial plan. Health care costs are a different story. If or when retirement income turns out to be insufficient either temporarily or permanently, some accommodations to Expenditure Stage behavior and new plans often can be made. A purchase can be delayed or canceled; an older couple or widow can move to less costly housing or move in with relatives.

For health care costs, by contrast, the options and behavioral adjustments are much more limited. As summarized in Chapter 9, Medicare provides virtually universal albeit limited health insurance coverage for older women and men. There can be substantial out-of-pocket health care costs even with Medicare. And the program's coverage does not start until age 65 even if retirement starts earlier. Unlike postponing a trip to see the grandchildren, putting off the purchase of a new television, or finding ways to lower the rent, unhealthy older people cannot simply decide to "put off being sick for a while. As a consequence of these dynamics, increased twenty-first century longevity means that health care emerges as an even more important component of Wealth Span planning and choices than it was in the past.

Security, Health, and the Five Legs of the Three-Legged Stool

Wealth Span planning is about financial security. Whether we use traditional language, *planning for retirement* or more simply *later life planning,* the goal is to work, accumulate, and plan for a secure financial future. The key word, of course, is *security.* Indeed, in one of the earliest discussions of the Wealth Span concept, Dr. Davis Gregg linked it both to security and to Rowe and Kahn's model of successful aging.

As noted above, Rowe and Kahn distinguish between normal aging and successful aging. The former, they argue, is the mistaken view that physical and mental decline, frailty, and dependence are all unavoidable normal aspects of aging. To the contrary, the MacArthur Aging Studies show unequivocally that these declines are not inevitable or normal. Rather, Rowe and Kahn focus on successful aging in which personal and lifestyle choices and behaviors maintain, and in many cases improve, mental and physical functioning in old age.

In describing the Wealth Span concept, Gregg noted the parallels between Rowe and Kahn's *mental and physical functioning* and *financial functioning* and behavior. The goals of Wealth Span planning, he said, are to "facilitate the maintenance of full financial function as nearly as possible to the end of our lives." But Gregg went a step further and extended the financial dimension of *full functioning* by adding the central importance of security:

> Fundamental to the development of sound research on the human Wealth Span is an understanding of the individual-level attitudes and behaviors underlying the concept. It can be argued that the need for security is fundamental and that economic security is a compelling goal for most persons.
>
> In the etymology of "security," the Latin *securus* means "without care," and is suggestive of broad human implications. Security can be thought of as peace of mind and freedom from uncertainty. Insecurity is characterized by feelings of doubt, anxiety, fear, and apprehension.

The traditional metaphor for retirement income security is that of the three-legged stool:

- Social Security
- Employer pensions
- Personal savings and investments

In recent years, many observers have added a fourth leg, that of income or wages from work. Changes in retirement patterns, elimination of mandatory retirement, and inflation in some years have brought many older persons back into the labor force, or influenced them not to leave at traditional retirement or early retirement ages. As noted with respect to Rowe and Kahn's Myth 6, almost half of people of traditional retirement age (65 to 75) are not fully retired. Some work because they want to, others because they have to. For all these reasons, it is now well established as a fourth leg of the stool.

- Income from work
- Health care costs

The data and discussion in this chapter, however, suggest that health care is the fifth leg of the three-legged stool. The first four legs are sources of income, and health care is an expenditure. But if the name of the stool is "Retirement Income *Security*," then to engage in Wealth Span planning aimed at a *secure* financial future means to understand attitudes and financial choices in the domain of health care. Since, as Gregg argued, security refers to peace of mind and freedom from uncertainty in contrast to anxiety, fear, and apprehension, then health care is a critical piece of the overall picture. The *security* in "retirement income security" comes from an evaluation of the accumulation of income sources (the first four legs of the stool) alongside a series of calculations of anticipated expenditures for health care.

Unfortunately, however, the magnitude and costs of future aging-related health care are not easily knowable. Consider the following five unknowns of health care and long-term care, questions that all middle-aged clients should ask and at least try to answer:

1. How long will I live?
2. Will I be healthy, or will my health decline . . . gradually?
3. What will health care and long-term care cost when I am elderly?
4. Will I be able to afford that care?
5. Will I be able to remain independent?

It is in large part due to our inability to answer these questions with much certainty that Wealth Span planning, in its attempt to increase peace of mind and decrease apprehension and anxiety, must be substantially involved with planning for the costs of health care and long-term care—the subjects of our next chapters.

CHAPTER 9

Health Insurance: Medicare and Medigap

There are probably no greater challenges for both client and practitioner in the art and science of financial counseling than navigating the connections between the Wealth Span and the future costs of health care. The world of health insurance is complex enough these days. In several ways, the emerging financial gerontological dynamics discussed in the previous chapters multiplies this complexity.

It is not only the case that old people are not all alike, but people become more dissimilar as they age. After all, people in their forties and fifties are (on average) generally working and reasonably healthy. But as people age into their seventies and eighties, both of these averages become less accurate. Some are working and some are not. As we saw in Chapter 5, recent trends show that many people in their sixties and seventies are *both* retired *and* working.

Retirement, Aging, and Getting Health Insurance

As to health, on the one hand we know that health begins to decline in older years, but here again averages are both misleading and historically changing.

Most older people are reasonably healthy, but a sizable minority begins to experience declines in functional capacity (Activities of Daily Living) and increasing illness, both acute and chronic.

On the other hand, we also know that people are on average living longer. It is not just the usually heralded life expectancy at birth that is dramatically increasing, but older-age longevity as well. The probability that a 60 year old will live to age 90 or beyond has doubled since John Kennedy was elected president. On the other hand, the squaring of the curve (see Figure 8.1) tells us that these added years are a period with a substantial range of good *and* poor health for the older people who will be living those longer lives.

On the other hand, the Six Debunked Myths of *Successful Aging* described by Drs. Rowe and Kahn tell us that poor and declining health are not normal aging and do not have to be usual aging. The doctors prescribe a range of diet and lifestyle interventions that can improve the health of older men and women well into their eighties and nineties. The medical demography research results recently reported by Professor Manton (in Chapter 2) tell us that Rowe and Kahn are right. The New England Centenarian Study suggests that longer life is both possible and feasible for an increasing number of us.

All of this makes planning for health insurance the complex issue that it has become. On the other hand, the existence of Medicare at first appears to simplify the connection between aging and the health insurance question somewhat. It would be nice if society had universal health insurance. This is not to take a political position as to who would pay for it or how it would be administered. But certainly the planning and decision processes would be simplified if we had some kind of universal health insurance.

Medicare Coverage and Noncoverage

Since 1965, older Americans have had something close to universal health insurance. Again, the political questions about how it should be paid for, who should be eligible or not eligible, and how it should be administered are not the issue here. From the perspective of Wealth Span planning, however, the presence of Medicare as a nationwide insurance system provides an important starting point. Making sure that your client understands the basic connections among health insurance, employment and early retirement, and Medicare eligibility is a critical first step that we explore in the first part of this chapter.

The second part of the chapter takes a brief look at Medicare. There are dozens upon dozens of books, manuals, guides, newsletters, and web sites about Medicare for consumers and for financial professionals. This chapter, of course, will not replace them. Rather, our targeted purpose is to identify the basic Medicare benefits and costs that define the context for the larger Wealth Span planning task of financing health care in older age.

The third section, a kind of addendum to Medicare, describes health insurance that is supplemental to Medicare, usually called *medigap* insurance. Such supplemental insurance can (1) reimburse the policyholder for many of the out-of-pocket costs that Medicare requires, and (2) pay for many of the medical services that Medicare does not cover at all. Because both Medicare and Medicaid are government-administered public health insurance programs, we purposely spell *medigap* with a lowercase *m* to emphasize that this is not a government-offered or -sponsored insurance.

Note that the purpose of this chapter is not to replace comprehensive or technically and financially specific sources of current costs and rules (the most complete and up-to-date of which is simply `www.medicare.gov`). Rather, the intent is to introduce key topics and point to resources that will be especially useful to financial professionals. Perhaps this introduction to these substantial topics is best characterized by a phrase that Texas-born Wharton-educated Davis Gregg was very fond of using: *This is a bird's-eye view, with the bird flying fast!*

Employment, Financial Literacy, and Health Insurance

Medicare Eligibility Versus Social Security Eligibility

Technically, the Medicare legislation of 1965 is an amendment to the Social Security Act of 1935. Both Medicare and Social Security are programs aimed at the well-being of the country's older population. As we all recognize, society's traditional cultural definition of "older" is the Social Security program's original age 65. Until the year 2000, when it began to rise, age 65 remained the age of full benefits for Social Security, even as the public's perceptions of when old age begins is changing.

So, for half a century or more, age 65 has been fairly well ingrained in the public mind as the sort-of-official definition of the beginning of old age. Yet most people, Jerry Beiderman included, know that you can retire as early as age 62 and still get your monthly Social Security check even if it is a bit reduced. In 1996, our *Financial Literacy 2000* project posed the early Social Security retirement issue to a national sample of adults (age 18+): Fact or Myth: If you are willing to receive a lower Social Security retirement check, Social Security allows you to retire as early as age 62. Over two-thirds of the American public correctly knew this to be a fact.

Another Story

Jerry Beiderman, 62, Early Retiring Chemist

Jerome Beiderman is a 62-year-old chemist who works for a midsized pharmaceutical research firm in New Brunswick, New Jersey. Ricky, age 54, his wife of 22 years, is a successful freelance photographer who sells her architectural renovation photo essays to several magazines and newspapers. Their daughter Tara, who is studying philosophy and drama, is in the middle of her sophomore year at Livingston College. Although he likes his job, Jerry recognizes that later this year he will become eligible for early Social Security retirement. He doesn't mind the reduction in his monthly Social Security check that he will incur by not waiting until age 65 plus 6 months. The few dollars will not make much of an overall difference because he will also start receiving his monthly defined benefit pension checks. The more important value is the idea of *being retired,* but still being healthy and productive. And having the time to play racquetball three times a week during the day will feel really good. Ricky's work is expanding, so Jerry plans to take on more of the production work in their basement darkroom. The company wants him to come in on a consulting basis at least a couple days a month, so really, whenever anyone asks him if he's retired or if he's working he can grin and say "BOTH!"

What is less clearly known within the public is the relationship between Medicare eligibility and early Social Security eligibility. Perhaps because retirement, Social Security, and Medicare have been seen for such a long time as a set of connected events and processes, a large portion of the public believes that when you become eligible to receive Social Security you are equally eligible for Medicare. In fact, Medicare eligibility is still linked to Social Security's original, traditional age 65, even as Social Security itself is available as early as age 62. To make matters even more confusing, as of this writing Medicare eligibility remains at 65 even as Social Security eligibility slowly rises to age 67 over the next two decades.

Financial Literacy 2000 asked: Fact or Myth: If you begin receiving Social Security benefits at age 62, you are eligible for Medicare benefits at the same time. Barely half (52%) the public correctly knew that this is a myth, al-

Another Story

**Social Security's Changing Retirement Age:
When Does *Your* Old Age Officially Begin?**

Even though most Americans do not wait until age 65 to retire (see Figure 5.2), the official Social Security full benefits retirement age is still important symbolically as well as financially. Because the rise from age 65 to age 67 is measured in monthly increments from 2003 to 2027, it hasn't always been clear when old age begins for people currently younger than 65.

So, here it is, officially: Your old age begins as follows, based on your year of birth:

Born	Old Age	Born	Old Age
1937 or earlier:	age 65	1955:	66 + 2 months
1938:	65 + 2 months	1956:	66 + 4 months
1939:	65 + 4 months	1957:	66 + 6 months
1940:	65 + 6 months	1958:	66 + 8 months
1941:	65 + 8 months	1959:	66 + 10 months
1942:	65 + 10 months	1960 and later:	67
1943–1954:	66		

The federal government now says that old age starts later in life. But that AARP envelope arrives in the mail on your 50th birthday. Go figure.

Check with `www.ssa.gov/retirechartred.htm` to get the latest changes and complete details.

though, fortunately, 72% of people age 55 to 64 answered correctly. So Jerry Beiderman, like most people who get their health insurance through their work, may become uninsured if he leaves work at age 62. (In some instances, retired or fired employees may have rights through the 1985 COBRA [Consolidated Omnibus Budget Reconciliation Act] legislation to individually purchase from or through their former employer the same basic health insurance they were receiving when employed, for as many as 18 months. The concern here, however, is the more direct linkage between retirement and Medicare eligibility.)

The magnitude of the employment connection is illustrated in Table 9.1. In 1995 64% of Americans under age 65 got their health insurance through their employer. Only 7% got their health insurance privately by buying it as individuals or through some other group, congregation, or affiliation. The importance of the workplace as the source of health insurance is seen even more clearly in the bottom section of the table. When uninsured persons and those who get their insurance through public programs such as Medicaid or civilians who get military or veteran-related health programs are deleted from the calculation, employers account for over 90% of health insurance.

Mr. Beiderman should do the insurance math before leaving his job. His Social Security age 62 early retirement benefit may be part of a reasonably comfortable income when added to his defined benefit monthly checks, along with his occasional consulting plus his wife's income. But he should do the health insurance math before making his final decision. Alternatively stated, when doing Wealth Span dollar calculations about the income and the costs of retirement life, people who retire early should recognize that Medicare will not be a source of health insurance until age 65.

TABLE 9.1 Employment Sources of Health Insurance Coverage (Adults under Age 65 in 1995)

Private—Employer	63.8%
Private—Not Employer	6.9
Public	16.6
Uninsured	17.4
	104.7%*
Private—Employer	90.2
Private—Not Employer	9.8
	100.0%

* Some individuals receive insurance from more than one source.

Source: Employee Benefit Research Institute, *EBRI Databook,* 4th ed., Table 26.1.

As a family, the Beidermans should also recognize that the overall issue is more complex than just Jerry's age and *his* Medicare eligibility. As a full-time undergraduate student, Tara is eligible to be covered on her father's company health insurance until she graduates. And at age 54, Ricky needs a decade of health insurance coverage until she becomes eligible for Medicare. So, the monthly retirement income will be there, but should Jerry think twice about leaving his job, given a loss of health insurance?

Employers, Retiree Health Insurance, and Financial Accounting Standard 106

Maybe Jerry has thought twice, and his second thoughts were that since his employers have such a nice pension they also will be providing retiree health insurance, at least until his Medicare kicks in (although his Medicare won't solve the problem of coverage for Ricky and Tara). Many companies provide some kind of help with retiree health insurance in the period before Medicare starts, either by continuing to provide and pay for health insurance or by offering retiree insurance on a company organized and subsidized basis.

It might happen that way, but it is much less likely these days than it used to be. Back then, in the postwar 1950s, it was relatively easy for companies to offer retiree health insurance benefits. The ratio of workers to retirees was favorable, longevity was shorter, health care costs were modest, and economic growth was generally substantial. In 1965, back then became even easier for employers. Employer funded retiree insurance could be integrated with the new Medicare program. Employers could offer their retirees secondary insurance providing what today would be defined as supplemental or medigap coverage.

As the costs of health care in the United States rose, so did the costs of company-provided retiree health insurance. Yet even as the numbers of both current retirees and future retirees with claims on health insurance benefits grew, companies did not have to detail their encumbered retiree health care costs in their current annual statements. The situation changed dramatically in 1990 when the private Financial Accounting Standards Board (FASB) approved a new corporate accounting rule. Under FAS 106 companies now had to list their health care cost liabilities in detail in their current year's accounting.

Some companies examined workforce, aging, and health care cost projections and concluded that they owed more in promised health care liabilities than they had in current profits. The consequence is that many companies began to constrict their retiree health benefits. In some cases this resulted in litigation, as current and near-future retirees thought they had been promised health care benefits. In some cases there were legal battles over the fine print in company health insurance pamphlets and brochures, because the matter had never been an issue in formal contract negotiations.

The American public is still somewhat unclear about the relationship between company-provided pensions and company-provided retiree health insurance. As pensions themselves continue to move toward defined contribution plans, the principle of "I am responsible" rather than "they are responsible" may help to clarify the health insurance issue. As of now, however, there is still some public ambiguity in the situation. *Financial Literacy 2000* asked respondents the following: Fact or Myth: Employers who provide pension plans are also required to provide health insurance to their retirees. Almost two-thirds (62%) correctly knew that this statement is a myth. Fortunately, a slightly higher percentage (69%) correctly answered the question among those age 45 to 64 for whom the issue is more imminent. But a third of American adults need additional advice.

Medicare

The Beidermans now understand their health insurance opportunities and limitations. They will purchase group health insurance through the National Association of Landscape Photographers. The family plan will insure Tara until she graduates from college. It will insure both Jerry and Ricky until each becomes eligible for Medicare at age 65.

Any misunderstandings about employer-sponsored retiree health insurance and age eligibility for Medicare have been corrected. They are taken care of prior to age 65, and Medicare benefits start after that. It appears that the Beidermans have more or less completed the health insurance component of their Wealth Span planning. *Less!*

Original Medicare Does Not Pay for Everything

As a traditional Blue Cross–type indemnity health insurance policy, *Original Medicare Plan* beneficiaries have a comprehensive range of costs that must be paid over and above what Medicare pays. These out-of-pocket costs can be substantial, and include monthly insurance premiums for part of Medicare coverage, annual deductibles, and co-payments for doctor and other covered services and supplies. In addition, Medicare health insurance doesn't cover everything. There are important health services that are not covered at all, which means that there are additional Wealth Span planning and budget issues to consider.

Medicare distinguishes between what is formally called the Original Medicare Plan and more recent plans. Over the past 20 years Medicare has allowed and encouraged older people to enroll in various kinds of Medicare-123 approved managed care programs, primarily health maintenance organizations (HMOs). By the end of the 1990s, however, Medicare payments to managed care plans were still less than one fifth of overall Medicare costs.

In the following discussion, as in most public discourse, unless otherwise specifically mentioned, the word *Medicare* refers to the Original Medicare Plan, the indemnity insurance plan originally developed from a Blue Cross insurance model with a schedule of deductibles and co-payments, covered and not covered hospital, doctor, and other medical services.

There is, as mentioned at the beginning of this chapter, a vast storehouse of readily available information on the strengths and limitations of Medicare coverage, including the newer nontraditional Medicare plans available in some but not all areas of the United States. More importantly, the rules, the limits, and the dollar levels both of the benefits and of the several categories of out-of-pocket costs change at least annually.

Consequently, both advisor and client should consult these sources, several of which are described later in this chapter. For now, and to provide a realistic introduction to these costs, we review the main categories of costs that consumers must pay and their current (2002) dollar levels. The literal bottom line of these facts and figures is to emphatically note that becoming eligible for Medicare at age 65 is only the end of the beginning of Wealth Span planning in the domain of family health care finance. Later in this chapter we describe the range of supplemental health insurance policies—medigap—that can be purchased to pay for many of the out-of-pocket costs.

Medicare Part A—Hospital Insurance

Medicare health insurance is divided into Part A and Part B. Part A covers hospitalization and a variety of hospital services. Every Social Security beneficiary is automatically enrolled in Medicare Part A, and there are no additional insurance premium costs to the beneficiary.

Part B—medical services—covers the costs of physicians and surgeons, lab fees, some medical equipment, and related services provided either in the hospital or in the doctor's office. As discussed later, Part B is optional, although over 95% of Social Security/Medicare beneficiaries choose to enroll. There is an additional monthly Part B insurance premium, which is automatically deducted from the beneficiary's monthly Social Security check.

Part A Hospital Insurance covers the cost of a semiprivate hospital room and pays for most hospital expenses such as lab tests, nursing services, pharmaceuticals provided by the hospital, x-ray and related services, and meals. If surgery is required, the cost of the operating room is covered, but not the costs of the surgeons, anesthesiologists, and other specialists (who are covered under Part B).

There are a number of direct costs that the beneficiary/patient must pay. It's only partially accurate to label these as out-of-pocket costs, as many consumers will have secondary medical insurance coverage as part of a retirement package, or will have purchased a supplemental medigap insurance policy to cover the costs not paid by Medicare.

The Good News and the Bad News of a Benefit Period

Medicare's Part A hospitalization insurance benefits are paid in terms of what is called a *benefit period.* The benefit period starts when the patient enters the hospital and ends after 60 *consecutive* days in which no Part A benefits have been used. For each benefit period the beneficiary pays a deductible, and Medicare Hospital Insurance (i.e., Part A) pays the rest of the hospital costs. In 2002, the deductible for each benefit period is $812.

If the cumulative (not consecutive) hospitalization lasts longer than 60 days within the same benefit period, then Medicare requires a co-payment per day before Part A will pay for the remainder of the hospital costs. From hospitalization day 61 to day 90 the 2002 co-payment for each day is $203. Beyond 90 accumulated hospitalization days every Medicare beneficiary has a lifetime of 60 *reserve days* for which there is a larger daily co-payment, $406 in 2002. Once the 60 reserve days are used they are gone forever, unlike the other Medicare Part A benefits which are renewed for each benefit period.

The benefit period is important to understand both for its protections and its costs. During a single benefit period there is only one deductible. Thus, if the patient enters the hospital for eight days and is discharged, but two weeks later becomes rehospitalized for another five days, the two hospitalization episodes are part of the same benefit period. The deductible paid as part of the first hospitalization remains in effect.

After the patient leaves the hospital, the same benefit period continues to be in effect until a period of 60 days has elapsed with no new Part A services (i.e., hospitalization and related services) being needed. Thus, if 20 days after the second hospitalization a third hospitalization of six more days is needed, the same already-incurred deductible continues to be in effect.

That's the financial protection given by the benefit period. However, since the same benefit period continues with multiple hospitalizations including posthospitalization Part A rehabilitation care (and does not end until after the patient has had a period of 60 days without any of these Part A benefits), the number of hospitalization days continues to accumulate. If the number of accumulated days *in the hospital* within a single benefit period goes beyond 60, then the daily Part A co-payments begin. As noted above, from day 61 through day 90 (successive or accumulated within the same benefit period), the patient must pay a daily co-payment of $203 (in 2002).

Another Story

Rosamay Brooks, Age 72

Consider Rosamay Brooks, a 72-year-old diabetic woman who is released from the hospital on June 30 after a four-day stay to treat a respiratory infection. On August 15, 46 days later, she is rehospitalized with a broken hip. She has a four-day hospitalization and then spends 12 days in a skilled nursing facility (SNF) for occupational and physical therapy, also paid by Part A.

Ms. Brooks seems to be doing fine; she has mastered the use of her walker, and her diabetes seems under control. But on September 22, three weeks later, she is back in the hospital for five days with an episode of congestive heart failure. On October 30, she forgets to take her insulin, falls into a comalike sleep, and is rushed to the hospital for six days of treatment to rebalance her sugars and the rest of her medicines. On December 10, she falls and breaks her other hip, requiring surgery and a hospitalization of five days, followed by another 15 days of rehabilitative care in a SNF.

She has been in and out of the hospital and the SNF from June 27 to December 30, but because there has not been a period of 60 consecutive days during which Part A benefits have not been used, it is all part of the same benefit period.

This good financial news for Ms. Brooks is that she is still working from the same deductible, and Medicare Part A continues to pay all of her covered hospitalization and skilled nursing rehab costs. Her potential bad financial news is that she has now accumulated 24 days of hospitalization in the same period (the SNF days are counted separately for reimbursement purposes but do serve to extend the benefit period). If this pattern of in and out of the hospital continues, the full Part A payments for hospitalization will continue only for a total of 60 accumulated hospital days, and on the 61st day of hospitalization (and through her 90th day) she will have an out-of-pocket *daily* co-payment of $203 (in 2002).

Part A Posthospitalization Rehabilitation

As we will emphasize in Chapter 11, although Medicare does not pay for long-term nursing home care, there continues to be an important public confusion on the matter. For example, in our first national Alzheimer's disease public opinion survey in 1985, and continuing through our recent 1998 poll, two-thirds of the public still don't know that Medicare does not pay for the nursing home care costs of Alzheimer's patients.

There is clearly a substantial need for more focused public education, especially as Boomers move through middle age with growing involvement with their elderly parents alongside Wealth Span consideration of their own future long-term care needs. There is, unfortunately, a somewhat rational basis for this confusion over the role of Medicare as a payer of nursing home care. The reason is that Medicare Part A does pay for posthospitalization rehabilitation care and such rehab typically takes place in skilled nursing facilities, (i.e., in nursing homes).

Many nursing homes provide both short-term posthospitalization rehabilitation to Medicare beneficiaries and at the same time, down the hall, provide long-term chronic nursing home care to others, that is not paid by Medicare. But this is just the first piece of the confusion.

In addition, this second group of long-term chronic care, non-Medicare residents of the nursing home continue to have their physician services and hospitalization (if they need it) paid for by Medicare. It is not surprising that many older people and their families, as well as the general public, draw the erroneous conclusion that Medicare pays for nursing home care.

Let's Do Away with Nursing Homes Forever!

For several reasons it would be nice if the phrase *nursing home* was zapped from our vocabulary. Instead, if we had *long-term care facilities* and *rehabilitation facilities* (or some more pleasant euphemisms for this pair of clumsy functional phrases), perhaps the public confusion over what Medicare does and does not pay for would be resolved and Wealth Span planning would be clarified. In addition, the past 40 years of negative emotional connotation of being in a nursing home can serve as an obstacle to the consideration and purchase of long-term care (LTC) insurance, even though most LTC insurance nowadays appropriately pays for long-term care services provided in places other than the traditional nursing home.

Skilled nursing facilities (SNFs) are nursing homes in which a variety of rehabilitative health services are provided to patients upon their discharge from the hospital. Typically, these services are medically called for after a heart attack or stroke, and especially after surgery.

Medicare Part A benefits include payment for physician-prescribed rehab that is medically called for after a Medicare-paid hospitalization. To qualify for Medicare-paid rehab services the hospitalization must have been for at least three days. In the context of this discussion of Medicare Part A, both the dollar costs and the counting of days in a single benefit period are important.

Within a single benefit period, Part A pays the entire cost of posthospitalization rehab in a Medicare-authorized SNF for the first 20 days of care. There is no additional deductible or any daily co-payment. For day 21 through day 99 there is a maximum $101.50 per day co-payment in 2002. Thus, if the daily charge in the SNF is $102 or more, then the patient pays $101.50 and Medicare Part A pays the rest. The patient pays the full cost starting on the 100th day of rehab care within the same benefit period.

The number of days in a rehab facility has important implications for the Part A hospitalization payments that Medicare will pay. As with Rosamay Brooks, an extended stay in a SNF serves to extend the life of a single benefit period, which is good financial news from the vantage point of not having to pay another deductible of $812. However, if there are repeated hospitalizations within a single now-lengthened benefit period, and if the accumulated hospitalization days exceed 60 days, then a hospitalization co-payment of $203 per day is triggered.

By and large, these procedures work to the advantage of the older Medicare beneficiary. Relatively few people accumulate 60 days of hospital stay in a single benefit period. For those who do, medigap insurance is likely to pay for the additional costs. Most medigap insurance also pays for required SNF co-payments.

Medicare Part B—Medical Insurance

The official name of Medicare Part B is "Medical Insurance" in an effort to distinguish it from Part A Hospital Insurance. For most families it is easier to think of Part B as *physician insurance* because most of the benefits paid will be for doctor services both in the office and in the hospital.

Enrollment Issues

Unlike Part A, Medicare Part B is optional, and requires a separate monthly insurance premium. In 2002, the Part B premium is $54 per month. Although it is optional, virtually all Medicare beneficiaries choose to enroll: Between 1970 and 1998, Part B enrollment ranged from 96% to 98% of all Part A beneficiaries.

There are some circumstances in which a client may choose to delay Part B enrollment, but it can be at a price. If, for example, a 65 year old is covered by health insurance at work or the spouse's work, the monthly Part B premium may seem like an unnecessary payment. If a person simply doesn't want to pay for the optional Part B coverage, the decision is fully optional. Procedurally, since most eligible beneficiaries do choose to enroll in Part B, Medicare has made the enrollment process automatic. When Medicare starts at age 65, the enrollee receives a card through which she or he can decline the Part B insurance. If the card is not mailed back, then Part B enrollment is automatic, and the premium—$54 per month in 2002—is deducted from the beneficiary's monthly Social Security check.

There are two forward planning conditions that affect the future cost of Part B insurance. If and when a Medicare (Part A) beneficiary later decides to enroll in Part B, the cost is increased by 10% for each 12-month period that the insurance was not purchased. For example, consider Mrs. Franny Ovitsky, who celebrated her 65th birthday in November 2000. She doesn't want to enroll in Part B when she first receives her Medicare packet, and so mails back her decline postcard. After a year she changes her mind and looks to the next General Enrollment Period. Medicare's General Enrollment Period is January through March of each year.

When she enrolls on February 7, 2002, her monthly premium is $59.40, that is, the current (2002) premium of $54 plus 10%. Next year, when the new Part B premium becomes effective on January 1, 2003, she will pay 110% of that premium, and she will pay 110% for the rest of her life. If her 65th birthday were in November 1999, and she enrolled on February 7, 2002, her premium would be 120% of the official monthly premium for the rest of her life.

There is an exception (there always is) that works to the advantage of the older person. If the reason for the postponement of the Part B enrollment was that the person was covered by group health insurance through work, or through the spouse's work, then there is a "Special Enrollment Period" that can be used. Use of this special period is important because the added 10% (per year) typically will not apply.

(*Note:* There is another set of circumstances for which delay of Part B enrollment would be advantageous. This has to do with legal protections involving a Medicare beneficiary's rights to purchase medigap insurance even with a preexisting health condition. These are discussed later in this chapter.)

Medicare Part B Coverage and Costs

Part B Medical Insurance primarily covers fees for doctors' services, including regular office visits to internists or specialists, as well as surgeons, anesthesiologists, and others involved in a hospitalization. As a traditional indemnity insurance policy, Part B involves both deductibles and co-payments. Note that both deductibles and co-payments are defined differently than in Part A.

In Part B there are no benefit periods as in the Part A Hospital Insurance. Rather, calculations are done on a calendar year basis. For all Part B covered services combined, there is a single calendar year deductible of $100 in 2002.

In addition to doctors' services, Part B covers outpatient medical services and supplies, diagnostic tests, prostate cancer screening, diabetes services (including diabetes self-management training and education provided by a visiting nurse in the patient's home), and second surgical opinions. Durable medical equipment is covered, including such things as wheelchairs, walkers, oxygen, and hospital-like beds for home use when prescribed by a physician.

For all these medical services, the general principle (with exceptions noted below) is that after the annual deductible, the beneficiary pays a 20% co-insurance of the costs and Medicare Part B pays the rest.

There are a number of other available services for which the costs are slightly different, with the differences favoring the patient. For example, for clinical laboratory tests such as blood tests and urinalysis, and for Medicare-approved home care, Medicare pays the entire cost; there is no 20% co-insurance. There typically is no charge to Medicare beneficiaries for annual flu shots or for a pneumonia vaccination (which research suggests may be needed only once in a lifetime).

To encourage diagnostic screening and examinations, especially for those Medicare beneficiaries whose good health means they have not had to pay the $100 annual deductible, Medicare pays for a number of tests with no Part B deductible required. These include mammogram screening and Pap smear examinations for women and prostate cancer exams for men (both requiring the 20% co-payment but not the deductible). For a prostate-specific antigen (PSA) screening blood test, Medicare pays 100% of the cost even when the annual deductible has not been paid.

Paying for Physicians

The major complexity in Part B coverage is how physicians are paid. Medicare has a national schedule of approved or allowable charges for different medical procedures. Most doctors who accept Medicare patients agree to bill at no more than the specified Medicare-approved rates. When billing for a medical procedure or visit (whether in the office, in a hospital, or in the patient's home), the physician bills for 80% of the approved amount. The other 20%, the co-insurance, is the patient's responsibility.

Medicare is thus the primary insurance for most beneficiaries. (Again, there are always exceptions. For example, if a Medicare enrollee is injured in a work-related accident, then Medicare is likely to be the secondary insurance to workers' compensation.) If an older person has secondary insurance, either as provided by a former employer or as privately purchased medigap insurance, then the secondary insurance typically will pay the 20% co-insurance amount. In many, if not most, situations, the physician will bill both the primary (Medicare) and the secondary insurance directly, with the patient receiving a statement of how much was billed to whom and for what.

Wealth Span Planning for Medical Administration

These comments have all focused on the financial costs of health care. But as our discussion of Medicare implies, Wealth Span planning should also take into consideration what we might call simply the administrative or bureaucratic complexity of health care costs and their payment. There are institutional ways to minimize the financial–medical–bureaucracy burdens. Managed care options within Medicare do away with deductibles and most complex co-payments. But only a minority of older people are currently enrolled in Medicare-approved HMOs and other managed care programs, and the number appears to be declining as many managed-care health insurance companies are either dropping or constricting their involvement with Medicare. As part of overall Wealth Span planning, some attention should be focused on who will work with the older client when dealing with financial and health bureaucracies becomes increasingly difficult and burdensome.

It is appropriate to emphasize this administration aspect of Wealth Span planning at many places in this book. Discussion of the complexities of Part B physician payment and reimbursement, however, offers an especially entangling illustration of the importance of administration in gerontological financial planning. If children or other family members are not present or likely to be available to help, then some other source of assistance with medical and financial bureaucracies should be built into the plan. Such help can be provided by financial advisors, accountants, elder law attorneys, or geriatric care managers. These specialists often work in partnerships or perhaps in teams or neighborhood alliances. The ELF model of such alliances is described in Chapter 12.

What Part B Medical Insurance Does Not Cover

There are a number of medical services that are not covered at all by current Medicare insurance (Original Medicare Plan), some of which are considered by gerontologists and geriatricians to be central to the good health of elderly persons. Some of these are likely to be covered by supplementary medigap insurance:

- Routine eye care (except for one pair of glasses after cataract surgery)
- Routine physical examinations (except for the preventative tests and screening exams mentioned above)
- Routine foot care and orthopedic shoes
- Routine dental care
- Hearing aids
- Outpatient pharmaceuticals (except for some oral cancer medications)
- Acupuncture
- Cosmetic surgery

Medigap Insurance

This listing of what Medicare does not cover offers a good segue to considering the financial protection offered by privately sold supplemental Medicare insurance, usually called *medigap* insurance. This insurance will reimburse the Medicare beneficiary for many of the out-of-pocket costs that Medicare requires, and will also pay for many of the medical services that Medicare does not cover. As mentioned at the beginning of this chapter, since Medicare and Medicaid are public health insurance programs, we purposely spell *medigap* with a lowercase *m* to identify it as not another form of government-administered insurance. However, since Congress mandated a standardization of 10 types of medigap policies in 1992, there is an important governmental involvement. Nonetheless, despite the presence of *medi,* consumers should be aware that the term *medigap* describes a generic type of private-sector supplemental health insurance within which is a substantial range of policy types, coverages, and costs.

Out-of-Pocket Medical Expenditures

Just as Social Security was never intended to be the full income source for retired people, official documents use the phrase "Medicare helps to pay for" to describe the intended partial rather than complete coverage for the country's older men and women. Using 2002 dollar figures, Table 9.2 summarizes the kinds of expenses that a beneficiary pays over and above what Medicare pays. Not included are the more unusual expenses of a 61st day in the hospital or a 21st day of rehab in a SNF.

TABLE 9.2 What the Beneficiary Pays

$648	Part B insurance premiums, per year
$812	Part A deductible, per each hospital benefit period
20%	Of the cost of durable medical equipment
$100	Part B deductible, per year
20%	Of all Medicare-approved amount of physician charges
100%	Of physician charges above Medicare-approved amount
100%	Of all outpatient prescription medicines
100%	Of all routine dental care and dentures
100%	Of all optician services and glasses
100%	Of all podiatry services and orthopedic shoes
100%	Of hearing aids

Medigap insurance was developed by private insurance companies to fill these gaps in what Medicare does not pay or pays only partially. The earlier years of medigap insurance were characterized by substantial financial abuse of older people. Some policies were advertised as having low-cost monthly or even weekly premiums, "pennies per day," but with print so fine that benefits to policyholders were virtually nonexistent. Some policies duplicated Medicare coverage, offering no real added value. In other situations, risk-averse older people were persuaded by confusing offers to purchase policies that duplicated other medigap policies they already owned.

After substantial investigation and congressional hearings, Congress mandated a standardized set of 10 medigap policy types, simply labeled as Plan A through Plan J. There is a basic or core set of benefits that every plan must include. The general pricing of these policies reflects the increasing number and value of benefits offered. In addition, premiums typically vary by the age of the insured, and sometimes by gender, smoking, marital status, and health condition.

As with health insurance and Medicare generally, medigap insurance is a large and detailed area of insurance and financial choice. So, again, we focus on the basics followed by recommended sources of more complete information. Three topics are considered: (1) the features of the different medigap plans, (2) a summary of key enrollment issues and factors that reduce policy cost, and (3) the use of Medigap Compare, an interactive web site through which consumers can find which medigap plans are available in their state or county, and by which companies.

The Basic and More Elaborate Medigap Plans

The 10 medigap plans are known simply as Plan A through Plan J. (These are available throughout the country except for Massachusetts, Minnesota, and Wisconsin. These state variations are described in the resources listed at the end of the chapter.)

The basic or core benefits must be included in all plans offered by all insurance companies. In turn, the specific set of benefits legally mandated for each plan type, A through J, must be included in every medigap policy sold by any company. Plan A, the set of core benefits, pays for:

- Part A (Hospital Insurance) co-payment for hospitalization days 61 through 90 ($203 per day in 2002), as well as days 91 through 150 ($406 per day in 2002)
- 100% of 365 additional hospitalization days as a lifetime benefit over and above any Medicare hospital benefits
- The Part B 20% co-payments (primarily physician payments) after the $100 annual deductible is paid
- The first three pints of blood—a kind of specialized deductible, since Part B pays for blood after the first three pints on the usual 80–20 basis

Plans B through J pay the Part A hospital deductible—$812 in 2002. Recall that this is not an annual deductible, but is payable for each benefit period. Thus, if a Medicare beneficiary is unfortunate to have three or four hospitalizations, each separated by 60 days of good health (defined in terms of Part A benefits paid), he or she could pay $2,400 to $3,200 in Part A hospital deductibles.

Plans C through J add reimbursement for the Part A SNF rehab co-payment. Within each benefit period, Part A pays all costs for the first 20 days of SNF care, but then requires that the beneficiary pay the first $101.50 of SNF care for days 21 through 100. Plans C through J reimburse that co-payment.

While there are other features of the different plans, the main other benefit is a prescription drug benefit, offered by Plans H, I, and J. All three plans require a $250 annual deductible, after which there is a 50% co-payment. Plans H and I have an annual maximum benefit of $1,250; Plan J has a maximum of $3,000 per year (a kind of prescription major medical plan).

Given the substantially higher annual premiums that these three medigap plans require, Medicare documents as well as the Consumers Union analysis strongly urge potential medigap customers to carefully assess their likely prescription costs. Given all three parameters—deductible, co-payment, and upper limit—an individualized cost–benefit analysis is an important aspect of deciding if an expensive pharmaceutical premium is cost-effective.

Selective Cost Comparisons

To get a good look at the substantial price range of different medigap plans sold in the same city, Appendix E of the Consumers Union's *Complete Guide to Health Services for Seniors* includes annual premium data for about three dozen cities. For example, to the basic benefits (Plan A summarized above) Plan C adds payment of the Medicare Part A hospitalization deductible ($812 in 2002). Plan I adds the prescription drug benefit with the lower annual maximum. The following illustrations are annual premiums purchased by a 65 year old; a 75 year old pays a substantially higher premium.

In Los Angeles, the Plan C premiums range from a low of $984 to $1,185 (a 20% difference). The Plan I premiums range from $1,920 to $2,812 (46%). The least expensive Plan I (prescription benefit included) costs 95% more than the least expensive Plan C. Your premiums may vary.

Medigap Insurance Rules and Shopping Tips

We conclude this part of the discussion by noting a few of the key medigap rules that can directly affect the cost of medigap insurance. As before, we caution that these are technical issues with details and costs subject to periodic change. Up-to-date rules, procedures, and costs can be found in the several sources listed at the end of this chapter and in the Resource Guide (Chapter 13).

The Open Enrollment Period

The best time to purchase medigap insurance is during a six-month period referred to as the Medigap Open Enrollment Period. This is a precisely defined period that starts at the time of Medicare Part B enrollment, lasts for six months only, and then closes forever.

Earlier, we mentioned that a delay in enrolling in Part B could cause a 10% increase in the premiums when Part B is eventually selected. However, because the Open Enrollment Period provides some very valuable protections, and because the start of the period is linked directly to Part B enrollment, it may be wise to delay Part B enrollment to reserve these medigap protections.

These protections include the following: During the six-month Open Enrollment Period, a medigap insurance company cannot deny the purchase of the insurance for medical reasons, including preexisting medical conditions.

The company cannot place conditions on the policy, such as a waiting period due to medical conditions, and the company cannot change the price of the policy because of past or present medical conditions. These protections are in force only for the six months after Part B enrollment, after which medical underwriting is permissible.

The clearest Wealth Span strategy is simply to anticipate these several time markers, do the shopping in advance, and then both enroll in Medicare Part B and purchase the chosen medigap insurance within that six-month period.

As also mentioned earlier, if the reason for not enrolling in Part B is that the Medicare beneficiary continues to have health insurance through employment (or spouse's employment), then both Part B and medigap can be postponed with no financial or health insurance consequences.

HMOs

The most comprehensive way of filling the gaps in Original Medicare Plan coverage is through a Medicare HMO. Every Medicare HMO must at a minimum provide the same benefits as Medicare Part A and Part B coverage. But built into the HMO model is much of the coverage provided by medigap insurance. Thus, Medicare HMO patients typically have no or very low co-payments for doctors and other medical services, and no 20% co-insurance of traditional indemnity Medicare. Most HMO plans offer some form of prescription medicine coverage, often with modest co-payments per prescription.

Medicare HMO insurance, like other health insurance, has produced multiple products. For example, although the older person must enroll in and pay for the Part B Medical Insurance coverage in order to join a Medicare HMO, most Medicare HMO plans do not charge any additional premium. For additional premiums, HMOs can offer additional or enhanced benefits such as glasses, hearing aids, and dental medicine and services. Thus, many of the gaps in the traditional Medicare program are filled.

Like the Medigap Compare web site, the government's Center for Medicare and Medicaid Services has also developed an interactive Medicare Health Plan Compare web site that allows Wealth Span advisors and their clients to learn what managed care plans are sold in their community, and directly compare the plans, their services, deductibles and co-payments if any, and their costs with the Original Medicare Plan.

Medicare HMOs around the country are having well-publicized financial problems, especially in areas with high concentrations of older beneficiaries. Consequently, the decision to substitute a Medicare HMO plan for the combination of original Medicare plus a medigap policy should be made in light of local HMO practices alongside the financial costs and benefits. Toward this end, Medicare has (1) developed detailed procedures for disenrolling in HMOs and reenrolling in Original Medicare, and vice versa, and (2) includes the number of older persons leaving each specific Medicare HMO in the Medicare Health Plan Compare web site.

Medigap Shopping Tips

Finally, when shopping for a medigap health insurance policy, consider the following tips, some obvious, others less so.

- Study the 10 types of medigap policies, knowing that insurance companies must identify their products by type, and that once so identified the policies must have the stipulated features. Price comparison then becomes more useful.
- As in most products, a more fully featured product will cost more than a policy with fewer features. An assessment of the real need for the various policy features should be made, especially for the expensive prescription drug benefits.
- Like auto insurance, a higher deductible typically comes with a lower premium, ceterus paribus. Within policy types, companies are allowed to create variations using different deductibles, and price their products accordingly.
- "Select medigap" policies incorporate managed care–type features, such as requiring use of physicians and hospitals from a specific list. Such medigap policies are less expensive.
- The Open Enrollment Period should be understood and integrated into the decision process to ensure that the Medicare beneficiary does not wind up being denied coverage due to a preexisting medical condition or have to pay a substantially higher premium because of that condition.

Medicare Health Plan Compare and Medigap Compare

The `www.medicare.gov` web site offers two interactive tools for comparing health insurance plans. Both are structured and work in a similar fashion. The user starts by indicating a state or zip code. In some cases the system asks for county. A selection of plans is listed, either medigap insurers or Medicare Health Plan providers. You then check off which ones you want to examine (or all). For medigap listing, the web site indicates which plan types (A through J) are offered by a particular company, alongside the company's contact information. Any special notes about the policy are also listed.

For the Health Plan comparisons—comparing original Medicare with managed care plans—the system provides three reports:

1. A list of the benefits and the associated costs, premiums, co-payments, and deductibles.

2. Quality and user satisfaction measures from studies of specific plans and their members, from research conducted under Medicare design and supervision. Each of the quality and satisfaction measures is defined, and the results graphically presented for the plans being compared.

3. Comparison across plans of members who disenrolled, along with a discussion of the meaning and limitations of the data.

Basic Medicare Information Resources

Amid the many books, guides, and articles available, we recommend the following for a very comprehensive beginning.

- *Consumers Union.* In 2000, the Consumers Union (CU), publisher of the widely respected *Consumer Reports,* published the *Complete Guide to Health Services for Seniors,* written by Trudy Lieberman and the editors of *Consumer Reports.* It includes a short but well-written introduction to Medicare. More importantly, it sets Medicare in the general context of health insurance, including medigap coverage and long-term care insurance. In true *Consumer Reports* fashion, half the book's almost 600 pages are appendices containing lists of specific agencies, insurance counseling programs, pharmaceutical assistance programs, and health resources for elderly persons of limited means. Many of the services and programs listed come with CU consumer-oriented evaluations. Appendix E illustrates the price variation in medigap policies in several dozen cities, naming specific companies and annual premiums. Appendix G supplies similar information for Medicare HMOs.

- *Medicare & You.* The most fundamental information source for all Wealth Span advisors and their clients is the official *Medicare & You* publication, updated and published annually by the Center for Medicare and Medicaid Services (until recently known as HCFA, the U.S. Health Care Financing Agency). Although every Medicare enrollee is sent a copy of the new handbook in the fall of each year, it is even more valuable as an advanced Wealth Span planning tool. It provides not only descriptions of the traditional and the new Medicare programs, but identifies the annually changed dollar costs and limitations within Medicare Part A and Part B. The latest version of the handbook is freely available on the Medicare web site, `www.medicare.gov`.

- *Medicare.gov.* Despite often-heard criticisms of government bureaucracy and inefficiency, the most comprehensive and at the same time user-friendly source of Medicare information is the CMS (Center for Medicare and Medicaid Services) web site at `www.medicare.gov`. Although developed for consumers and health practitioners, the comprehensiveness of the information resources make the site a welcome tool for financial professionals. In addition to *Medicare & You,* available Acrobat (.pdf format) documents describe second opinions, women and Medicare benefits, hospice care, rehabilitation at skilled nursing homes, and detailed descriptions of recent and pending changes in Medicare plan availability (including new managed care options, medical savings accounts, and HMO changes). In addition, the web site includes the Medigap Compare and the Medicare Health Plan Compare online interactive software described earlier. The (some would say *unexpected*) attractiveness and usefulness of this government web site brings to mind the loud comment of an apparently very angry senior citizen during a 2000 presidential election campaign stop at a senior center in West Palm Beach. Shouted the old man at Candidate Bush, "And if you're elected you damn well better tell the government to stay out of my Medicare!" The candidate promised that he would.

CHAPTER 10

Long-Term Care Services: Nursing Homes, Home Care, and Assisted Living

In the context of the human Wealth Span, the question of health and long-term care in old age poses a special challenge to the financial advisor for three reasons:

1. Many middle-aged and older adults are more worried about the costs of long-term care than they are about the more basic issue of outliving their pension and other retirement resources.
2. Long-term care nowadays is much more varied than simply the much-dreaded nursing home.
3. Much of the concern and worry in (1) is due to a lack of information about (2).

Consequently, an important dimension of strategic Wealth Span planning for middle-aged and older clients is the financial psychology of long-term care.

Worries and Concerns: The Financial Psychology of Long-Term Care

Wealth Span planning traditionally emphasizes savings and investment, pensions, and retirement income security. But as we noted in Chapter 8, from a financial psychological perspective, the *security* in "retirement income security" refers not only to the number of dollars received or available in the client's older years, but to the psychological comfort and knowledge that those dollars will be sufficient to cover all necessary costs. As the previous chapters also demonstrate, health care comprises a central component of those necessary costs that need to be financially covered.

Most older people can afford to pay for their general health care costs through some combination of Medicare, employer-connected health insurance (paid, subsidized, or organized), and medigap insurance. Such is not the case for long-term care. None of these kinds of health insurance cover long-term chronic residential care. Further, because long-term care represents a "distant" future health care situation, neither the need for long-term care nor its cost can be easily predicted. Because of these uncertainties, Wealth Span planning for long-term care requires a greater attention to the financial psychology of the situation. This worry is not simply a matter of wealth versus poverty. In fact, our research documents that wealthier people have greater concerns about the financial implications of long-term care than do less wealthy people.

The 1996 National Council on the Aging (NCOA)–Hancock national long-term care survey asked respondents to agree or disagree with the following statement: The costs of long-term care will reduce my retirement income and assets. Table 10.1 shows that there is a substantial national consensus on this issue—approximately 80% of every age group agrees.

Interestingly, Boomers are even more concerned than everyone else. It may be that middle-agers are worried not only about the costs of their own future care but about the long-term care needs, including financial needs, of their aging parents.

Furthermore, the results at the bottom of the table show, people with higher income are more concerned than lower-income respondents. It may be that they have more future retirement income to protect, or perhaps they anticipate that public programs (such as Medicaid) will not be available to them. Whatever the reason, their financial long-term care concerns are clearly in evidence.

Four years later, the NCOA's *American Perceptions of Aging in the 21st Century* study examined the same issue using a more focused way of asking the question. The results demonstrate the same basic picture but with an interesting twist that demonstrates how critical the long-term care issue can be in overall

Table 10.1 The Cost of Long-Term Care Will Reduce My Retirement Income & Assets

	Agree	Disagree
18–31	75%	19
32–42*	86%	12
43–50*	88%	10
51–71	79%	17
72+	78%	18
Below $50,000	81%	15
$50,000 and above	85%	13

* Boomers in 1966.
Source: The NCOA–Hancock Long-Term Care Survey (1996).

Wealth Span planning. Respondents were asked to think ahead to when they would be 75 years old, and then to identify their worries about that future time:

Think about your life at age 75.

How worried are you that you will:

- Outlive your pension and savings?
- Spend all your money on long-term care?

The significance of these financial worries is seen in the comparison of the responses of three age groups for whom long-term care planning is especially salient: the older half of the Boomers (age 44-53); traditionally defined pre-retirees (54-64); and the young-old (65-74). As seen in the top section of Table 10.2, middle-aged and older respondents are more worried about spending their money on long-term care than they are worried about outliving their pension and savings. From 49% to 58% are worried about spending all their money on long-term care compared to 34% to 53% worried about outliving their pension and savings.

An interesting variation is seen when the results are examined by income. We again divided respondents into those above and below $50,000 annual household income. The results in the lower section of the table show that people in the $50,000+ income group are relatively *more* worried about the costs of long-term care than are people in the lower income group.

TABLE 10.2 Financial Worries at age 75: Pension Income versus Long-Term Care

		% worried		
	Age	Outlive My Pension	Spend It All on LTC	Greater LTC Worry %
ALL	44–53	53	58	+5
	54–64	46	58	+12
	65–75	34	49	+15
Below $50,000	44–53	57	59	+2
	54–64	54	62	+8
	65–75	39	51	+12
$50,000 and above	44–53	47	57	+10
	54–64	39	54	+15
	65–75	23	36	+13

Rich People Have Worries Too

Table 10.2 paints an important Wealth Span picture of the interaction of wealth and health in older age. In their late fifties to mid-sixties most people are beginning their Expenditure Stage—receiving their pension payments, minimum defined contribution withdrawals, and Social Security checks.

- At age 65, whether retired or working, most people are automatically enrolled in Medicare Part A Hospital Insurance and Part B Medical/Physician Insurance, and have investigated employer-offered supplemental insurance or medigap insurance policies.
- At any age, when we compare people in the two income levels, not surprisingly wealthier people are not as worried as less wealthy people.
- Looking across the rows in the bottom part of the table, the more interesting pattern is that in every income–age subgroup, worries about the costs of long-term care are greater than worries about outliving one's pension.
- Finally, it is especially interesting that for every age group the *worry gap* is greater for the wealthier respondents (+2 versus +10 for the older Boomers, +8 versus +15 for the pre-retirees, and +12 versus +13 for the 65 to 75 age group). That is, wealthier people are more concerned that they will spend all their retirement money on long-term care than are less wealthy people.

Why so? When entering their Expenditure Stage, most older people can have a reasonably clear idea about their income and health expenses and health insurance. What we cannot know so clearly is the risk of long-term illness and the costs of long-term care. Higher income does provide insulation from this kind of worry.

Consumer Preferences and the Continuum of Long-Term Care

For many older adults the phrase *long-term care* is virtually synonymous with *nursing homes.* Whatever may have been the case in the past, however, defining long-term care simply as nursing home care is incorrect. This is a bigger problem than simply a poor or outdated definition: It is a financial psychology issue and a Wealth Span planning issue. It continues to be an important problem because the lingering but false linkage that many people perceive between nursing home and long-term care can have negative consequences for Wealth Span planning.

Fortunately, nursing homes are no longer the only form of long-term care. We now have what is gerontologically referred to as the *continuum of long-term care.* Generally speaking, the continuum ranges from assistance in one's own home (or the home of an adult child or other relative), to assisted living facilities, to nursing homes. Nursing homes remain an important part of the continuum, but they certainly are not necessarily the entry point.

Another Story

No Nursing Home Insurance for This Mother

A few years ago I made the following proposal to my mother: Since we had run out of birthday and holiday presents to give each other, this year we would buy long-term care insurance for her. My gift to her would be arranging and paying for the purchase of the insurance. Her gift to me would be in accepting the insurance. She absolutely refused. Her unmovable argument was simply that she would have no part of nursing home insurance, that such insurance would simply "grease the skids" into a nursing home, and she would have no part of it. Period. It didn't matter that her son the doctor was a professor of financial gerontology. Case closed.

All planning and counseling professionals—financial, legal, social, and health—need to provide their clients with more complete and accurate information about the continuum of available options in long-term care. Financial planners have a special responsibility, however, since the costs of paying for future long-term care are a major Wealth Span concern of middle-aged as well as older consumers.

This chapter discusses the continuum of long-term care services—nursing homes, assisted living facilities, and home care—and Chapter 11 discusses long-term care finance.

Nursing Homes

As my brief Mother Case Study illustrates, from a Wealth Span perspective the publicly perceived connection between long-term care and nursing homes is unfortunate because it can act as a obstacle to important planning. It may not matter, as social gerontologist Robert Atchley has written, that "part of the dread elders experience at the prospect of entering a nursing home is based on an outdated picture of it as a 'last home for the aged.'" On the other hand, as he also points out, over half of nursing home residents are age 80 or older.

Nursing Homes as the Last Home for the Aged

It may be an ironic consequence of the improvements in geriatric health care that the image of the nursing home as the dreaded last home for the aged is becoming more statistically accurate. People are living longer, some more healthy and some less healthy. As the Squared Mortality Curve in Figure 8.1 illustrates, for many elders the new patterns of longevity imply that when frailty and functional limitation finally come, they come at a later age than in years past. At the same time, expanded systems of social and residential care such as senior centers, home-delivered Meals on Wheels, home health care, and the expansion of assisted living suggest that nursing homes are in many cases a residence for the most frail elderly.

A study published in March 2001 by the U.S. Centers for Disease Control and Prevention (CDC) documented that the nursing home population in the United States is more frail and older in 1997 than it was in 1985. In 1997, 51% of nursing home residents were 85 years of age or older, compared to 45% twelve years earlier. This trend reflects the fact that people are entering nursing homes at an older age. The average age of admission was 81.1 in 1985 and 82.6 in 1997.

The level of functional disabilities is also increasing. More residents required assistance with Activities of Daily Living (ADLs) in 1997 than in 1985 (see Table 2.2). For example, help with taking a bath is often the first indicator of the need for personal daily assistance: 96% of nursing home residents required this assistance in 1997 compared to 92% in 1985. At the other end of the scale, help with eating is generally the least and the last needed assistance: 45% needed this daily assistance in 1997 compared to 40% in 1985. Overall, the average nursing home resident required assistance with 4.4 ADLs in 1997 compared to 3.8 in 1985, a 22% increase.

In reviewing these notable trends in the role of nursing homes in the larger picture of American long-term care, a recent U.S. Administration on Aging report summarized it succinctly: "As a consequence of new housing options such as assisted living and community and in-home long term care services, the demographic profile of nursing home residents has significantly changed to a population which is older, more disabled and in greater need of medical attention." The implication of these trends is that the role of the dreaded nursing home has shifted to a later stage in the Health Span (and therefore in the Wealth Span). The parallel implication is that nursing homes are clearly not synonymous with long-term care.

The Continuum of Long-Term Care

To more precisely identify the placement of nursing homes on the continuum of long-term care—and, by implication, their role in Wealth Span planning—we start with a definition of long-term care, in order to distinguish it from health and medical care more generally. Consider the straightforward definition offered by Professor H. R. Moody, who teaches biomedical ethics and health care at the Brookdale Center on Aging in New York. Dr. Moody defines long-term care as the "support given to individuals suffering from chronic illness or disability that limits their ability to live independently."

The key word is *chronic*. Long-term care implies the sustained and continuing assistance that a person may need. The distinctive nature of nursing homes in the overall picture of chronic care is the medical intensity of that care. The CDC nursing home report mentioned earlier defines nursing home care as being more like hospital care than residential chronic assistance: "Nursing homes or skilled nursing facilities provide 24-hour care to sick or disabled individuals who do not require expensive inpatient hospital services but cannot be cared for at home through home care or other community agencies."

The continuum of long-term care includes not only the intense hospital-like services delivered in nursing homes, but the more low-intensity kind of daily care associated with the concept of Activities of Daily Living described in Chapter 2 in our discussion of individual aging. Robert Atchley, for example, uses the phrases *health care* versus *personal care* to distinguish between medically oriented nursing care in contrast to the help with bathing, eating, and dressing that is included in measures of ADLs.

Needing the help of someone else to get dressed or take a bath is certainly no one's preferred image of old age. But such assistance is different from the image of life in a nursing home and the fear that this image symbolizes. Such fears can be a deterrent to important long-term care planning. Consequently, it is especially important to Wealth Span planning that clients fully understand the nature and content (alongside the relative costs) of different kinds of long-term care services and know that nursing homes are only one end of the continuum.

Some analysts estimate that an older person has a 25% chance of living in a nursing home. Whether such estimates are seen as optimistic or pessimistic, they offer little guidance for sound Wealth Span planning for at least two reasons.

First, the future validity or predictive value of any such estimates is certainly open to question. With people living longer, the number or the percentage of nursing home residents may well increase. But tomorrow's Baby Boom elderly will have lived through very different social health and personal health conditions than their parents and grandparents experienced. Consequently, today's middle-agers are likely to have a smaller probability of needing the kind of intense hospital-like medical care for which nursing homes have been designed.

Rowe and Kahn's *Six Myths of Aging Debunked* (summarized in Chapter 8) and their recommendations for midlife and even late-life health interventions, are based on Health Span research discovered and validated in only the past two decades. Taking the New England Centenarian Study's diagnostic test at `www.livingto100.com` (Chapter 2) and acting on the results could also produce a healthier population of old Boomers than Boomer parents and grandparents. In other words, the elderly years of today's middle-agers may well require long-term care, but current and recent rates of nursing home need are not good guides to that future.

Second, no matter what the future trends in nursing home utilization may be, few people have a crystal ball that can accurately predict health 20, 10, or even 5 years into the future. When it comes to long-term care, prudent Wealth Span planning tells us to plan for the worst even as we hope for the best. While clients should know that nursing homes nowadays are just one part of the long-term care continuum, understanding nursing homes still remains a significant piece of the picture. Once such discussion is brought into the planning process, consideration of alternative financial strategies (discussed in Chapter 11) will be better informed.

Advising Clients about Nursing Home Choices

There are many personal and emotional, financial and bureaucratic, immediate and longer-term factors involved in the process of choosing a nursing home. Most of the time this decision becomes the responsibility of the middle-aged children of sick or frail parents. Because financial issues are almost always associated with the nursing home decision, it's not surprising that a middle-aged client will turn to a trusted Wealth Span advisor, even with questions that are outside the usual realm of financial plans and choices.

In advising about issues of long-term care finance (Chapter 11), there also may be legal questions that call for the input of a family law or elder law specialist. But on the more urgent and emotionally charged issue of selecting a nursing home, the best strategy is to be able to direct your middle-aged client to easily accessible sources of local information relevant to specific community options and choices.

Information about trends in age-related worries about future health and long-term care needs, and about the general nature and cost of nursing homes, provide an important informational context for making a nursing home choice. But we can again turn to the insightful words of Eldon Weisheit, who was quoted poetically at the end of Chapter 4. On the matter of making a nursing home decision, Weisheit simply reminds us that "your decision needs a zip code."

In addition to the financial gerontology resources discussed throughout this book and those listed in the Resource Guide (Chapter 13), your should consider working with other local community specialists as described in Chapter 12 (e.g., Geriatric Care Managers). Beyond these, however, the following tools can be of value in evaluating and choosing a nursing home.

- Whether a nursing home is a privately owned, stand-alone business or part of a national chain, run by a for-profit company or a nonprofit fraternal or religious organization, ultimately your client's choice will be a specific and local one. A good place to start the local search is with the Information and Referral service that is offered by the local Area Agency on Aging (AAA) that serves your county or city. As discussed in Chapter 12, AAAs are the local node of a national network of local, state, and federal agencies that organize and provide a variety of aging-related services. The name and contact information of your local AAA (prounced "triple-A") can be found in the government listings (the blue pages) of your local phone book, or by contacting your State Unit on Aging (see the next paragraph). Information also can be obtained from the National Association of Area Agencies on Aging at `www.N4A.org`.

- Nursing homes are highly regulated, but regulated primarily at the state rather than at the federal level. As discussed in Chapter 12, every state has a State Unit on Aging (SUA) to coordinate a broad range of statewide and local aging programs. Nursing homes are one of their primary regulatory concerns, and each state's SUA is an important source of professional and consumer information about nursing home standards and patient rights, and of official reports of current nursing home abuses, investigations, and censures. Contact `www.nasua.org`. More detailed information on how to find the current address and complete contact information for all State Units on Aging is provided in Chapter 12.

- Federal regulations require every state to establish a long-term care ombudsman program to hear, collect, and investigate consumer complaints about specific nursing homes. Some states have placed this officer or office in the State Unit on Aging, some in the health department, and in others it is an extension of the governor's office. The U.S. Administration on Aging web site (`www.aoa.gov`), described more fully in Chapter 13, includes links to the contact information for the ombudsman program in each state.

- There are two national trade associations of nursing homes. The American Health Care Association (`www.ahca.org`) primarily represents the for-profit nursing home industry, and the American Association of Homes and Services for the Aging (`www.aahsa.org`) primarily represents the not-for-profit industry. Their web sites not only provide information about their member institutions, but include articles and background information about nursing home services more generally. Each web site offers its own version of a Consumer Guide to choosing a nursing home.

- Not quite an antitrade association but a useful complement to the two organizations just mentioned is the National Citizens' Coalition for Nursing Home Reform (NCCNHR) (`www.nursinghomeaction.org`). Founded in 1975 by people working with Ralph Nader investigators, it focuses on abuse of the elderly in nursing homes. NCCNHR's main financial issue concerns how nursing homes treat Medicaid residents. It too offers a freely available guide on how to choose a nursing home. While it is not dramatically different from the guides offered by the trade associations, all these materials should be viewed as pieces of the same textbook.

- Financial professionals and consumers alike will benefit from several recent articles on nursing home choice published in *Consumer Reports* magazine. However, a much more comprehensive resource is the *Complete Guide to Health Services for Seniors,* a 600-page book written by Trudy Lieberman and the editors of *Consumer Reports.* The book includes two very valuable resources on nursing home selection. First, it includes a comprehensive section on reviewing different kinds of long-term care services in general, with a separate chapter on nursing home choice—all presented with the *Consumer Reports* traditional style of buyer-beware skepticism. Second, because your client's father needs a zip code, Appendix M is the Consumers Union's 52-page *Nursing Home Watch List,* listing over 1,500 nursing homes that have been found in official state inspections to have a high level of deficiencies. The list is very specific, organized by state, and includes the name, city, and street address of the watched nursing home. (Only the zip code is missing!) A description of the deficiencies rating criteria is given; the following summarizes the criteria:

> GUIDE TO THE RATINGS: The following facilities had state inspection surveys during the period from July 1995 to October 1998 that we have judged to raise questions about the quality of care delivered to residents. . . . Because some facilities historically have a "yo-yo" pattern of compliance, meaning that inspectors found no deficiencies one year and many the next, it is possible that a facility listed here now has a current survey showing no deficiencies. If you are using or considering one of these facilities, check surveys reported over a four-year period to assure yourself that prior problems have indeed been corrected.

The (Nursing) Home Shopping Network: Using the Interactive Nursing Home Compare

Beyond these books and guides, one of the best ways to explore the range of available nursing home services in your client's community is the hands-on use of the Nursing Home Compare web site. Nursing Home Compare (NHC) is a free Internet service provided by the Centers for Medicare and Medicaid Services (CMS, the new name for HCFA, the Health Care Financing Administration). The web site states that "it contains information on every Medicare and Medicaid-certified nursing home in the country, including over 17,000 nationwide." The address is `www.medicare.gov/NHCompare`.

We briefly describe this valuable service, introducing how it can be used and how the information can be applied to a client's needs. The best approach, however, is old-fashioned learn-by-doing. As I continually remind my daughter about these kinds of things, it's free and you can't break it.

What the Web Site Offers

The opening screen asks if you want to search by state, county, city, zip code, or by the name of a specific nursing home. After being told that there are 774 nursing homes in Pennsylvania, I narrowed the search by entering my zip code and was told there was only one nursing home in the selected area. (By the way, it had zero health deficiencies; see following.)

When more than one nursing home is retrieved, they are compared side by side as columns on the page/screen. Separate sets of information describe the nursing home, the residents, and officially documented discrepancies. Alas, no cost information is included.

Nursing home information starts with the facility's name, address, phone number, and Medicare provider number. The number of beds, of residents, whether or not it has both Medicare and Medicaid participation, and date of most recent state inspection are listed. The ownership status is described (e.g., nonprofit or for-profit, part of a chain, located within a hospital).

Resident information indicates the percentage of residents who have various kinds of health problems and care needs. For each of a dozen or so problems, the percentage of *this* nursing home's residents with the problem is compared via a bar chart to all facilities in the state and in the nation as a whole. Each of these health problems is accompanied by a clear statement describing why this piece of patient information is useful. For example, if a large percentage of the residents are incontinent, it means a greater workload for the staff. The consumer should then judge if the staff appears large enough to handle the burden.

Perhaps most useful is the information on deficiencies based on Medicare-directed state inspections of nursing homes. Deficiencies are listed (and tallied) about mistreatment, quality of care, healthful environment, nursing and administrative staff response deficiencies, and whether residents' rights are being violated. Each deficiency is rated on a four-point intensity scale measuring the level of harm to residents.

The beginning of the report for each nursing home includes the total number of deficiencies and the date of the most recent inspection. CMS requires that states inspect their nursing homes at least once every 15 months. In our trial use of Nursing Home Compare in mid-2001, none of the listed inspections was older than 2000.

How the Information Can Be Used

If a client needs to know where nearby nursing homes are located, the Nursing Home Compare service is an excellent sources of names and address. But there are other big picture Wealth Span planning functions that the web site can serve. Consider just a few:

- Your Yellow Pages will provide names, addresses, and phone numbers, but NHC can identify them in terms of size, ownership, and other information not provided in a phone book.

- Discovering the actual number of nursing homes in an area can be an important early-stage piece of information when your middle-aged client is contemplating decisions about an elderly parent. If your client, who lives in Chicago and has a sister in Knoxville, has a widowed father in failing health in Denver, one piece of the overall planning process is the availability of desirable nursing homes in the three cities. Of course, this is only one piece of a complex Wealth Span family decision, but if there are no suitable nursing homes in Denver, then the decision process becomes more focused.

- Medicare participation is an important variable, indicating that the nursing home meets specified standards of care. You might wonder why Medicare issues are relevant since Medicare does not pay for long-term chronic care in nursing homes (see Chapter 9). Because Medicare does pay for more intense posthospitalization rehabilitation care, most nursing homes want to receive Medicare certification. Your client would want to know that (1) the nursing home in Knoxville is good enough to meet Medicare standards, and also (2) if her father does need postsurgical rehabilitation services, he will be in a place that has been certified to offer them.

- Most nursing homes are Medicare certified. Some are only Medicaid certified, meaning that they meet standards for chronic custodial care but not the higher standards for physical and occupational therapy required for Medicare certification. If your client is given a brochure about a nursing home that is *not* listed in NHC, this means that it is neither Medicaid nor Medicare certified. Maybe the place has such a wealthy clientele that they never use Medicare-reimbursed rehab services. Such is unlikely but not impossible. In any event, not being either Medicare or Medicaid certified raises a red flag.

- The inspection and deficiency information can be critical, and certainly will not be listed either in the Yellow Page ad or in the nursing home's brochure. The NHC deficiency ratings will tell if the facility has many or is free of deficiencies, how long ago the deficiencies were reported by the state, and whether they are threats to health or administrative snafus.

- Your client might also look at patterns of deficiencies across several nursing homes. For example, if your client is interested in a relatively new and not-yet-inspected facility that is part of a nursing home chain, NHC will show how other facilities owned or managed by that company in your state and around the country have fared in state inspections. Given recent mergers and acquisitions in the nursing home industry, find out if behind the familiar Happy Terrace Care Center name carved on the entry arch [*Note:*

A Continuing Story

As part of this research I used NHC to check out the Medicare-certified rehab center where my mother spent 12 days after hip surgery a couple of years ago. She found the place disgusting, but it was recommended by the hospital discharge nurse. It was on the CU Watch List (1995–1998 data), and NHC reported a May 2000 inspection with over a dozen deficiencies. Mother was right again! If we had known about the deficiencies, we would have asked the discharge nurse to keep looking. Better yet, I could have logged on to Nursing Home Compare.

this is intended to be fictitious] there is a parent corporation that operates nursing homes under different names in various states—and learn what *their* deficiency record is.

Following on Consumers Union's comment about a "yo-yo" pattern of deficiencies, I looked at a quick and dirty sampling of two nursing homes in each of five states listed on their Watch List. CU used 1995 to 1998 data, and current NHC data are from more recent state inspections in 2000 or 2001. I verified that these were the same facilities by name, address, and Medicare number. Currently nine of the ten had from 3 to 21 current health deficiencies. The tenth home had disappeared.

Home Care

At the other end of the long-term care continuum is home care. If possible, it would always be preferable to live out one's life at home. For many older people, as health declines and functional disabilities accumulate, it may not be feasible to stay at home. In the context of long-term care, one way to assess the likelihood that home care is realistic is to contrast care at the two ends of the continuum.

Why and When Home Care?

Why would a person move into the dreaded nursing home? If an older person's illness, disability, or frailty is so substantial that hospital-like services and environment are necessary, then the nursing home is appropriate. Another scenario involves cognitive decline. An older person may be physically strong enough to take care of himself, including taking his medications, but if he forgets how or when to do so, then the functional capacity for independent living may be gone. It should be kept in mind that although Alzheimer's disease starts out as a decline in memory and cognitive capacity, in its later stages it is a physical health disease as well.

Another scenario focuses on family as a support system. We know that most care provided to older people is from family, sometimes the spouse and more often from adult children. But what happens when the need for care moves from household social and personal supports to more substantial health needs?

Much family and aging research in recent years tell us that the single most important predictor of moving into a nursing home is neither mental nor physical decline, but the absence of another person to assist in either providing or coordinating daily care. This well-documented principle can be combined with a more formal definition presented in the *Encyclopedia of Home Care for the Elderly:* Home care is a program of services provided under health leadership at home for the chronically impaired who do not require 24-hour institutional care but who are incapable of full-time independent living due to physical or mental impairment.

Home Care as the Alternative

In other words, in many cases the key to home care as a viable alternative to the nursing home is a family member (or other caregiver) and an appropriate set of outside health and personal care services brought into the home. These services can be brought into either the parent's own home or to the daughter's home. If the parent can still live relatively independently in his or her own home, the home care services can include housekeeping, delivered meals, companions, and transportation services.

Whether the parent stays in her own home or moves in with a child, services more directly identified as long-term care can be brought into the home including personal assistance (such as the ADLs discussed in Chapter 2) and a range of health and rehabilitative services. Home care can include companion and transportation services, as well as respite services for the home-based caregiver—care for the caregiver.

There are over 8,000 home care and home health care agencies in the United States. While there have always been some home health services (the rumor is that doctors used to make house calls), the substantial growth in the number of agencies, as noted in the following section, is mainly due to Medicare's use of home health services as part of posthospitalization rehabilitation (recall that Medicare does not support chronic long-term care). This dramatic expansion over the past 20 years in Medicare reimbursement of home health services in turn has expanded an industry that now also provides some long-term care at home services.

Among the thousands of home care agencies are for-profit and volunteer nonprofit agencies, programs administered from inside hospitals, and some services provided by state and local health departments. Interestingly, in the past few years nursing homes (and some assisted living companies) also have begun to offer in-home health and long-term care services.

Visiting home health professionals include nurse practitioners who are registered nurses with master's level nursing training, usually with a specialty. In recent years, the Geriatric Nurse Practitioner has become a specialization certified by the American Nurses Association. Home care agencies can also provide nursing aides, physical therapists, diabetes and other pharmaceutical educators, nutrition counselors, clinical psychologists, social workers, and companions.

The Medicare–Home Care–Long-Term Care Connection

From a client perspective the impact of Medicare on home care is important to long-term care in three ways:

1. Medicare policy fostered the expansion of the number and kind of geriatric health services that can be administered in the home and not just in a hospital setting.

2. It stimulated the development of the home health care industry, such that these health services are available throughout the country.

3. Because Medicare pays for (reimburses) these services, it has also established a home health certification system.

The situation is similar to the connection between nursing homes and Medicare described earlier in this chapter. Although Medicare doesn't pay for long-term nursing home care, it certifies nursing homes because of the Medicare-reimbursed short-term rehabilitation care they provide.

A connection between Medicare-certified home health agencies and long-term care came about as Congress took notice of the rapidly increasing *Medicaid* payments for the long-term care of older poor people in nursing homes. In 1981, Congress authorized a few states to pay for home-delivered long-term care services on a trial basis. By 1995, such pilot programs were available in all 50 states. Thus, it became established that long-term care could be provided as home care.

Whether home care actually saves money, for the family or for the country, is still being researched and debated. The result of these programs, however, is that in both the public and private sectors there is now a widespread national availability of Medicare-certified home care agencies that have developed the capacity to deliver personal and medical long-term care services away from the nursing home.

Advising Clients about Home Care Choices

- Although Medicare certifies home care agencies, the results are not as publicly accessible as are the nursing inspection data. An especially good consumer resource is the *Consumer Reports* Health Guide described above. The authors offer a comprehensive set of questions to guide the selection of a home care agency. CU also discusses the tax implications of hiring an individual (versus an agency), recommends a written contract, and provides a model contract to start the process.
- If your client will be involved in the caregiving, the one-volume *Encyclopedia of Home Care for the Elderly* published in 1995 by Greenwood Press is a comprehensive source. It focuses substantially on how to work and cope with such health issues as cancer and cardiac patient care, hearing impairment, Alzheimer's and Parkinson's diseases, and diabetes. Another set of articles focuses on how various professions can be used in home-based long-term care (e.g., clinical social workers and geriatric nurse practitioners).
- The Eldercare Locator is a public service of the Administration on Aging (see Chapter 12). It operates as a national call-in referral service to locate local-level agencies and companies that specialize in providing home care (and other services) to older people. The hotline is open Monday through Friday, 9 A.M. to 8 P.M., Eastern time. `1-800-677-1116`.
- Because, as noted above, Medicare has become a substantial payer of home services, the "Alternatives to Nursing Homes" section of its consumer web site (`www.medicare.gov/nursing/alternatives`) offers additional information on the circumstances under which Part A will pay for home care services.
- The most comprehensive consumer-oriented resource is the web site of the National Association of Home Care (NAHC), the industry's main trade association (`www.nahc.org/Consumer`). While NAHC honestly discloses that it is "dedicated to making home care and hospice providers' lives easier," the site also includes valuable consumer information. The "How to Choose a Home Care Provider" section of the web site includes definitions of home care, a listing of accreditation agencies, a summary of how home

care can be paid for by either private or public sources, and a national home care locator. The agency locator asks for city, state, and zip code, and then allows the consumer to specify the kind of home care needed. The online questionnaire also allows the consumer to specify such services as physical therapy, dietitian service, respiratory therapy, and nursing services. As an extension of this guidance, the web site offers an extensive checklist of questions the consumer should ask of the candidate agencies, and further recommends that these agencies be reviewed with physicians, hospital discharge planners, and the local Area Agency on Aging.

Assisted Living

On the continuum of long-term care, between the nursing home and home care is a relatively new kind of long-term care known as *assisted care* or more usually as *assisted living.* Like home care, assisted living focuses more on residential and *personal care* rather than *health care* (to again use Professor Robert Atchley's distinction). Like nursing homes, however, assisted living means living in a group context with similar financial and administrative considerations to be understood and choices to be made.

Board and Care

Before there was large-scale, commercial, long-term residential care now known as assisted living, there was smaller-scale residential care for relatively independent elderly known as *board and care.*

A board and care home is fundamentally a relatively small (five to eight residents) group residence with meals provided for older persons who are pretty much able to take care of themselves. The *care* in board and care is usually quite minimal, including housekeeping, laundry, and help getting to the dining room as needed. Board and care is traditionally found in the large homes of families who rent out their unused bedrooms to functionally independent elderly women and sometimes men.

These group homes are not intended to be health facilities, and the staff is likely to include mainly housekeepers and cooks, with no trained nursing or health care professionals on the premises. They vary substantially in size and quality, are basically "mom and pop" sole proprietorship small businesses, and are unregulated as a kind of geriatric residence.

The Need for Larger-Scale Assisted Living

The image of board and care services provided in an elegant old mansion-like house suggests a kind of permanent senior citizen bed and breakfast. Despite this idyllic picture, at least three factors contribute to the development of the modern larger-scale assisted living facility.

The first is simply gerontological demographics. The size of the elderly population will continue to grow substantially. Second, the different kinds of required personal care and the levels of that care in group residences are also expanding. A facility with 50 to 150 residents can afford to have the staff, facilities, and equipment to provide such care.

The third factor is a kind of multiplier of the previous two factors. We again refer to increasing life expectancy accompanied by extended number of years of potential frailty for many older persons—described by the Squaring of the Curve in Figure 8.1. An increasing proportion of a larger older population will live longer independently, but then require a higher level of personal assistance.

Table 2.2 documented the higher levels of assistance with ADLs that are associated with advanced older age. Earlier in this chapter, we noted that the average age at which people first enter a nursing home is getting older. Overall, the dynamics of individual aging and population aging are producing an increasingly large population of older people who may not be able to live totally independently in their own homes but do not need the medical care and intensive hospital-like health care that is characteristic of the nursing home.

What, Then, Is Assisted Living?

There is no clearer definition of *assisted living* than the one offered by Professor Victor A. Regnier. Regnier is especially qualified to speak on the subject: He holds a unique joint appointment as Professor of Gerontology *and* Professor of Architecture at the University of Southern California. He is a Fellow both of the Gerontological Society of America and of the American Institute of Architects.

In *Assisted Living Housing for the Elderly: Design Innovations from the United States and Europe* (1994) he writes:

> Simply stated, assisted living is a long-term care alternative that involves the delivery of professionally managed personal and health care services in a group setting that is residential in character and appearance in ways that optimize the physical and psychological independence of residents.

Regnier extends the definition by noting that the goal of assisted living is to keep older adults out of nursing homes and hospitals as long as possible. The primary set of services are personal care with a strong dimension of personal self-management as long as this is feasible, extended by a range of health care assistance. The professional nature of the assistance provided is an important contrast to most board and care homes, senior apartment buildings, sheltered housing, and other places whose primary goal is limited to providing residence and meals for older persons.

Within the assisted living building, residence is typically in a private or a shared room. Although most of the time it would be appropriate to refer to a *room* rather than an *apartment,* in some facilities the room is much like an efficiency apartment in many urban apartment buildings. That is, the space is one room with a bedroom area separate from a den or living room area, and with its own bathroom.

Many of the newer facilities have some kind of kitchenette-like space including a sink, small built-in refrigerator, and kitchen-like cabinets. In some older places, a refrigerator can be brought in. Because meals are part of the basic assisted living services, few if any have stoves but many allow microwave ovens. Any or all of these kitchen-like amenities can be turned off or removed if and when they pose a safety hazard.

Safety features include emergency pull-cords in the bathroom and in other parts of the room. Some use the telephone as part of the emergency response system, and others have intercom systems. While some older assisted living places are in converted hotels, newly built facilities have wider hallways and doorways for wheelchairs and walkers, grab-bars in the bathroom, and handles rather than round doorknobs.

Other physical features include the group dining room, living room or den areas for social interaction, places for games and television viewing, and other features to provide a home like rather than an institutional environment.

A Wealth Span Question: Should the Place Look Nice?

Before we proceed to a brief summary of the kinds and costs of personal and health services that are part of assisted living, let's take a look at an issue that appears to be controversial but probably shouldn't be—a combined Wealth Span and consumer beware issue. How important should the appearance of the place be? Are assisted living facilities purposely designed and decorated to encourage unnecessary, frivolous family expenditures whose real purpose is to fatten the assisted living company's bottom line?

As with several of the other health-related issues discussed in these chapters, the Consumers Union's *Complete Guide* to senior health services does a pretty good job of guiding the advisor and the client in locating and evaluating an assisted living facility—with one important exception. The *Guide's* collective authorship seems very concerned, almost to the point of being offended, with private companies' efforts to make their facilities look nice.

CU's concern is that the entrepreneurs that build assisted living facilities are constructing facilities that appeal to the aesthetics of adult children. CU quotes a speaker at an assisted living trade association meeting who said that first impressions are the key to marketability. The *Guide* then seems almost offended by the fact that in one facility a snack area is called the butlery, and that specialized Alzheimer's units are given kinder, gentler names such as reminiscence center or memory support center.

To be sure, and with quite appropriate consumer protection concerns, the *Guide* states that "a fancy front room with Georgian-style furniture and an ice cream parlor do not guarantee that a resident needing a bath every day will get one. . . ." The *Guide* observes that it is often the middle-aged child who is selecting a facility for the parent, but concludes that the outward design of these facilities is directed to appeal to the child, rather than to what older residents really find important. The result is, in the Consumers Union's view, that "adult children, lured by clever marketing and the classy appearance of many facilities, are coaxing their often reluctant parents into this relatively new kind of care arrangement."

In contrast, recall that *residential in character and appearance* is one of the central components of Professor Regnier's definition of assisted living, a concept that is not made casually. Later in his book, Regnier notes that the design of an assisted living place serves two purposes. The first is functionality, for example, how well room layouts, lighting, and furnishings will facilitate safety and accessibility. But the second purpose is how the design of the place influences the attitudes and the behavior of all the participants in the process, including the residents, visitors, staff, and family members.

> If a setting is viewed as an institution, then residents are often seen as sick, feeble, or unhealthy. Viewed from the perspective of a residential environment, expectations regarding competency, independence, vulnerability, and dependence are often different. The environment becomes a frame that establishes expectations and beliefs.

For the Wealth Span advisor, both the consumer vigilance perspective and the gerontological architect's perspective have merit. A fancy lobby and dining room should not mask poor services and broken promises. The amenities should not be shallow marketing devices to appeal to the tastes of middle-class middle-agers. However, older parents, like their adult children, might like the amenities.

Unlike the crisis atmosphere in which nursing home choices often have to be made, assisted living decisions should and often can be part of a decision process that unfolds over months or weeks, rather than hours and minutes.

The older person should be a full member of this process, and the choice should reflect her values and preferences, as well as financial and gerontological opportunities and constraints. After all, this will now be your client's mother's home, and possibly her last one.

And so the ambience, the furniture, and the pleasant decor are part of a very important set of residential and lifestyle choices. Indeed, even the Consumers Union *Guide* acknowledges that those old-fashioned ice cream parlors and 1940s-style jukeboxes are designed to make the World War II generation feel at home.

Assisted Living Services

The basic services included in assisted living are housekeeping and meals. Transportation (to doctors, shopping malls, and entertainment) is typically included also. For many older persons, such assistance may be sufficient. They are freed from shopping, cooking, housekeeping, house maintenance, all within a sheltered living environment where help is available when the cord is pulled or the button is pushed. To be sure, some of these basic services can be provided in the form of home care discussed earlier in this chapter. In assisted living, however, the older person and his family are freed from what Chapter 9 refers to as "Wealth Span Planning for Medical Administration"—the responsibility of coordinating and monitoring the different services.

Surveillance services are an especially important aspect of the assistance, although not always easy to spot. The pull-cords, buttons, and other emergency response systems are physical devices, some of which can be installed in a private home or apartment.

The congregate aspects of assisted living, however, add an additional layer of *passive surveillance.* If a resident does not show up for breakfast when she usually does, this will be noticed by staff right away. The failure to pick up the mail or a daily newspaper offers a similar kind of unobtrusive monitoring. Showing up for breakfast in her bathrobe when she is usually dressed meticulously can be another red flag. Housekeepers on their daily rounds can notice many signs of decline.

Beyond these basic levels of assisted living, the higher levels of care focus on help with the ADLs discussed earlier. Help with taking a bath is often one of the first kinds of assistance needed, as the list and the percentages in Table 2.2 indicate. Help with getting dressed may follow.

Again, the home care alternative offers an important contrast. Much of this assistance can be brought into the home through visiting nurses, companions, aides, and others. One of the values of the assisted living facility is that the staff to perform these services is already on site, again freeing the family from the administrative burdens of hiring and monitoring care providers. If the need for the bathing and dressing assistance is temporary or episodic, purchasing such help in the form of home care can be especially costly, both financially and psychologically.

Along with increased personal help with daily assistance, assisted living facilities can offer a range of health assistance. Here, however, the distinction with nursing homes becomes important because assisted living facilities are not licensed by state or federal authorities as skilled nursing facilities. Thus, unless the facility has hired a registered nurse to be a part of the staff, such medical needs as administration of injectable medicines may not be available. However, volunteer or paid visiting nurses can be brought into an assisted living resident's home just as they can be brought into a private home (see the Medicare discussion below). Catheters and intravenous medicines on a continuing basis are also typically beyond the staff and the regulatory capacity of assisted living facilities; should such needs arise, it may signal the need for a move to a nursing home.

Assisted living can provide assistance with the administration of prescription and nonprescription medicines. [*Note:* Some states' regulations may curtail or prohibit this service.] As needed, the resident can be freed from the tasks of filling the prescriptions and refills, of counting and sorting the daily regimen of tablets, and worrying about the time and coordination of taking the medicines. Specialized pharmacies are used to fill the prescriptions with single pills packaged with the name of the patient and the drug, the dosage and frequency, and instructions. Assisted living staff then take the responsibility of bringing the medicine to the resident.

These can be costly services not only because of the cost of the additional staff, but because 30 individually packaged pills are more expensive than a bottle of 30 pills. However, supplementary retiree health insurance or privately purchased medigap insurance with a pharmaceutical benefit may cover the increased cost of these medicines.

Models of Assisted Living

From a financial perspective, most assisted living can be described as a kind of apartment hotel model of living. Like an apartment, the room (or apartment) is the permanent residence of its occupant, often with much of her own furniture, books, television, and decorations. Like a hotel, however, there is regular housekeeping, linen service, and other basics. Also like a hotel, there can be room service for meals when going to the dining room is difficult. Like an apartment, there is a monthly rental, and contracts are usually on a month-to-month basis, although sometimes there is a minimum three- or four-month stay. And more like an apartment than a hotel, there also may be a 30-day notice required before the resident leaves.

The Condo Model versus the Apartment Model

We use the term *apartment* for an additional reason: Its rental context separates it from the *condo* model. As in residential real estate, in the condo model of assisted living, the resident purchases her apartment (or townhouse). In the assisted living context, the condo model is known as the *continuing care retirement community* (CCRC). The down payment or purchase price for a CCRC unit is in the thousands and can be in the hundreds of thousands of dollars.

In earlier years, the CCRC was typically known as the *life care community.* Life care meant that the resident was purchasing (1) an upscale condo unit as a residence in a place specially designed for older residents; (2) an array of assisted living services similar to those described above; and (3) nursing home care either on the CCRC campus or in a nearby nursing home. In a very real sense, then, the condo model reflects the full long-term care continuum, from residence to home care to assisted living to long-term care insurance to nursing home care.

While some continuing care advocates argue that CCRCs can be developed for middle- and even lower-income residents, to date this model represents a major Wealth Span *set* of choices and decisions. It is a set of substantial real estate, investment, and family finance choices as well as long-term care and insurance decisions. While the CCRC is beyond the scope of this discussion, we include some basic sources of information and analysis at the end of this section.

Services, Costs, and Levels of Care

Given the apartment–hotel model of assisted living services, payment is typically assessed in terms of levels of care. Because there are seemingly countless ways that this principle can be implemented (e.g., how levels of care are defined and distinguished, or how different units or levels of services are priced), this is clearly a situation of Wealth Span consumer awareness and continuing vigilance.

Most assisted living facilities use a level-of-care approach. A basic or entry level of care and cost reflects the monthly rental, housekeeping, meals, and perhaps transportation and entertainment/event costs. Before moving into the facility the older person is evaluated by the social work and health staff to assess how much assistive care is needed (i.e., to determine what services above the basic entry level might be needed).

A second level of care and cost might include help with one or two ADLs. Some facilities define this assistance in terms of hours of daily care, sometimes in quarter- or half-hour units of daily time. The Consumers Union *Guide* found that some commercial assisted living chains automatically assign a new resident to a higher (and more expensive) level of care, promising to reevaluate and possible downgrade the level and cost after three to six months; clearly a buyer beware issue. Third or fourth levels of care are also possible using the same process.

Some not-for-profit assisted living facilities, operated by religious denominations or fraternal organizations, may use a single cost for all residents, a financial approach that implies an insurance logic. All residents pay the same underlying care rate (although the specific monthly rental will reflect the size and location of the apartment). The risk-pooling idea is that all or most residents will eventually need higher-intensity, higher-cost assistance as they get older (Table 2.2 and Figure 8.1 again). At any one time the less dependent residents are subsidizing the more service-dependent residents, but eventually the costs even out.

Because of all these kinds of variations, and a lack of standard packages of services (akin to the standardized features in medigap insurance policies), average costs may not be usefully accurate. CU anecdotally mentions monthly fees ranging from $1,800 to $4,000. In illustrating price changes, CU describes a person who paid $2,400 per month in 1990 whose cost rose to $3,400 by 1999. The Assisted Living Federation of America and the National Center for Assisted Living, both trade associations for the assisted living industry, report ranges of $25 to $200 per day and $500 to $3,500 per month. Again, these are only broad suggestive numbers, since the basic price of an apartment or room varies with its location in the facility, and monthly charges vary in terms of levels of care and services that may cost extra in one facility but be included in the monthly price in another.

Medicare and Assisted Living

Earlier in this chapter, we noted that Medicare does not pay for chronic long-term care, either in nursing homes or in assisted living facilities. However, when counseling a family about the financial aspects of assisted living, Wealth Span advisers should remind the client that Dad retains all his Medicare benefits whether he lives in his own apartment, in their home, or in a commercial assisted living facility.

If the older person has to go into the hospital, Medicare Part A will pay the same hospital bills and require the same deductibles and co-payments no matter where he resides. Primary care physicians as well as surgeons and other specialists are reimbursed by Medicare Part B, again independent of where the patient resides.

As usual, however, there are the good news–bad news exceptions. The good news is that, as noted in Chapter 9, much of the posthospitalization rehabilitation that Medicare Part A covers can now be received as home care rather than in skilled nursing facilities (nursing homes, SNFs). Visiting nurses, visiting physical therapists, and diabetes education are all Medicare-covered services that can be provided in the home, and therefore in the assisted living facility. The facility itself may have administrative specialists who can help the resident and the family navigate the Medicare rules and reimbursement procedures, and also help organize and schedule the home care visits.

Some physicians still make house calls—to older patients in assisted living facilities. If your client's mother does not have a continuing relationship with a physician, the facility may suggest physicians who make regular visits to the place. Medicare Part B will cover these doctor's appointments whether in the doctor's office or in the patient's assisted living home.

But some potential bad news: The resident or a family member should be confident that the physician contact is substantial and medically valuable. Among the nursing home scandals of the 1970s were stories of physicians who saw (quite literally, probably) 20 patients per hour in a single nursing home, and charged Medicare for full office visits.

As a related occasion for awareness, in its *Guide,* CU described some assisted living facilities that were part of an HMO-like managed care organization, and thus include the use of their group physicians as a required part of the contract. If using these doctors is the resident's choice, it may be convenient and medically preferable. But if she has her own long-standing doctor or she belongs to a different HMO, then her Medicare benefits may be redundant to the newly required physician use.

Advising Clients About Assisted Living Choices

- *The assisted living decision as a deliberative process.* The choice of a nursing home is often a choice made in the context of a medical crisis, not a deliberative decision. By contrast, the need for the move from one's own home to assisted care often can be anticipated months in advance and therefore can truly be a deliberative decision process. My own focus group research validates the commonsense view that the process directly must include the older person who will be the resident. We studied focus groups of elders, of middle-aged children, and of parent–child dyads. The kids often misread their parents who typically wanted independence with an acknowledged need for assistance, but not to be fully insulated and coddled. When Wealth Span advisors are asked for guidance, the middle-aged children should be advised to ask their parents about all their preferences and their dislikes, and then learn which are the non-negotiable demands and which are the malleable preferences, for example: living near the kids or not; in a new warm climate or back in the old neighborhood; with religious or ethnic comrades or in the midst of heterogeneity; must be able to keep the cat and be near the church or it doesn't matter.

- *The neighborhood Geriatric Care Manager.* Chapter 12 describes the Wealth Span professional as a gerontology team member. When it comes to selecting an assisted living facility, the local Geriatric Care Manager, also described in Chapter 12, is another key professional team member. She is not only a nurse, social worker, psychologist, or gerontologist, but has substantial knowledge of the local community. As a fee-for-service professional, she should talk with your client and the elder family member, help to assess the values and preferences, and work with the Wealth Span advisor concerning the financial opportunities and constraints. Then she will identify the possibly appropriate assisted living facilities, help to refine the list, narrow the choices, and arrange for visits to the finalists. If your client's mother lives halfway across the country, a geriatric care manager out there can be engaged, and the same kinds of services can be provided, again capitalizing on her experience with that local community. Unfortunately, there is no government-organized comparison directory, such as Medicare's Nursing Home Compare described earlier, for assisted living. Chapter 12, however, describes in more detail the National Association of Professional Geriatric Care Managers and its useful web site.
- *Assisted Living Federation of America (ALFA) and the National Center for Assisted Living (NCAL).* The two primary trade associations for assisted living facilities are ALFA and NCAL. While both organizations' web sites are primarily focused on their industry and members, both also offer two sets of consumer-oriented services. The first is general consumer information describing the structure, philosophy, services, and public policy issues surrounding assisted living. Second, like the nursing home association web sites described earlier in this chapter, both of these web sites offer search facilities. NCAL is actually the assisted living subsidiary of the American Health Care Association (AHCA), the trade association for for-profit nursing homes, which now includes for-profit assisted living companies. ALFA's directory search is based on its *Careguide* magazine. Although the magazine is available on a paid subscription basis, many of its

consumer-oriented how-to-do-it articles are freely available on the ALFA web site (www.alfa.org). NCAL offers more assisted living consumer information on its web site (www.ncal.org) than does ALFA, including a very consumer-friendly and informative analysis of long-term care insurance in general, and how such insurance connects to assisted living.

- As with the resources described in the nursing home section of this chapter, in the assisted living area the trade associations are also balanced by the activities of a consumer organization. The Consumer Consortium on Assisted Living (CCAL) focuses on the rights of frail elderly residents of assisted living facilities. In addition to providing consumer education, CCAL is concerned with the degree to which state regulations of the industry vary, providing some elderly with substantially less regulatory protections than others. Not surprisingly, its web site (www.ccal.org) offers its own version of checklists, questions, and warnings to older persons and their families. In fact, the elements of the assisted living decision process offered by CCAL are noticeably more detailed than the decision checklists offered on the industry web sites.

- The Consumers Union *Complete Guide to Health Services for Seniors* is again a valuable place to start reading. It lists a series of questions consumers should ask about any assisted living contract, with each question described with at least a paragraph of detail (e.g., where will the resident live, are meals included, will privacy be protected, who is in charge of medications, what about transportation, can they kick you out). CU includes a financial checklist to record the costs of specific items, such as additional charges for meals, cable TV hookup, and local phone service. The overall value of CU's tour through the personal and financial process of assisted living choice is substantial, despite what appears to be an overstated and unsubstantiated view that assisted living companies invest in fancy furniture at the expense of quality geriatric services.

- *Continuing care retirement communities.* A brief but comprehensive introduction to CCRCs as a form of long-term care can be found in the CCRC article in the *Encyclopedia of Financial Gerontology* (described in the Chapter 13 Resource Guide). A more consumer-oriented introduction is offered by the AARP web site (www.aarp.org/confacts/housing/ccrc.html), which also offers two additional CCRC-related resources: links to federal government and Better Business Bureau documents, and internal links to AARP discussions of such related topics as home sharing, home modification, and nursing home choice. As noted in the Nursing Homes section of this chapter, the American Association of Homes and Services for the Aged (AAHSA) is the primary industry association of nonprofit nursing homes. It is also represents CCRCs, and its web site (`www.aahsa.org/public/ccrc.htm`) includes an article contrasting nursing homes with CCRCs. The site also advertises AAHSA's directory of over 500 CCRCs in the country, but does not provide online access to the information.

CHAPTER 11

Long-Term Care Finance: Medicaid, Long-Term Care Insurance, and Reverse Mortgages

Wealth Span planning for retirement, or later life in general, is relatively straightforward. Most of the factors involved are knowable and are more or less under one's personal control. Most people nowadays can choose when and how they retire, earlier or later, fully or partially. Most clients know the value of their pensions, investments, Social Security, and other accumulated wealth. As seen in Chapter 9, either in early retirement or by age 65 the personal and family situation with regard to health insurance is fairly well known.

By contrast, planning for long-term care is planning for the unknown. Whether you will be among the 20% who someday will need daily assistance with getting dressed and taking a bath or will be healthy enough to die on the tennis court at age 100 cannot be predicted with much validity or certainty.

Most of us, advisors as well as clients, would like to ignore the likelihood of needing long-term care. This is especially influenced by the traditional view of long-term care as being sent to a nursing home. However, both the content and the context of long-term care are dramatically changing.

Content

Long-term care is no longer only, or even primarily, nursing home care. As Chapter 10 illustrated, the kinds of services that comprise chronic long-term assistive care can be met in a number of different ways, including home care and assisted living facilities.

Context

As society experiences both individual aging (discussed in Chapter 2) and population aging (Chapter 3), the needs for chronic assistance are not limited to the kind of 24-hour, hospital-like medically intensive care that is the hallmark of the nursing home. Rather, as the Squaring of the Curve (Chapter 8) implies, many aging persons will experience incremental changes in their needs for care, relatively slow decreases in functional limitations spread over several years, and never require intensive nursing care.

Given this modern pattern of the content and context of aging and long-term care services, the financing planning for long-term care should also take these new patterns into account. For example, an insurance policy that pays for nursing home care only would be inadequate no matter how little it costs in premiums or how much it pays in benefits. This is less a problem than it was as recently as five years ago, as many long-term care insurance companies now recognize the need to pay for different kinds of long-term care. Nonetheless, from a Wealth Span perspective, the changing terrain of long-term care needs and services means that long-term care financial plans also must be kept up to date.

Public Worry and Misunderstanding About Long-Term Care Finance

Chapter 10 documented the degree to which the American public is concerned and worried about the costs of long-term care. As the pattern in Table 10.1 indicates, 80% of the public is worried that the costs of long-term care will reduce their retirement income and assets, with middle-agers even more worried than others. Measured in a different way in Table 10.2, when asked about their worries about living to age 75, more people are more worried about spending all your money on long-term care than are worried about outliving your pension and savings.

Despite these concerns, relatively few people are well informed about how long-term care can be delivered other than in nursing homes. And over many years surveys continue to find that the public erroneously expects Medicare to pay for their long-term care.

This chapter examines three ways to pay for long-term care: Medicaid, long-term care insurance, and reverse mortgages. Reverse mortgages might be considered as part of a plan to self-insure for future long-term care costs since for many older people a home with a paid-up mortgage is their largest family financial asset.

Our primary focus is to introduce each of these in terms of how comprehensive (or not) each is in light of contemporary long-term care services. The administrative and financial details of long-term care financing are constantly changing (e.g., Medicaid reimbursement rules, or long-term care policy features and premiums). As before, use this chapter as a guide to the basic concepts and controversies; the resources listed at the end of each section and in the Resource Guide should be used to find current details.

Medicaid

Medicaid and Medicare were enacted into law at the same time in 1965. Both share the fundamental American compromise concerning government and health care: governmental structure with individual choice, and private sector insurance mechanisms administered by public-sector agencies. Unlike the British and other European governmental health systems that were seen as threatening American medicine and society in the late 1950s, these programs were modeled on the principles and practices of American private-sector health insurance.

Fundamental to the system is free choice by consumers of their doctors and other health providers, with payment for covered health services as reimbursement by the insurance company in a context of deductibles, co-payments, and specifically covered and excluded services. Medicare is the insurance company for older Americans. Medicaid is the insurance company for poor people of any age.

Why should professional Wealth Span advisors be concerned about Medicaid? After all, Medicaid is a welfare program and few clients of financial counselors are on welfare. For long-term care financial planning, however, the situation is not so simple. Medicaid has become the single largest payer of nursing home bills in the United States. And while the eligibility definitions and procedures may be complex (as suggested below), it turns out that under definable circumstances, middle-class, middle-income elderly can qualify to have their nursing home bills paid by Medicaid. This summary of the technical aspects of Medicaid eligibility processes is drawn from a series of three highly readable and available studies issued in 1999 by the Kaiser Family Foundation. The citations of the reports, which are available both in print and on the Foundation's web site, are noted at the end of this section.

Medicare versus Medicaid: Two Differences

Difference 1: Eligibility

Medicare health insurance is designed to be available to all persons regardless of income, with eligibility based on age. Medicaid health insurance is designed to be available to all persons regardless of age, but with eligibility defined by a means-tested low-income requirement.

The connection between poverty versus medically needy is especially relevant to the issue of long-term care and older people. Medicare does not pay for chronic, long-term care. Medicaid, by contrast, can pay for nursing home care for people who qualify under a state's definitions and guidelines for ascertaining a person's or a family's poverty. Because many older people cannot afford the costs of chronic, long-term care in nursing homes on a sustained basis, they often move into or spend down into poverty because of these long-term care costs. People who become impoverished as a consequence of their residence in a nursing home can qualify for Medicaid benefits. Therefore, understanding these rules and regulations of Medicaid eligibility in advance is critical to the Wealth Span planning for long-term care for a potentially large number of older Americans.

Difference 2: State (Not National) Administration

The other major difference between Medicare and Medicaid concerns program administration. Medicare is a national program. Eligibility for Medicare benefits at age 65 is the same throughout the country. Costs of Medicare insurance, including premiums, deductibles, and co-payments, and the profile of Medicare Part A Hospital Insurance and Part B Medical (physician) Insurance benefits are the same throughout the country.

By contrast, Medicaid is a cooperative program jointly administered by the states and the federal government. The state role is central in establishing the specific definitions, rules, and procedures by which individuals qualify for Medicaid benefits, including nursing home payments. In the Kaiser Foundation's more formal definition of Medicaid, the state's central role is seen in how federal funds are spent: Medicaid makes federal matching funds available to states for the costs the states incur in paying health care providers for covered services to eligible individuals. Low-income individuals who meet their state's Medicaid eligibility criteria are entitled to have the state pay for the covered services. In turn, states are entitled to federal matching funds for these costs.

In other words, within federal guidelines it is the states that establish eligibility criteria and the states that pay for covered health services, and then get reimbursed via matching funds from the federal government.

Medicaid is designed as a welfare program, an insurance program to pay certain medical bills of people whose income and assets fall below an established poverty level. The program is means-tested; that is, eligibility for benefits is based on comparing a person's financial means with a financial standard established by the state.

Medicaid Eligibility for Middle-Income People?

But the story is more complex than this. How is it that Medicaid will pay for the long-term care of middle-income older people? If the devil is in the details, perhaps the angel is in the analysis. Medicaid rules allow for different pathways to eligibility. One major pathway is mandatory or categorical eligibility. If an older person receives payments from SSI (Supplemental Security Income), the national income-welfare program for older persons administered by the Social Security Administration, then he or she is considered categorically (i.e., automatically) eligible for Medicaid benefits including long-term care benefits. (Eleven states have more restrictive eligibility rules but these too must comply with federal requirements.)

The second pathway is directly relevant to the question of Medicaid benefits for middle-income individuals and couples: the medically needy pathway. In this approach, eligibility comes if the costs of medical expenses—including nursing home expenses—causes impoverishment. As of 1998, 35 states (and Washington, D.C.) elected to offer the medically needy pathway to Medicaid benefits. However, the required comparison of family income and asset resources to medical expenses itself is complex, suggesting that the angel is in the analysis. Wealth Span planning should examine such an analysis in advance to determine if a medically needy status is possible or strategically desirable.

The Details and the Analysis

To summarize, all older (age 65+) persons can be considered for Medicaid eligibility through one of three pathways:

1. If they are poor by way of receiving federal SSI payments, they are automatically eligible for their state's Medicaid benefits.

2. If a person is not an SSI recipient, then his or her poverty status must be assessed in terms of the state's Medicaid poverty definitions and procedures.

3. If the person is not judged to be poor by way of the state's poverty definitions, then the medically needy pathway may be available.

In both the state poverty and the medically needy pathways, Medicaid eligibility is determined through analysis of two sets of financial criteria: income tests and resource tests. In turn, for both of these tests there are two components, a *standard* and a *methodology.* For example, a state's income test might stipulate that to be judged poor in that state and thereby eligible for Medicaid an older person must have an income less than $700 per month (the federal poverty level). Another state might use a more lenient 125% of poverty, or $875 per month. These are their standards.

The methodology, however, describes how an older person's income is counted or measured, in comparison to the standard. Social Security benefits, pension payments, interest and dividends, and wages are all potentially countable components of an older person's income. Each state makes its own choices as to which of these income components, and how much, to include or exclude. The same monthly income might qualify for Medicaid benefits in one state but not another.

The same kinds of analysis, a standard and a methodology, apply to the resource test. An elderly person must have resources that are less than the specified standard amount to be eligible for Medicaid benefits. Resources include real estate, stocks and bonds, savings accounts, and cars. A typical Medicaid resource standard is about $2,000 for individuals or $3,000 for an elderly couple.

The methodology, however, determines which items are counted as resources, and how they are valued for purposes of the resource test. A person's home is typically not included regardless of its dollar value. In addition, the first $2,000 of personal effects and the first $4,500 of a car's value may be excluded.

This process moves us closer to answering the Wealth Span planning question of how middle-income elders might qualify for a welfare-oriented public program. The answer is that parallel to this application of the state's old-age poverty definition, the medically needy pathway operates in the same fashion, that is, applying a standard and a methodology to an income test and a resource test.

While most older persons and couples do not have incomes low enough to qualify for Medicaid under the state's income definitions of poverty, 35 states have chosen to establish the medically needy pathway. In this pathway's methodology, income is compared to the person's overall medical expenses over a specified number of months. If income minus medical costs produces a net income that is less than the state's medically needy standard, then the elderly person or couple is eligible for Medicaid-covered services.

Federal regulations mandate that all states include nursing home care as a covered Medicaid benefit. And since the cost of nursing home care can easily exceed monthly income for even moderate or middle-income couples, the medically needy pathway can be useful to many older people in the 35 states.

The Magnitudes and the Moral Dilemma

In light of all this, it should not be surprising that Medicaid has become the single largest payer of nursing home care. According to the Kaiser Foundation reports, Medicaid spending on long-term care was $44 billion in 1997, financing the care of nearly 70% of all nursing home residents. Medicaid spends an average of $7,800 per year (1995 data) on long-term care per elderly beneficiary. Not surprisingly, however, this national Medicaid average hides substantial variation, since each state can develop its own standards and methodologies: from a high of over $15,000 per elderly person in Connecticut, New York, and Washington, D.C., to less than $5,000 in South Carolina, Mississippi, and Oklahoma.

Given these large numbers of dollars, there are now—as always—exceptions to the rules. The medically needy pathway enables, or at least implies, a situation that could allow relatively higher-income older people to obtain Medicaid payment for their nursing home care. Assume a state-defined medically needy income standard of $500 per month—meaning that when an older person's income net of medical expenses falls to $500 or less, he or she has met the standard and becomes eligible for Medicaid benefits.

An older person who has a $4,000 monthly income and who is resident in a $3,300 per month nursing home (less than the current $42,000 annual national average) and has another $300 of monthly out-of-pocket medical expenses, would arithmetically meet the state's income standard that defines *medically needy.* In response to such a situation, 33 states have set an upper limit on income, a *special income rule* methodology for people living in nursing homes. Federal rules allow states to establish their rule as high as 300% of the SSI benefit (about $1,500 per month in 1999). Thus, nursing home residents whose total monthly income is greater than this amount will not qualify for Medicaid, even if their income net of total medical costs is less than the income standard. The devil is in the details after all.

Four general conclusions emerge from this discussion of the complexities of Medicaid eligibility:

1. Medicaid eligibility is a complex financial and procedural process. The specific dollar and percentage numbers shown here are for illustration only. The complexity of the real numbers is due to differences across states in their designation of standards and methodologies, and to continuing changes in national rules and state implementation of those rules.

2. While Medicaid primarily is a welfare program, over the years policy makers have come to recognize that the high costs of medical care and long-term care can cause otherwise middle-income families to become medically needy. Medicaid policy and practice now finance nursing home and related health care benefits for such people. At the same time, in response to or in anticipation of inappropriate use of the medically needy pathway, social policy also includes the special income rule for nursing home residents. [*Note:* A 40-year-old securities analyst with a solidly middle-class income and lifestyle who incurs over $650,000 in hospital and medical bills during her husband's eight-month losing battle with leukemia also qualifies as medically needy. It's not just old people who can become medically needy and qualify for Medicaid benefits.]

3. All financial planners should assess the degree to which their clients, either for themselves or for their parents, may want to attitudinally consider qualifying for Medicaid benefits to help pay for the family's impending or future long-term care costs. In so doing, the next step is recognition that the technical complexity of the process typically requires the involvement of one or more specialists. Whether the specialist is an elder law attorney, a specially trained accountant, or a geriatric care manager, it is an area that goes beyond the everyday expertise of most financial advisors.

4. There is, however, a special challenge for Wealth Span counselors. In addition to the income test, each state also uses a resource test to assess eligibility for the medically needy pathway. For middle-income families the issue of concern here is sometimes referred to as hiding assets or divesting assets in order to qualify under a state's resource test guidelines.

To be sure, Medicaid processes include rules designed to inhibit people from divesting their assets on the eve of entering a nursing home in order to qualify for Medicaid benefits. For example, if the assets are disposed of within 36 months of applying for Medicaid, then (under current law) eligibility is delayed by 36 months, but can start thereafter.

As long as the rules are followed—in other words, with appropriate advance planning—a middle-class elder (or her family on her behalf) can legally meet all the state's resource and income tests including the special income rule, and qualify for Medicaid nursing home benefits. For many older persons and their families, this scenario offers a financial–moral Wealth Span dilemma.

ONE OLDER PERSON ARGUES: I've worked all my life to pass this wealth on to my children. So why should I now have to spend down my resources for long-term care when there is a public program—financed over the years *with my tax dollars*—that will legally pay for my long-term care?

REPLIES ANOTHER OLDER PERSON: I managed to live through the Depression by scrimping and saving and hard work. Didn't go on welfare then or ever. I've always paid my own way. Now I get my Social Security, my automatic COLAs (cost of living allowances), and my Medicare. Medicaid is a welfare program for those poor people. I have no business exploiting a legal loophole and taking that money. And anyhow, I'm not going on welfare!

For some people there is no moral dilemma—they have a clear position, either one of the above. For others whose financial resources in terms of long-term care are marginal, the desire to preserve assets for their family may be paramount. In some cases it may be younger family members who need those inheritable resources who work to see that their elder family member qualifies for Medicare.

Recall again the 2000 public opinion patterns presented at the beginning of Chapter 10. Table 10.2 documents that people of all ages are more worried about spending all their retirement money on long-term care than they are about just outliving their pension and savings. This comparative "worry gap" is larger for higher-income people. For individuals and families for whom these choices are not morally directed, there are no easy financial answers. From a Wealth Span planning perspective, perhaps the answer is a combination of more accumulation, greater financial literacy, and more advanced wise planning.

Hands-On Information and More

- One of the most useful and accessible sources of both professional and consumer information about Medicaid are reports of the Kaiser Family Foundation–Kaiser Commission's *Medicaid and the Uninsured* Project. A series of three reports published in 1999 (May, August, and November) offers both detailed and general information. The reports are freely available for downloading in Acrobat pdf-format at `www.kff.org`. At the site, following a click on the Medicaid button, you can either search or just scan a full list of publications that is organized by date. The November 1999 report on Medicaid's role in long-term care is a comparison of the role of Medicaid, Medicare, and long-term care insurance in paying for the care of older beneficiaries. The May report is a professionals' guide to Medicaid eligibility for the elderly. The full explication of state variations in Medicaid eligibility (the income and the resource tests) on which this chapter's comments are based is presented in this report. The August 1999 report is a consumer's Medicaid primer. This 14-page primer defines Medicaid, describes who is eligible and what it pays for, and provides an excellent (and official) glossary of Medicare–Medicaid language.

- While Medicare has a straightforward web address (`www.medicare.gov`), the Medicaid web site is less easy to find, and not as useful. The entry is through the Health Care Financing Agency (HCFA) (now called the Centers for Medicare and Medicaid Services [CMS]) and from there to Medicaid. The Medicaid articles are directed to professionals, including Wealth Span advisors who may need to know the basics of what Medicaid covers, why, for whom, and with what restrictions. However, because Medicaid national policies are ultimately administered at the state level, the information presented here (`www.hcfa.gov/medicaid/ltchomep.htm`) is general in nature, but does include links and e-mail addresses to direct the user to the necessary state information.

- As in other areas of health, finance, and aging, `www.Elderweb.com` is a very valuable resource. The best parts of the Medicaid section are its Medicaid eligibility and long-term care links to navigate official HCFA/Medicaid information. Issues of state differences in asset transfer, spousal impoverishment, state toll-free 800 telephone numbers, and other program issues are well represented here.

Long-Term Care Insurance

If a family does not qualify for Medicaid, or does not want to try to qualify for publicly funded long-term care, the alternative would typically be phrased as *self-insured,* and so the major alternative focuses on commercially available long-term care insurance.

It is possible to self-insure without purchasing an insurance policy. As many insurance guides suggest, very wealthy families may not want to spend money on insurance if they can pay for the long-term care out of other assets. However, many families either cannot or prefer not to earmark $160,000 or more for this single purpose.

A more practical way for most middle-income families to self-insure is to use the equity in their home. The sale of the home in old age could provide the capital that will pay for long-term care for the rest of the husband's and wife's life. Alternatively, the development of the Home Equity Conversion Mortgage, more generally known as the *reverse mortgage,* now makes it feasible for older families with a paid-up mortgage to use the equity in the home while continuing to live in it as a kind of self-insurance. After considering commercial long-term care insurance, we will conclude this chapter with a brief look at reverse mortgages.

The Costs of Long-Term Care

Throughout these comments about long-term care we have emphasized the fact that long-term care is not simply or only nursing home care. The dreaded nursing home is one part of a continuum of long-term care that also includes assisted living and home care. This point is especially relevant here because a long-term insurance policy that covers only nursing home care is simply insufficient.

That being more or less obvious by now, I will reverse myself (but only for a brief and focused purpose) and direct our attention to the recent and current *cost of nursing home care* in the United States. The purpose is to identify a financial yardstick by which we measure the dollar need for long-term care insurance.

Table 11.1 shows the trend in the average monthly nursing home costs from 1985 to 1997 as compiled by the U.S. Centers for Disease Control and Prevention (CDC). CDC reports that in 1997 the national average month in a nursing home cost $3,609. The more useful average is actually closer to $3,800 as will seen below, but either number is a reasonably good basis for discussing what long-term care insurance should cover, now and in the future.

The cost of nursing home care varies across the regions of the country, being highest in the Northeast and lowest in the Midwest and South. In 17 years the average cost of a month in a nursing home has increased by 145% nationally, which is reflected in all the regions.

Table 11.1 Nursing Home Average Monthly Costs, 1985–1997

	1985	1997	% Change
All facilities	$1,456	$3,609	148%
Northeast	$1,781	$4,589	158%
Midwest	$1,399	$3,203	129%
South	$1,256	$3,225	157%
West	$1,458	$3,791	160%
Ownership			
Private, for-profit	$1,379	$3,508	154%
Non-profit, government	$1,624	$3,792	133%
Certification			
Medicare Only	3%*	$4,221	
Medicaid Only	10%	$2,436	
Both	85%	$3,765	
Neither	2%	$2,422	

* Percentage of all nursing home residents in each kind of facility in 1997.

Source: U.S. Centers for Disease Control and Prevention, 1997.

There is little difference in cost between private for-profit compared to non-profit and government nursing homes, although interestingly the nonprofit group costs a bit more. Both sets of nursing homes experienced the same level of price increase.

The only other distinction we abstracted from the CDC data concerns Medicare versus Medicaid certification. Recall from Chapter 10 that Medicare pays for rehabilitative care that takes place in a skilled nursing facility (SNF) as a follow-up to Medicare-paid hospitalization. Thus, if a nursing home wants to be certified to receive Medicare payments for medically intensive short-term care (and virtually all nursing homes in the United States do), it must be staffed and equipped to provide such care.

It is Medicaid that is the largest U.S. payer of chronic long-term care. To be certified to receive such Medicaid payments nursing homes do not have to have the Medicare-SNF level of nursing staff and other hospital-like medical and health services.

As it turns out, however, most nursing homes that are Medicaid certified are also designed and developed to qualify for Medicare certification as well. This is not only medically convenient for the older beneficiary, but it is good business for the nursing home. Living in a dually certified facility for chronic long-term care purposes, the patient can also receive medical and health-related rehabilitation services, and the SNF can be paid for both kinds of services.

The cost implications are seen in the bottom part of Table 11.1. In 1997, Medicaid-certified-only homes had an average monthly cost of $2,436 and Medicare-only facilities had a cost of $4,221, reflecting their capacity for providing the higher-level short-term medical care in contrast to less intensive chronic long-term care.

Because the CDC monthly cost data were not sorted for this Medicare–Medicaid certification distinction in 1985, we used this space in the table to indicate the percentage of all nursing home residents who, in 1997, lived in each type of nursing home (indicated by the box around the numbers). As it turns out, only 3% are in Medicare-only certified homes and less than 10% are in Medicaid-only certified homes. Since the preponderance (85%) of nursing home residents are in facilities with dual certification, the monthly average of $3,765 is a more accurate estimate of the 1997 national average.

How does the current cost information affect a client's estimate of the need for long-term care insurance? Over the last 17 years the average cost of nursing home care has increased by 148%, a trend that also is seen in the regional and ownership categories. Some might argue that this was an atypically large increase, reflecting in part the impact of expanding federal and state funding of nursing home care.

However, there are several other gerontological and demographic trends that affect the situation. This period experienced increases in population aging, which influence the demand side of the supply and demand of nursing homes. As noted in Chapter 10, people are entering nursing homes for chronic long-term care at older ages and at a higher level of need for personal assistance. Such needs would increase the demand for staff and other health services.

But to the extent that these shorter-term demographic trends may exert an upward pressure on nursing home costs, then we should consider the trends over the next 30 years or so. Even if the rate of nursing home needs does not change much, American society will experience substantial increases in the need for nursing home use simply because of the older aging of the Baby Boom.

There were approximately 1.5 million older (age 65+) nursing home residents in 1997. The CDC estimates that due to Boomer aging there will be 3 million nursing home residents in 2030. "Even if the percent of elderly requiring nursing home care were *reduced* by one-third over the next 30 years, older persons would still need two million beds in traditional long-term care facilities," the CDC concluded. For all these reasons, then, decisions about long-term care insurance should reflect the likelihood that compared to current costs, future costs are likely to be substantially higher.

Who Should Buy Long-Term Care Insurance and Why?

Despite the logical connection between *long-term care* and *health,* long-term care insurance is not seen by everyone as health insurance. In a very real sense it is *estate protection* insurance. Generally, we buy insurance to protect us from the financial consequences of a negative event—car accident, house fire, broken hip, early death, or long-term care. Insurance can't stop the event from happening, it only softens the financial consequences.

The previous paragraphs identified the likely future high costs of long-term care, using trends in nursing home costs as the yardstick. And so the question arises: Under what circumstances should a client purchase insurance to protect against the financial consequences of this expensive risk?

The October 1997 issue of *Consumer Reports* presented a four-article special report on long-term care insurance titled "How Will You Pay for Your Old Age?" The subheading stated: "Long-term-care insurance is one option—an expensive one. Do you need it?" Fair question. The articles contain much valuable information and, in good Consumers Union (CU) style, end with a set of ratings for over 100 specific policies available at that time, each explicitly rated on a five-point scale from excellent to poor.

While the factual information is useful, many Wealth Span advisors might question the strategic orientation of the articles. CU agrees that long-term care insurance plays an important estate protection or estate preservation role. Their working premise, however, is that Medicaid is the first line of financial protection, and that other planning activities should be oriented toward gaining access to Medicaid long-term care benefits. Indeed, the CU worksheet provided in the article titled "Do You Need Insurance?" is structured to separate Medicaid assets from total assets, with the literal bottom line being "your assets subject to spend-down."

As we noted earlier, for many older men and women who survived the Depression, the use of Medicaid poses a question of personal values, an ethical question about using a social policy initially created as a welfare program. At a less philosophical but more practical level, however, reliance on Medicaid could be strategically shortsighted since it is a public program whose rules can be (and have been) changed.

Furthermore, unlike Medicare, Medicaid is a joint federal–state-funded and -administered program, so that the rules can be changed at two levels of public administration. At the beginning of this section, we identified trends that suggest the demand and probable cost of nursing home care are likely to increase over the next few decades. These same dynamics could also motivate national and state politicians to change the rules and benefit structures of Medicaid payments for long-term care.

People who have an estate to protect, and who assume that all or much of that estate might be required to pay for needed long-term care, may not want to link that protection to future Medicaid rules and payments.

Self-insurance is another approach. One kind of self-insurance is to set aside a large chunk of wealth and earmark it for future long-term care. The Consumers Union analysis states: "Nor do you need [long-term care] insurance if you can set aside roughly $160,000 at compound interest solely to pay for nursing-home care. These funds would pay for about four years of care." What CU should have added is that this amount might pay for four or five years at *current* nursing home average costs.

A second kind of self-insurance is to use the equity in one's home. As mentioned, most older people in the United States own their own home, and most older homeowners have paid off their mortgage. Reverse mortgages are a relatively new way for an older couple to retain ownership of their home but still be able to get cash out of the equity to pay for long-term care (not just nursing home care).

Reverse mortgages are not simply second mortgages (or new first mortgages). Traditional mortgages focus on the creditworthiness of the borrower, a test that many older people may not pass. By contrast, eligibility criteria for reverse mortgages, discussed in the following section of this chapter, focus on the equity in the home rather than the income of the borrower. A third kind of self-insurance is a variation on the first, but does not require a $160,000 set-aside from family assets. Rather, we propose a small *investment depletion* technique to pay for long-term care insurance premiums.

And so we return to the previously posed question. Who should purchase long-term care insurance and why? The following are not definitive answers but conversations that Wealth Span advisors should have with their clients. These are not simply insurance Q&A, but strategic issues of Wealth Span importance.

- *The Medicaid financial–moral issue.* If spend-down is possible and realistic, then to what extent does the client have a position on the issue? For potential Medicaid-eligible families this should be one of the first long-term care conversations between advisor and client.

- *Estate protection.* If the client cannot or does not want to earmark $160,000 from the estate for long-term care, then insurance may be the better estate protection approach. The conversation should note that if both husband and wife are to be protected in this way, then $320,000 might be needed for the four years of care suggested by CU.

- *Risk tolerance.* Resistance to long-term care insurance is often expressed by the question: Why should I buy insurance for something I may never need and certainly am working hard (exercise, diet, etc.) to avoid? We buy car insurance and home insurance and hope never to need them. To be honest, car insurance is required by law in most states to financially protect the other guy, and homeowners insurance is required by the lending institution to protect them, not the home owner. Still, the conversation needs to focus on the degree to which the client wants to expose the estate to the unknown future costs of long-term care.

- *Risk tolerance II.* A second risk conversation should be held with families thinking seriously about the Medicaid solution. Here, the risk is that the future rules governing Medicaid eligibility and Medicaid payment levels will not be adequate to provide long-term care. For example, current Medicaid practice includes a 36-month *look-back rule.* Medicaid benefits will not start until three years after the family has divested itself of assets so as to pass the resource test—a rule to prevent wealthy people from moving their assets today and acquiring Medicaid benefits tomorrow. Before 1991 the look-back rule was only 24 months, and there is no reason to believe that it won't be a 48-month rule in the future.

- There are other conversations to be held, but one especially important one concerns the current and anticipated health of the older client. Unlike Medicare, or medigap insurance purchased during the Medigap Open Enrollment period, long-term care insurance does have medical underwriting requirements. Stephan Leimberg, former Professor of Taxation and Estate Planning at the American College, notes that most companies use detailed medical questionnaires and/or physician statements before issuing policies, and thus do the underwriting at the time of application rather than when the benefits are claimed. Long-term care insurance applications that are not accompanied by detailed questions about health and health history, Leimberg says, may be a warning that the company will be underwriting at the time of a claim. The question of risk and risk tolerance are relevant again here. Once a person has experienced or suffered a major health problem, she or he may not be eligible for long-term care insurance benefits.

Policy Features of Long-Term Care Insurance

Long-term care insurance is a relatively new insurance product, and policies have changed substantially over the past five years. The following is a list of basic features and coverages, but substantial advisor and client investigation are certainly called for. This list reflects the key points suggested by the United Seniors Health Council (USHC), a nonprofit long-term care educational organization in Washington, D.C., that has been providing counseling for over 15 years both to individuals and in the form of books and articles for the public at large.

- *Services covered.* Long-term care is no longer just nursing home care, and insurance policies should cover care in whatever venue the consumer prefers. The better policy benefits provide a pool of funds that can be spent in nursing homes, at home, or in assisted living facilities. Some policies stipulate that the *full* benefit can be received only in a nursing home, with the home care benefit calculated at 50% or 75% of the full daily amount. Better policies pay 100% of the stipulated daily benefit without restriction as to where the long-term care is received. CU warns that because assisted living is a relatively new industry with varying kinds and levels of residential and health assistance, all insurance policies do not treat all assisted living facilities in the same way; read the fine print, CU suggests. In earlier years long-term care insurance policies did not pay benefits for Alzheimer's disease; no acceptable policy includes such a limitation these days.
- *Benefits and benefit periods.* Most policies are structured to (1) pay a specific number of dollars per day of long-term care, usually about $120 per day; and (2) pay that amount for a maximum number of years. Of course, the higher the daily dollar amount or number of years, the higher the annual premium. Three to six years of care is currently seen as the appropriate level of insurance coverage, but aging Boomers may need more or less, depending on where they are likely to be on the squared curve.
- *Inflation Protection.* Long-term care insurance is purchased to pay for needs that are 30 years or more in the future. Clearly, $120 will not likely pay for a day of care in 2032. Most policies offer inflation protection for additional premium cost. This additional insurance is usually for 5% compound inflation. USHC recommends compounded inflation protection for people under age 70, and the simple 5% inflation coverage for those over 70. Professor Leimberg notes that some companies offer cost-of-living inflation protection, but with the cost of the additional premiums itself indexed to increases in the consumer price index. A $120 benefit with 5%

compounding purchased in 2002 would be worth about $519 per day in 2032. The financial planner's *Rule of 72* is useful here. At 5%, the originally purchased daily amount will double every 14.4 years.

- *Benefit triggers.* It is important to know what it will take to trigger the receipt of long-term care benefits. Most often, these triggers are connected to the Activities of Daily Living (ADLs) discussed in Chapter 2. If an older person needs help with three ADLs, in some policies, then the full daily benefit amount can be paid. Once again, the fine print is critical. *Any 3 ADLs* is a more lenient trigger than, say, *Eating plus one other.* As Table 2.2 shows, daily help with eating or going to the toilet is a relatively rare need even for 85 year olds. Such a trigger could withhold benefits when they are really needed.

- *Deductibles and waiting periods.* As with other kinds of insurance, long-term care policies have a deductible, called *waiting periods* or *elimination periods.* If the policyholder pays her own daily long-term care costs for the first week, month, or other period, the premiums will be less. CU appropriately notes, however, that inflation is likely to override any savings from the lower premiums of a high-deductible policy. The cost of those two weeks or one month of care may not be large at today's rate of $120 per day, but will be substantial when today's 55 year old needs long-term care in 30 years.

- *Renewal and waiver of premium.* Most policies offer to waive continuing premiums when the policyholder begins to receive long-term care benefits, and most policies are guaranteed renewable without additional medical examination.

What Policies Cost and At What Age to Buy Them

Given the policy variables mentioned above (plus other features) there is quite a range in annual long-term care insurance premiums. Unlike medigap insurance, there is no publicly mandated set of policy features that would make features-and-cost shopping easier. The best guide to current premiums is presented in CU's *Complete Guide to Health Services for Seniors.* Appendix S gives the 1999 annual premium for about 90 policies that offer comprehensive coverage, meaning that they do not limit where the policyholder can receive his or her long-term care.

One of the more notable aspects of long-term care insurance is that premiums are established at the age of initial purchase and do not increase as the policyholder ages. Since the insurance company will be collecting premiums from a 55 year old for many more years than from a 75 year old before benefits are paid at age 82 (on average), annual premium levels are much less for younger purchasers. Annual premiums can rise for all policies in a given class (e.g., that offer the same benefit or package of benefits), but an individual's premiums cannot increase because of his or her aging.

CU thus reports the premiums for its sample of 90 policies for three ages: purchase at 55, 65, and 75. Table 11.2 presents the highest and lowest premiums for the three ages for policies with the following characteristics: The cost in 1999 of a policy with lifetime coverage, $120 [daily] maximum and $120 maximum home care and assisted living benefit when available; a 90- or 100-day waiting period; and a 5% compounded inflation protection coverage. CU says that this profile of coverage gives a flavor of how much a good policy costs.

When to purchase long-term care insurance is a fundamental Wealth Span question. Many specialists suggest that younger than age 55 is probably too young, and as the CU sample of premiums in 1999 shows, age 75 is expensive.

For purposes of illustration, let's look at a client age 65 who will start receiving long-term care benefits at age 82 (the current average age of entry to a nursing home). He pays insurance premiums for 17 years (age 65 through age 81). Using the numbers in Table 11.2, this man would have paid between $24,000 and $71,000 in premiums.

In evaluating an investment, financial planners use a safe alternative such as an account that pays a steady average 5% compound growth over the period. So, at 5%, at the end of the 17-year period the value of these premiums (excluding tax details for the illustration) would be approximately $38,000 to $113,000 before any benefits are received at age 82.

Whether or not this is a good deal, however, is a larger Wealth Span judgment and not just a financial one. Table 11.1 says that in 1997 the average national nursing home cost was about $3,800 per month, or $45,600 per year.

Table 11.2 Annual Premium Range (Consumers Union 1999 Sample)

Purchased at Age:	Low	High
55	$ 864	$ 3,451
65	$1,416	$ 4,176
75	$3,917	$12,077

Note: See text for definition of policy features that define these comparisons.

The $113,000 investment value (using the high age 65 long-term care insurance premiums in Table 11.2) would pay for about two and a half years of average-cost care. This assumes, moreover, that the monthly cost of the long-term care stays at $3,800 for 17 years, which of course it will not: With an annual increase of 5%, after 17 years a $3,800 monthly cost rises to $8,300.

There are, however, Wealth Span issues beyond the financial calculations at varying rates of return, different tax treatments, and the like. Risk tolerance, as mentioned earlier, is important. What happens if long-term care is needed before age 82? Few 65 year olds have intense needs for assistance with ADLs (seen in Table 2.2), but some do. Aside from premature need for long-term care, a younger-old person can become uninsurable, from diabetes, a driving accident, Parkinson's disease, asthma, or a seizure.

Overall, long-term care and long-term care insurance are important Wealth Span choices. Financial considerations are important, but the cost of premiums and even the investment alternative values are not the only issue. Perhaps one way of summarizing these various health and estate protection considerations is simply to observe that given the increasing costs of long-term care, the larger the estate the more valuable the estate protection insurance.

A Little Proposal

Finally, consider the following somewhat simpler approach to earmarking a small part of the current estate to purchase long-term care insurance. Rather than putting $160,000 aside to pay for future long-term care, as CU estimated, why not put only about $20,000 aside to pay for long-term care insurance premiums?

Let's consider the same scenario of a 65 year old who starts using long-term care at age 82, i.e., 17 years of premium payments and investing. Because the financial inputs can be reasonably modest, the nonfinancial Wealth Span goals of long-term care funding are more easily seen, and met with less anxiety. Let's assume a $2,000 annual premium (a premium 40% above the low age 65 premium in Table 11.2).

We will again assume an investment return of 5% compounded and ignore any tax worries. If $22,000 is placed into an investment account at the beginning of year 1 and the $2,000 premium is paid at the end of each year, the account would be depleted at the end of the sixteenth year with no additional deposits. In year 17, the now 82 year old begins long-term care, the policy pays the bills, and the waiver of premium feature means he doesn't have to pay any further premiums. If the insurance company raises the premiums by 10% in year 5, an additional deposit of $1,500 at the end of year 5 would rebalance the picture.

The main point is that an investment account can be established to purchase a substantial amount of long-term care estate protection without freezing a large part of that estate. If he needs long-term care before age 82, the insurance is there. If he survives a concussion from a skiing accident at age 72 but as a consequence becomes uninsurable, his insurance is already there. If he dies at age 75, no further long-term care insurance premiums are paid and the balance of the account remains part of the estate.

Hands-On Information and More

- The major source of independent long-term care information, for both professionals and consumers, is the nonproft United Seniors Health Council of Washington, D.C. USHC has been involved in public education through seminars, direct hotline counseling, and publications for 15 years. *Long Term Care Planning: A Dollar and Sense Guide* (2001) is the third edition of a guidebook for the consumer. *Long-Term Care Insurance: A Professional's Guide to Selecting Policies* (2002) is the fourth edition of a guide first published in 1991. Both books provide background to long-term care needs of the elderly, focusing on the role of private insurance along with other sources of long-term care funding, including Medicaid. The USHC website, `www.unitedseniorshealth.org`, provides updates of long-term care public policy events that affect insurance issues, such as changes in tax policies.
- A second very useful source, as in other health subjects, is the CU's *Complete Guide to Health Services for Seniors* (2000), authored by Trudy Lieberman and the editors of *Consumer Reports.* Much of the *Guide*'s Chapter 14 on long-term care insurance is a reprint of the *Consumer Reports* special report published in 1997. The unique value of both the magazine report and the book's Appendix S are the detailed evaluations of dozens of specific policies (identified by 1997 policy code number), including annual premium information. CU notes that while the specific policies and dollar costs may have changed, the general features and price information, as well as CU's consumer ratings, are still valid consumer guides. It is the only easily accessible source that reviews and evaluates specific companies and policies.
- The AARP web site's (`www.aarp.org/confacts/health/privltc.html`) section on "Private Long-Term Care Insurance" is an excellent set of guides and questions aimed at understanding and selecting insurance policy features. The AARP information is one of the few such discussions that explic-

itly starts with the continuum of long-term care and starts with a presumption that home care rather than nursing home care is the preferred solution for most older people.

- The Health Insurance Association of America (HIAA) is the trade association of the major insurance companies that offer health and medigap insurance, as well as long-term care insurance. The web site (`www.hiaa.org`) offers a very readable guide to long-term care insurance that includes a number of tax and other legislative and regulatory issues not found in most insurance guides written for consumers. Of special value are the directories of HIAA's insurance company members that offer either individual or group long-term care insurance. HIAA does not recommend or endorse any company. The listing for most companies includes their consumer web sites, so that comparative Windows shopping is quite feasible.
- The ElderWeb (`www.elderweb.com/finance&law`) is an especially valuable source of tax and political news about long-term care. Articles from ElderWeb's online *Newsletter* over the past 15 months on long-term care insurance are identified. While articles on pending and new tax treatment of policies, congressional investigations, corporate changes, and the like, may be a year old, like summer TV reruns, if you haven't seen them then they're news to you.

Reverse Mortgages: When Your Client Is Cash-Poor but Equity-Rich

Ken Scholen begins his book *Your New Retirement Nest Egg* (1996) with the following conversation. "Do you own a home? If you do, you have a retirement nest egg that you didn't have just a few years ago. Even if you've owned your home for a long time, it has only recently become a true retirement nest egg."

Scholen is founding director of the nonprofit National Center for Home Equity Conversion. Reverse mortgages are mortgages by which older people can borrow against the existing equity in their homes without going through the borrower qualification processes that are part of a traditional mortgage.

In a traditional forward mortgage (including home equity loans), it is the borrower's personal (or family or business) creditworthiness that is assessed by the lending institution. The approved customer–borrower then pays the bank each month. In a reverse mortgage, it is the property that qualifies for the loan, and the bank pays the customer.

An often-used phrase to describe many older families is, simply, *cash-poor but equity-rich.* They may have substantial equity in their paid-up mortgages but a relatively small cash flow from their monthly Social Security and pension checks, hence the potential value of reverse mortgage.

As convenient as all this seems, however, from a gerontological perspective, it is not difficult to understand why older couples are reluctant to sell their home to unlock the equity for day-to-day living expenses:

- A home is symbolic as well as real estate; being independent in old age includes not being forced to sell and move for financial reasons.
- Changing residence is always disruptive, but to be forced to move for cash flow purposes is a substantial attack on one's feelings of independence.
- It may not be possible to find a new residence in the same or a different desired neighborhood at a price affordable to an older couple.
- Even if a new house's sale price is affordable, Social Security and pension income would not likely qualify the older borrower for a new first mortgage.
- For many older families, the family home represents a central asset to be bequeathed to the children or grandchildren.

ANOTHER STORY

The Potential Senior Market for Reverse Mortgages

The potential value of reverse mortgages can be seen in the following results from the National Council on the Aging's *APA21* year 2000 national survey. Of the 80% of Americans age 65 and older who currently own (versus rent) their homes, 85% have paid off their mortgage. More importantly, older-old and less wealthy people are more likely to have paid-up mortgages. This is especially noteworthy since it is older people and those with less annual income who are more likely to benefit from the availability of a reverse mortgage.

	Mortgage	
	Paid-Up	**Not**
65–69	77%	23%
70–74	84%	16%
75+	90%	10%

	Mortgage	
	Paid-Up	**Not**
Under $50,000	86%	14%
Over $50,000	73%	27%

A reverse mortgage is a valuable financial tool that can respond to most of these obstacles. More to the point, reverse mortgages have been explicitly invented to allow cash-poor, equity-rich older people to draw cash from their home equity, while continuing to live in and own their homes.

Like all real estate transactions, reverse mortgages are complex private business contracts between borrowers and lenders, insurance agents, and other third parties that require a range of specialized advice as well as consumer awareness. The total cost of a reverse mortgage is influenced by both (1) financial variables such as the loan's starting costs, possible variable interest rates, and real estate market dynamics; and (2) gerontological variables such as your client's age and likely longevity, marital status and estate situation, and health status and long-term care preferences. Because of this complexity, we later describe specialized software that allows you and your client to simulate a variety of over-time scenarios in order to estimate the total costs of a reverse mortgage.

Reverse Mortgages and Long-Term Care

Why is a mortgage included in a discussion of long-term care? The simple answer is that most older people prefer to live in their own homes for the rest of their lives and not move to a nursing home or an assisted living facility if at all possible. As much gerontological research demonstrates, even with accumulating disabilities, many older people in their eighties and older can maintain an independent lifestyle with a variety of home health care services and products and home modifications.

Although Medicare's home care benefit pays for some durable medical equipment and visiting health services, usually after a hospitalization episode, more generally home care services, products, and home modifications come with substantial out-of-pocket expenses. For cash-poor, equity-rich elderly couples the reverse mortgage can be the only predictable continuous source of their financial well-being *and* residential independence. Such independence may last three years or 13, a period of time made possible by unlocking the wealth of a lifetime of financially responsible behavior—via the mechanism of a reverse mortgage.

Who or What Qualifies for the Loan?

Why not simply refinance the house or arrange a home-equity line of credit in order to:

- Continue to own and live in the home
- Pay for aging-related structural modifications

- Purchase needed medical equipment and services
- Arrange for transportation and shopping services
- Have additional money for vacations, gifts, or a new VCR
- And still bequeath any remaining house value to heirs

The basic answer is that first and second mortgages typically require the borrower to be creditworthy, and many older, retired persons no longer have sufficient regular income to qualify. By contrast, in the reverse mortgage the real estate—not the borrower—qualifies for the loan. The lending institution evaluates both the equity and the current market value of the house in determining the potential amount of the loan. The age of the borrower then shapes the details of the overall amount and terms of the loan.

A second fundamental principle of the reverse mortgage is protection of the house as the older client's residence for as long as he or she can live there. Thus, repayment of the loan is triggered by sale of the property, but the property cannot be sold as long as the older borrower (including surviving spouse) still lives there.

How Can the Money Be Received?

The older client can receive loan payments any of three ways (or combinations): in a lump sum, in monthly advances, or by a line of credit.

Lump Sum

The borrower can receive the entire cash amount in a single lump sum payment, at which time interest starts accruing at the agreed-upon interest rate (fixed or variable). The principal plus accrued interest is repayable only when the surviving elder permanently leaves the house. *Permanent* is usually defined as not living in the house for six months, as when the surviving spouse moves to a nursing home. Intermittent medical circumstances or "snowbird" residential patterns may be acceptable, but the Wealth Span advisor should make sure that *permanent* is explicitly defined in the loan agreement.

Monthly Advances

Scholen identifies three kinds of fixed monthly payments differing by how long the payments are made: (1) *term:* a fixed term, number of months, selected when the loan is made; (2) *tenure:* as long as the surviving owner permanently lives in the house; or (3) *lifetime:* payments continue after leaving the home.

Term payments can be received for a relatively short number of years, after which no additional payments are received. The fewer the number of payments, the larger each payment can be. As with a lump sum, even after the payments stop, interest continues to accrue until the surviving borrower permanently leave the house, triggering repayment—typically sale of the property.

Tenure payments are almost a lifetime annuity in that they are guaranteed for as long as the surviving spouse lives in the house. As Ken Scholen notes, "No matter how long you live, no matter what happens to value of your home, you continue getting fixed monthly payments until you die, sell your home, or permanently move away."

The *lifetime* approach is a true annuity in that payments will be made even after the owner leaves the house, for example, to live in a nursing home. The reverse mortgage produces a lump-sum payment, which is then used to purchase a third-party lifetime annuity. In this approach the annuity is purchased with the borrowed funds, and the loan does not have to be repaid until the older person permanently leaves the house. The lifetime annuity payments, however, continue no matter where the client resides.

Note that the purchased lifetime annuity is a separate financial–legal contract from the reverse mortgage, so that the older client and his or her Wealth Span advisor have to keep track of both financial transactions. All of the consumer issues surrounding annuities come into play, including the risks involved, fixed versus variable, commissions and servicing costs, stability of the insurance or annuity company, and beneficiary and inheritance issues.

Line of Credit

The mortgage amount can define the limit of a line of credit, and the interest owed is on only the amount actually borrowed. The National Association of Reverse Mortgage Lenders estimates that in recent years 60% of all reverse mortgages are written in this way. Among the cautions included below, note that given the start-up costs in initiating the reverse mortgage, a line of credit can be very expensive if the credit is not substantially used in the first years of the loan.

Costs and Cautions

However the older borrower chooses to receive the funds, it should be clearly kept in mind that reverse mortgages are mortgages. As such, there will be origination fees, service fees, possible escrow and title search fees, anticipated closing fees, and mortgage insurance. For example, it is financially inefficient to take out a reverse mortgage to set up a line of credit if the line of credit is not used for several years. [*Note:* In December 2000, the online *ElderWeb Newsletter* reported that HUD reverse mortgages taken out to purchase long-term care insurance are exempt from certain loan origination and other start-up fees.]

The same kinds of cautions are especially relevant because of the fundamental gerontological nature of the transaction. Serious consideration should be made of the health of the older couple. They may very much want to stay in their own home for as long as both are in fairly good health. The reverse mortgage funds can pay for home renovation and help to purchase monthly health aides and visiting nurse services not covered by Medicare.

Here, too, the time factor is relevant to amortization of mortgage fees and related costs. In my gerontological research I have talked with wives who are more than willing to provide loving care to a frail husband in the house that has been their home for over 30 years. But often she does not want to maintain the large house after he dies, but plans to sell the house and buy a condo where the garden is maintained and the snow is removed by someone else, or move into a castle-like assisted living facility near London, or move in with her son and daughter-in-law in Santa Barbara. If her move takes place relatively soon after the loan is started then the several start-up costs of the new mortgage will represent a larger percentage of the overall cost of the loan. Thus, Wealth Span planning here, as in financial gerontology more generally, requires a sensitive consideration of personal and family concerns along with the financial choices.

Payback: When? And How Much?

Payback is not required until the surviving spouse dies or permanently moves away from the house. Payback is also triggered by sale or lease of the house even if the older borrower continues to live there. Payback is not required even if the bank has stopped making its contractual payments, as long as the borrower is still living in the house.

In considering the events that can trigger payback, Wealth Span planning again requires consideration of both financial and gerontological circumstances. For example, the elderly borrower still has all the financial and physical responsibilities of home ownership, including property taxes, community fees, regular maintenance and repairs, and the insurance routinely required by real estate lenders. Because most reverse mortgages stipulate that repayment can be triggered by failure to do these things, the preference for "aging in place" must be weighed against the capacity of the older borrower to complete these responsibilities—financially, physically, and administratively.

When repayment is triggered, the usual process is that the house is sold and the debt repaid from the net proceeds. If these net proceeds are larger than the total debt, the client or the client's estate receives the difference. The property does not have to be sold, however. If the owner's family wants to get a new traditional mortgage (or has the cash), they can simply repay the debt and retain ownership.

What happens if the net proceeds from the sale are less than the accumulated debt—for example, if the surviving borrower lives to be 97 years old and receives more tenure payments accruing more interest than originally estimated, or if the market value of the house has declined substantially since the reverse mortgage was issued?

Of course, the lending institution would have tried to account for such issues by means of mortgage limits linked to the borrower's age, condition of the house, and the local real estate market. Still, what is your client's liability if the debt is larger than the net value of the sale? The client's or her estate's debt obligation is limited to the home's net proceeds after sale. By definition, a reverse mortgage is a nonrecourse loan. At the time of repayment the individual or the estate never owes more than the home value, and the lender may not seek additional repayment from other assets, the estate, or the heirs.

The AARP Reverse Mortgage Comparison Software

Based in part on Ken Scholen's discussions of total annual loan cost, AARP has developed a computer model for comparing costs of different reverse mortgages. The model assumes that the total cost of the loan only begins with origination costs, starting interest rates, and current home value. Since accrued interest is added to deferred debt, the amount owed is compounded and can grow substantially over time. Unlike in a fixed mortgage in which time is a fixed parameter of the loan, here time is a variable reflecting the older person's life expectancy or life expectation of living in the house, which adds a variable health dimension to the scenario.

Consequently, the AARP simulation model starts with variables for total amount borrowed, initial interest rate, and current house value, and then includes variables for home value changes and variable interest rates if relevant. The crucial time variable starts with the borrower's statistical life expectancy at the time of the loan, and then simulates the full set of financial variables using 20%, 40%, 60%, 100%, and 140% of that life expectancy. The result is a simulation model that shows the interaction of financial variables with gerontological variables. Summary outcomes such as the Total Annual Loan Cost (TALC) produce direct comparisons across different kinds of loans, or the same loan structures using different life expectancies.

The AARP web site (`www.aarp.org/revmort`) includes a list of lenders currently using software based on the AARP specifications, and the specifications themselves are freely available by e-mailing to `Rminfo@aarp.org` and asking for the reverse mortgage model specifications.

Hands-on Information and More

In years past, the primary source of information was Ken Scholen's book. Currently, however, on his web site Scholen recommends that the beginning reader start with AARP's new publication *Home Made Money: A Consumer's Guide to Reverse Mortgages,* and then graduate to his newer book and web site. In fact, much of the 1996 Scholen book has been reprinted and updated for the AARP publication. In what must be considered as a gold standard of ease of public availability, at `www.aarp.org/revmort`, *Home Made Money* is available as directly printable pages or as a fully downloadable Acrobat .pdf file of 72 pages or call 1-800-424-3410 to request publication #D12894, or e-mail to `RMinfo@aarp.org` and request the publication. Scholen's more advanced information, data, analysis, and list of his latest publications are available at `www.reverse.org`. The web site also describes HUD-FHA, Fannie Mae, and other lending agencies and institutions that offer reverse mortgages.

- Housing and Urban Development (HUD) information begins with the "Top Ten Things to Know if You're Interested in a Reverse Mortgage," and then includes links to HUD information materials including directories of HUD-approved lenders and HUD-approved housing counseling agencies (`www.hud.gov/buying/rmtopten.cfm`)

- Fannie Mae (Federal National Mortgage Association) offers detailed information on the specifications of their Home-Keeper Mortgage; directories of lenders are linked to this home page (`www.fanniemae.com/single family/reverse/`)

- The National Reverse Mortgage Lenders Association (NRMLA) is the trade association of financial services firms that offer reverse mortgages in the United States and Canada. Their home page, `www.reversemortgage.com`, includes links to a variety of both consumer and financial services professional pages, including directories of lenders and mortgage counselors. The NRMLA site is also a good source of new bulletins about ongoing developments in this business.

- Finally, the nonprofit, nonpartisan ElderWeb (`www.elderweb.com`), includes a comprehensive set of articles plus links to reverse mortgage issues in its "Financial and Law/Home Equity" section. In addition, the weekly *ElderWeb Newsletter* reports changes in mortgage limits, fees, and other rules. As mentioned earlier, ElderWeb.com is free and does not require registration to read or download its substantial finance and aging materials.

CHAPTER 12

The Wealth Span Advisor as a Gerontology Team Member

As we hope these chapters illustrate, the practice of applied gerontology is an emerging and a complex field with multiple connections to personal and family finance. As the trusted professional Wealth Span advisor, you will be called on to listen, to provide information, and to counsel on issues that are sometimes a bit removed from your usual financial experience.

To be sure, in times of a geriatric medical crisis it will be the family physician or a surgeon who will be the primary advisor. At other times it will be the attorney—sometimes in planning mode but often in crisis mode—who has to deal with matters of estates, wills, guardianships, and competence. But more often it will be the financial professional, as you advise on longer-term Wealth Span strategies and choices, who has the more enduring personal relationship with the family.

As the story in Chapter 4 about 50-year-old and even 60-year-old children of elderly parents emphasizes, it's becoming increasingly likely that it is the middle-aged client who will seek advice and counsel on questions of aging and gerontology. And when you are asked questions by a nervous, even frightened, middle-aged son, you are not only a member of that family's gerontological advisory team, but you may become one of the co-captains.

More to the point, the *team* imagery emphasizes the fact that you are not expected to be a gerontology expert. Consequently, the purpose of this chapter is to introduce several kinds of community resources and other team members. In the second section of the chapter, we mention the ELF concept that was described to me several years ago by a financial planner who is very much involved in working with older clients in an interdisciplinary team context.

We start with a description of the national aging network, a broad and valuable community-based information and referral network to which you and your clients can turn to get local advice and consultation. We then look at the ELF model of community alliances, teamwork, in working with the multidimensional problems facing aging families. Finally, we look at how you can locate geriatric health specialists when clients become especially concerned about Alzheimer's disease.

The Resources of the Older Americans Act's National Aging Network

1965 was a watershed year for pubic policy and aging in America. After a decade-long political battle, a national program of health insurance for older men and women—Medicare—was enacted into law. At the same time Medicaid was also enacted, which would become the country's biggest payer of nursing home care for poor and medically needy elderly. The national debate over Medicare gave political legitimacy to the elderly as a recognizable constituency in the country's national politics. During the congressional and public debates in the early 1960s that surrounded the passage of these two landmark pieces of legislation, there was also talk about the active elderly and the nonmedical needs of the *wellderly* in addition to the health care needs of the *illderly.*

The postwar years had seen the growth of the older Americans from 9.0 million in 1940 to 17.7 million in 1960, an increase of 86% in just 20 years. At the same time, the older population was moving, migrating to southern Florida and southern California. In response, many states and localities were developing a range of nonmedical services for their wellderly citizens. Most prominent were two categories of what became known as *social services* in contrast to health and medical services:

- Social interaction was promoted through the activities of senior centers.
- Nutritional services came in the form of both home-delivered Meals on Wheels and congregate meals typically served in senior centers.

Interestingly, research on the impact of the congregate meals programs demonstrated that the opportunities for social interaction provided by the programs had as much positive impact on the well-being and quality of life of older persons as did the meals themselves.

And so the community social services–oriented Older Americans Act was signed into law in 1965. Medicare was and remains a nationally administered program, and Medicaid continues as a joint state–national program. From the beginning, however, the Older Americans Act focused on local community programs and reflected the local–state–national complexity of American government and politics.

Known simply as the *aging network,* this nationwide system of governmental and some private-sector organizations at the community level is a "federalized" network that includes national, state, and local agencies. The aging network is a federalized system in the uniquely American sense of the word: This is a *nationally* mandated set of programs that is implemented largely at the *local* community level, but through legislation, regulations, and budgetary authority of 50 separate *states* (plus the District of Columbia and Puerto Rico).

In many ways the aging network is a microcosm of the very essence of federalism. Political scientists often describe American federalism using the metaphor of a pendulum: Sometimes the pendulum swings in the direction that gives greater authority and responsibility to the federal government in Washington, and at other times it swings toward state and local authority and responsibility. Certainly, the rhetoric of the national Republican and Democratic parties over the past 70 years reflects ideological disagreements about which side of the continuum should tax, regulate, spend, and generally be responsible for social policy.

Of course, this continuing national debate over federalism goes back much further and much deeper than recent debates over social services. In many textbooks the Civil War is labeled as the War between the States. Depending on one's point of view, that war was fought over slavery or it was fought over states' rights. Although enacted 100 years after the Civil War, the brief political history of the Older Americans Act of 1965 is a reasonably accurate microcosm of the fundamental debate about federalism.

The Older Americans Act was signed into law on July 14, 1965, as part of Lyndon Johnson's Great Society initiatives, a time when the pendulum was swinging toward Washington, D.C. The aging network was substantially transformed in the early 1970s by Richard Nixon's New Federalism, which moved the pendulum in the direction of the states, and so it remains today a federalized network. The local, state, and national levels of government share responsibility for designing, funding, and implementing a system or a collection of services and programs that are available to all older men and women and their families, regardless of income. Interestingly, the eligibility definition of *old* in the Older Americans Act is *60 years and older,* another attempt to distinguish social services for the wellderly from Medicare's hospital and medical benefits.

Wealth Span Advisors and the Older Americans Act

Later in this chapter we take a look at the role of the financial professional as part of local alliances. The ELF model of teamwork among *E*motional, *L*egal, and *F*inancial professionals illustrates how the Wealth Span advisor can both benefit from and contribute to these kinds of local partnerships. Because of the growing gerontological concerns of your financial clients, you will be confronted with an expanding array of issues and questions, many of which will come from worried middle-agers. Only some of these will be narrowly financial in origin or solution. More likely, these questions about aging will require a broader effort involving community agencies and other professional expertise. For example, as the trusted Wealth Span advisor you are likely to get the following questions from your middle-aged client:

- How can I arrange for temporary in-home nursing care for Mother?
- How do I get an assessment to learn if Father really does have Alzheimer's disease?
- What if Mother needs to have meals delivered to her apartment?
- Where do I go to learn about the quality of nursing homes in this city?
- What about "little things" like house cleaning and maintenance chores?
- Who can fill Mother's insulin syringes if I'm out of town for three months?
- How can I find a good geriatric care manager or elder law attorney?

The Older Americans Act, and the local–state–national network of agencies it has created, is the first place to go for community-based answers to these questions. The key social service that every local Area Agency on Aging (AAA—pronounced *triple A* just like the auto club) in the country is mandated to provide is an information and referral service.

The subject matter of the information and local referrals is as broad as the goals of the Older Americans Act itself. The basic goals of the Act read like a kind of Declaration of Human Rights for older Americans. Listed below, these 10 basic goals are not only consistent with the larger goals of Wealth Span planning, but to a large extent are dependent on successful planning.

1. An adequate income in retirement
2. The best possible physical and mental health
3. Suitable housing
4. Full restorative services for those who require institutional care
5. Opportunity for employment with no discrimination because of age
6. Retirement in health, honor, and dignity
7. Pursuit of meaningful activity
8. Efficient community service
9. Immediate benefit from proven research
10. Freedom, independence, and the free exercise of individual initiative

The Agencies of the Aging Network

The 1965 legislation established the Administration on Aging (AoA) as an administrative agency within the Department of Health, Education, and Welfare (now Health and Human Services). One of the AoA's primary roles was to act as a coordinator of existing programs distributed across other federal agencies, in housing, transportation, job training, education, and health. The idea was, for example, that if a housing program and a transportation program each had aging requirements, there should be a specific office in the national government, a focal point, that would have responsibility to see that the programs in different Cabinet Departments were at least talking to each other. Thus, the information and referral responsibilities of the local AAAs are historically rooted in the Older Americans Act's national responsibilities to coordinate a broad array of social programs and services.

The establishment of an agency in Washington was a positive development for older people at the national level, but the 50 states also had programs serving the needs of elders. State programs that had been developed over many years, across different governors and budgets, like national programs, were likely to be distributed across many different state agencies and departments. Consequently, the Older Americans Act mandated the establishment of a State Unit on Aging (SUA) in every state. The role of the SUAs was parallel to the AoA's role at the national level—to oversee and coordinate programs so as to maximize their effectiveness in providing services to older citizens.

In some states the SUA is an office within an existing government department, such as the state's department of health or social services. Some states simply created a governor's office for aging matters. But most states have passed their own enabling legislation that establishes a separate department of aging. Over the years, the social, financial, and political importance of aging programs have grown to such an extent that many states have accorded these departments cabinet-level status within the executive branch. Similarly, at the federal level in 1993, the office of the Commissioner on Aging was elevated to the status of Assistant Secretary for Aging in the Department of Health and Human Services.

A listing of addresses and other contact information for all SUAs is included on the web site of the National Association of State Units on Aging (NASUA) at www.nasua.org. A printed list is included as Appendix B in the Consumer Union's *Complete Guide to Health Services for Seniors.* However, see our description below of the AoA web site (www.aoa.gov) for more accessible, comprehensive, and up-to-date information about individual state units and their programs.

There are approximately 660 AAAs across the country. In less populated areas, one AAA may serve several counties. In urban areas, there can be a city and a separate county agency. Some AAAs have branch offices that coordinate services in their neighborhood.

Most AAAs are units of local city or county government. In other communities, the AAA may be part of or affiliated with a United Way organization. Still others are stand-alone nonprofit corporations. If the local area is relatively rich in resources, the AAA may serve primarily as a coordinator of community services, with the services themselves delivered by others, such as congregate meals provided by senior centers or churches and synagogues. In smaller or less wealthy communities, the AAA might use its federal and state funds to be the actual provider of services.

Of more central importance to the Wealth Span advisor, however, is the fact that all AAAs offer an information and referral service, an invaluable first place to search. In addition to this general community-based information, AAAs may coordinate or provide health insurance counseling, geriatric assessment, employment services, household chores services, and meals for homebound elderly. It should be emphasized that the information and services offered by the Older Americans Act are not limited to old people. As mentioned, the official eligibility for these programs begins at age 60—in keeping with the original concern with the wellderly. Of special value to financial advisors and families of older persons, AAAs provide services to caregivers of older persons even if the caregivers are younger than 60.

A direct way to locate the AAA where you work or live is in the green or blue governmental pages of the local phone book. Some phone books these days have orange pages listing nongovernmental community agencies. Even the Yellow Pages might be useful, under such headings as social services, aging services, or senior centers. A senior center, local chapter of AARP, or the seniors program of a local church or synagogue should also know the address and phone number of the local AAA. And there is always the web. A list of current addresses and telephone numbers for all AAAs is provided by the National Association of Area Agencies on Aging (N4A) at www.n4a.org, but see Another Story below describing the AoA web site.

The State Long-Term Care Ombudsman Program

While the original responsibilities of the State Units on Aging were primarily to coordinate existing state-level and local-level services, over the years states were mandated to establish additional programs. One is the Long-Term Care Ombudsman Programs. If advisors or clients have either general questions about the quality of nursing homes in the community or want to register complaints about a specific long-term care facility, the state ombudsman program or a staffer at the local branch office is the appropriate point of contact. As long-term care becomes increasingly needed as well as an increasingly complex issue for aging families, the state ombudsman becomes a more valuable source of information and guidance. A printed list of all state ombudsman programs, as of 2000, is included as Appendix O in the Consumers Union health *Guide.* A more interactive list with direct hyperlinks to the agencies can be accessed from the AoA web site described below.

Another Story

The U.S. Administration on Aging Web Site

In a display of substantial user friendliness to older and middle-aged consumers and the professionals who work with them, AoA has developed an especially valuable web site. As mentioned earlier, the state and local agencies that are part of the national aging network are listed on the web sites of their respective membership organizations, NASUA and N4A. However, more complete information is offered by the national AoA at www.aoa.gov. This is especially important if you are working with a client whose mother or father lives in a different area (i.e., your local phone book isn't very useful).

(continued)

On the AoA home page, the first item under "Welcome" is "About AoA and the Aging Network." Clicking on this item leads to a concise listing of aging network links. The most valuable is labeled simply "Area Agencies on Aging" but includes substantially more information than just a passive list of phone numbers and addresses. The result is a Table of Contents in hyperlink format with every state listed. Clicking on a state's name takes you to a page that links to the State Unit on Aging's own web site (every state has one), and also to a hypertext list of those local AAAs that have their own web site.

If you don't see the AAA that you need on this list, then click to the state SUA's web site. You may not know which AAA serves the city, county, or town in which you are interested, especially if it is in another part of the country. It is very useful, then, that many of the SUA web sites have interactive maps, zip code search capacity, or other ways to help you find the AAA of concern.

The aging network home page also includes a link to a complete list of the names and contact information of the person who currently serves as the director of the long-term care ombudsman program in each state.

Finally, the AoA web site does an excellent job in describing its own history, program, current activities, and news with respect to national aging politics and policy. For advisors interested in more general finance, health, and demographic facts about aging, the AoA web site provides direct links to age-related materials in many other federal agencies, including the Census Bureau, the Bureau of Labor Statistics, and the National Institute on Aging. Many consumer-oriented documents from these agencies, relevant to aging, are available as Acrobat .pdf files. A modest set of finance and retirement planning links is also included on the AoA site.

Strategic Neighborhood Alliances: The ELF Model

You are the trusted financial advisor to the Cranstons, a successful fifty-something family. Steve is the director of the Computers and Business Program at the local community college and Margaret is chief pharmacist in a local drugstore. You've helped them fund Danny and Keri's college education, helped establish supplementary retirement accounts, made sure that they have appropriate life insurance, and remind them regularly to update their wills and reexamine their estate planning. You've introduced the subject of long-term care insurance, but the relevance seems such a long way off that nothing yet has happened.

Margaret's father, John Wilson, has successfully been living alone out in Kansas City since being widowed a few years ago, but last month he suffered what appears to be a fairly serious heart attack. He is nowhere near ready for a nursing home, but his doctors say that he shouldn't live alone, at least not for the next six months until the extent of the damage and his capacity for recuperation are more fully assessed.

The Professional Geriatric Care Manager

Mr. Wilson is medically stable now, and the Cranstons have returned from Kansas City and are now asking you for advice. Where, in turn, do you turn? Locating appropriate care, arranging for it, and monitoring it is not only a time-consuming task but an emotionally draining one if Steve or Margaret have to fly back and forth to Missouri several times to arrange the care. Even if Father moves in with the kids, both of them work so there's still the challenge of finding the right home care and services.

Enter the professional geriatric care manager (GCM). Care managers are professionals who may have been trained as nurses, social workers, family therapists, clinical psychologists, or even financial planners. They have additional training or experience with the problems of older people. There is currently no special licensing of GCMs at the state or national level, but they should have a professional degree or license in their home professional field.

In addition to professional experience, the value of a GCM is her (usually) knowledge of the local community. The GCM is almost always a fee-for-service provider, being paid to identify, negotiate for, and sometimes monitor the health, social, and other caregiving services provided by others. Other than fee-for-service, care managers sometimes work for local community agencies (some AAAs have care managers on staff). Sometimes hospital discharge planners provide similar kinds of services.

As you will learn when Margaret, Steve, and you first talk with the care manager, some of the early issues are clearly financial, once the medical and health crises have been dealt with. The discussion will focus on such things as health care services *apparently* not covered by Medicare or health insurance, medical equipment, home modification, visiting health services, and visiting companion and homemaker services. We say *apparently* not covered because a knowledgeable GCM will have the experience and the skill to navigate the often Byzantine world of public and private eligibility and reimbursement rules.

Geriatric care managers offer advice and insights on the administration of required health care services beyond just describing the costs of those services. Mr. Wilson wants to stay in his long-time home in Kansas City, and for the time being the kids want to facilitate it. Designing a care plan involves more than just funding it. Using `www.caremanager.org` (see below) the kids have located a locally knowledgeable and professionally qualified GCM in Kansas City who has both a nursing degree and is a licensed clinical social worker (LCSW). The care manager has described the kinds of things she can do and recommend, all in the context of her fairly detailed knowledge of the local community:

- Locating personnel to shop, cook, and generally help a homebound older person
- Arranging for transportation and companion service to medical appointments
- Arranging home nursing and physical therapy services both in general and for specific procedures
- Using an Activities of Daily Living (ADL) assessment to determine if and how much the client needs daily assistance with dressing, bathing, and other ADLs
- Finding someone to work with the medical bureaucracies, seeing that forms get filled in or filled out and filed, that bills get paid or routed to the kids, seeing that reimbursements get requested

As frailty and disabilities increase, the patient may not be able to live alone even with the highest-quality and most efficiently administered home care services. When the move to assisted living or to a nursing home becomes undeniable, the GCM can provide a range of services using her professional experience and her local community knowledge. This can include identifying which facilities meet the personal values, health, and financial preferences of the client, arranging for the older person and his family to visit those places, and making recommendations. In this context, the Consumers Union's health *Guide* cautions that the family must still play an active role in evaluation and decisions, since some care managers may receive fees from the nursing home or assisted living facility for directing consumers to the places.

Finally, when other families live far away, as in the case of the Cranstons, the GCM can monitor Mr. Wilson's care after he moves into his assisted living residence. She will be on call if he has an accident or if his health declines significantly, will generally serve as his *personal ombudsman* in the facility and local health system, and will be a professional liaison to his children.

Emotional, Legal, and Financial Teamwork

Whether Mr. Wilson continues to live in Kansas City or moves closer to Steve and Margaret, eventually there will be the need to discuss finances and legal issues. In other situations, the GCM may need to call in the expertise of a financial advisor, but in this case it was the financial advisor who contacted the care manager. Sometimes it is the family lawyer who is, after the medical crisis has subsided, the professional first contacted by the middle-aged kids. In turn, the lawyer may contact the care manager or financial advisor.

After writing about these kinds of issues in the *Journal of the American Society of CLU & ChFC* a few years ago, I got a phone call from a financial planner who acknowledged the importance of this kind of financial–gerontological teamwork by describing how he and two of his professional friends were already engaged in a kind of formalization of this process. They dubbed their teamwork as the ELF approach.

Three different professionals in the same community, they kept their independent practices but worked together in providing their clients with the needed other expertise. Along with her administrative services and community knowledge the care manager provides the *E*motional supports when the family first turns to professional advice. Often, there is some need for *L*egal intervention, either now or later in the Wealth Span. And, clearly, there is a *F*inancial dimension involved in all of these services. Hence, the ELF model.

The value of this approach, and its memorable acronym, is that it offers the client (whether the older person or the middle-aged children) the particular expertise when it is needed at a given moment in the overall process. Some GCMs are part of companies or agencies that include health, social, financial, and legal counseling in the same office. In my earlier investigation of these services I met a man who had been an army nurse who became a Chartered Life Underwriter (CLU) and a Chartered Financial Consultant (ChFC), and later established a multiperson office that specialized in gerontological services. More likely, however, the environment is still characterized by independent practitioners.

Where can Wealth Span advisors find these other professionals to work with on a basis that has the potential to grow into an enduring team? There are always the local Yellow Pages, although most phone books don't include the category of geriatric care managers (validated by my not-so-scientific survey of 15 cities while waiting in airports around the country over the past couple of years).

Even if your local phone book does identify a local GCM, often the bigger challenge is a client who, like Steve and Margaret Cranston, want guidance for a parent who lives halfway across the country. The National Association of Professional Geriatric Care Managers (NAPGCM) was established in 1986 as the professional membership association of GCMs. While there is as yet no separate license, curriculum, or separate exam process, NAPGCM members must subscribe to the organization's code of ethics as well as show evidence of professional education and certification in their home discipline.

The NAPGCM web site, `www.caremanager.org,` provides information concerning the nature of services provided and a guide to selecting a care manager. It offers a national directory, searchable by city, state, or zip code Members are described in terms of their educational and professional degrees and designations, as well as the specialties they offer. No fee information is included in the directory.

Elder Law

Another member of the ELF team is the lawyer. General practice attorneys and family law specialists deal on a daily basis with many of the Wealth Span issues discussed here, such as wills, trusts, and estate and retirement planning. But there are several gerontological issues that are likely to require elder law specialists. Guardianships, conservatorships, and civil commitment proceedings are likely to bring the lawyer and the Wealth Span advisor into either close collaboration or anguishing conflict. Two of the long-term care finance issues discussed in Chapter 11, Medicaid planning and reverse mortgages, benefit from legal specialists who understand and follow recent state and federal rules and procedures. Matters of elder abuse, financial as well as physical, and issues of age discrimination are all part of the elder law specialization.

There are three major ways to find a local elder law attorney. Indeed, the fact that there are at least three relevant organizational pathways testifies to the growing importance of the connections between legal practice and gerontological practice. And as the ELF model implies, Wealth Span decisions are often in the center of the controversies.

The American Bar Association (ABA) has a Commission on Legal Problems of the Elderly, described at `www.abanet.org/elderly.` The larger purpose of the web site is to inform lawyers, other professionals, and the public about developing issues of law and aging. The "community" button on this home page connects to a national Lawyer Locator. After selecting elder law from the list of specialties you can then specify state, city, or name of a lawyer or firm. A recent search for all of the United States and Canada indicated that 1,193 attorneys identify elder law as one of their specializations.

The National Senior Citizens Law Center (NSCLC) is a nonprofit legal research and advocacy organization that does not directly handle many client cases. Rather, it focuses on the legal analysis of current and pending issues of law and aging. As part of its advocacy and consumer orientation, the NSCLC web site (www.nsclc.org) offers a set of consumer guidelines for selecting an elder law specialist.

Last but not least, the National Academy of Elder Law Attorneys (NAELA) is the primary membership association of elder law specialists. The NAELA web site also includes a locator function, but provides for greater specificity than the ABA locator. That is, where elder law is a single ABA specialty, the NAELA site (www.naela.org) allows you to search for any one of 20 specializations within elder law.

Neighborhood alliances are not, of course, limited to the ELF combination of care managers, lawyers, and financial advisors. Clinical psychologists, physical therapists, dietitians, and others should all be added to the team as the situation requires. The main point of the memorable ELF metaphor and model is simply to emphasize that as part of the overall practice of Wealth Span planning, the establishment of teams or alliances will prove to be valuable both to the client and to the financial professional.

Another Story

Local Advice by Internet: Benefits Check*Up*

In mid-2001, the National Council on the Aging launched a new nationwide free Internet service (www.benefitscheckup.org) to allow consumers to learn what public benefits program they *might be* eligible to receive from state as well as federal programs. (The instructions emphasize *might be* because the consumer still must go through all formal applications procedures.) The basic premise of Benefits Check*Up* is that there are hundreds and hundreds of programs out there at the national, state, and local level that older people might not recognize as being of benefit to them. Some of these have low-income eligibility requirements, and some do not. The input to the online software consists of a questionnaire asking about the user's age, residence, and health; the kind of home and amount of rent or house payment; household monthly income, wealth (other than car and home), and monthly expenses; and current program benefits now being received (such as Medicare, Medicaid, Social Security, or Unemployment Insurance).

(continued)

The software emphasizes that all information is strictly confidential—no name, Social Security number, other identifying information is ever requested. Further, the responses to the online questionnaire can be estimates, and the matching of program to eligibility will still work. While many public benefits are targeted to people with lower income, there are many others that are not, in such areas as travel, educational programs, and various kind of tax credits. Finally, even when specific benefits are not being sought, trying out the program using various "simulated" old people can inform consumers, family members, and financial advisors about important state and federal agencies that they might not have considered.

To get a flavor of the kind of information Benefits Check*Up* can provide, I simulated a 73-year old lower-middle-income woman living alone in Chicago. After about four minutes of entering her data, the output was a list of 22 programs that provide social service and financial benefits. Each of these 22 items was presented as a hyperlink connected to more detail about the benefit, including where the older person should go or call to sign up for the program. When clicking on one of these links she received the following information: The program/benefit was explained, a link to the federal or state consumer pamphlet or blank forms or other consumer background information was presented, and a reminder was given of what documents she should bring to the local governmental office when she went to apply. One of the useful little surprises was how the software used her zip code which she entered at the beginning of the questionnaire. For each of the benefits, the program output listed the address in Chicago of the closest state or federal office where she could apply for the benefit. Six examples from her 22 are as follows; the first two are income-related benefits, the other four are not:

1. Tax credits for low-income elderly. Chicago IRS offices are listed.
2. Federal Weatherization Program, to fix the old houses of lower-income older people. A Cook County office is listed.
3. Senior Citizen Real Estate Assessment Freeze. An Illinois program to freeze the assessed value of senior citizens' residential property; a relatively close-by Cook County Tax Assessor's office is listed with address and phone number.

(continued)

4. The Senior Health Insurance Program is a state program that provides no-cost counseling to people over age 60 who want to know about medigap insurance policies sold in Illinois. The Illinois Department of Insurance web site is given as a link.
5. Golden Age Passport is a discount card for entry to U.S. national parks and historic sites, available to people age 62 and older.
6. And if she wants to be a volunteer, the local office of the federal RSVP (Retired and Senior Volunteer Program) is provided.

The Wealth Span Advisor as Medical Consultant

Despite all your specialized training and the several initials after your name (plus the expanded expertise from reading these chapters), you probably don't think of yourself as a geriatric medical consultant. The odds are, however, that you will be. It is a basic thesis of this book that as a Wealth Span professional you will develop a long-standing trusting and friendship relationship with many of your clients. The essence of Wealth Span planning is a look toward the future, a look toward life and financial security in older age. As suggested several times, middle-aged clients are likely to turn to you with questions not only about their own aging, but about issues related to their parents' older aging.

While most of the questions you are asked are financial, in gerontological matters many financial questions are either the consequences of aging or are dealt with in anticipation of aging. It should not be surprising, then, that Wealth Span conversations with your middle-aged client move from their own planning and aging to the aging of elderly parents. If a client's mother breaks her hip or has a heart attack, the medical responses are fairly clear and your client's family will have already seen the surgeon or the cardiologist. Cognitive decline in old age is not as clear, is gradual, and is saturated with many questions, unknowns, and fears. You should not be surprised if your client's Wealth Span questions move from financial security to personal and parental aging to long-term care issues and costs, and to medical issues such as the universally feared Alzheimer's disease (AD).

Consequently, the final section of this teamwork chapter has two basic purposes:

1. To provide some background for your conversations with clients about geriatrics with a special focus on AD. Another Story will provide a brief overview of what Alzheimer's Disease is and is not, including questions of diagnosis and treatment. When using these bits of information, keep in mind that AD is a swiftly changing field of clinical and laboratory research, and any of these facts may be outdated tomorrow.

2. To offer some organizational and Internet sources of further information, including how you can advise your client about locating a geriatric specialist if and when needed.

Another Story

What Alzheimer's Disease Is and Is Not

- Alzheimer's disease is a progressive irreversible degenerative disease that attacks the brain and affects memory, cognitive abilities, behavior, and eventually results in death; the progressive pattern is not uniform, varies substantially across individuals, and can range from 3 to 20 years from the time symptoms are first verified.
- Other than age, there are no established sociological correlates of AD. Old people of different race, social class, or gender are equally likely to get AD.
- AD is a disease; it is not a part of normal aging.
- Some memory loss is a normal part of aging, short-term memory decline is usual.
- While an early symptom of AD is memory loss, memory loss by itself is not a predictive indicator of the onset of AD.
- AD is a kind of dementia; dementia includes memory loss but also includes language difficulties, difficulty in performing routine tasks (such as driving or cooking), personality change, and loss of intellectual functioning. *Not all dementias are irreversible AD.*
- Since both memory loss and dementia can be symptoms of other treatable, medical problems (that is, not AD), it is critical that clients, patients, and families seek medical expertise for diagnosis, and not

(continued)

throw up their hands in despair in the belief that incurable Alzheimer's disease has arrived (thus ignoring or postponing important medical treatment of those conditions). In fact, many AD-like symptoms are caused by fixable, reversible, curable conditions, including:

- Adverse reaction to medicines
- Adverse reaction to alcohol
- Mixing of medicine and alcohol (the metabolism of old people works differently from the metabolism of younger adults)
- Vitamin and other nutritional deficiencies
- High fever
- Thyroid conditions
- TIA (transient ischemic attack) *invisible* or *mini-strokes*
- Minor head injuries, concussions
- Depression (e.g., widowhood)

- *Diagnosis.* (1) Systematic medical and psychological assessment to eliminate all other possible causes of the dementia; (2) monitoring over time to see if symptoms get worse as measured clinically and professionally; (3) as of now, brain autopsy is the only certain diagnosis; (4) research continues to find blood proteins (i.e., a blood test) that can identify the presence of AD.

- *Treatment.* As of now there is no cure for AD. It is irreversible and leads to physical as well as mental deterioration, and eventually to death. There is, however, an increasing number of pharmaceuticals that can slow down the progression of the disease when it is in its early stages (hence the critical importance of early diagnosis). Other medications can help to manage some of the behavioral symptoms.

How Realistic Is the Fear of Alzheimer's Disease?

The statistics describing the incidence or rate of AD in the population are necessarily a bit fuzzy since the nature of diagnosis—*eliminate everything else*—is imprecise. There's even a social class distortion to the numbers: Research shows that people with more education, married persons, and those who live in supportive family environments can mask their AD symptoms for a longer time than can other people. Based on an analysis of several community-based studies that used both observational and medical testing, the general consensus is that about half of people over age 85 have AD or another form of dementia.

Even aside from the fuzziness of these estimates, there can be no doubt that the general prevalence of AD in the population will increase substantially over the next several decades as millions of Boomers age into their eighties and older. From a Wealth Span perspective, population aging (as noted in Chapter 3) shapes the health and financial environment of the next several decades. In this context, then, the number of Alzheimer's patients and the corresponding need for long-term care (whether at home, in nursing homes, or in assisted living facilities) will rise because of Boomer aging. And if centenarians are more vulnerable to AD than 80 year olds, then the overall population rate of AD may also increase as longevity improves.

Whether or not these numbers are accurate and realistic, the personal fear of aging and mental decline is very real. Certainly, in this sense, Wealth Span counseling should include discussion of aging and long-term care financing, but also other preparations in anticipation of these problems. Once again the planner's mantra: Hope for the Best but Plan for the Worst.

In 2000, the National Council on the Aging (NCOA) asked a representative sample of Americans the following question: Think about your life at age 75. How worried are you about the following problems—very worried, somewhat worried, or not worried at all? The list of problems included:

- Being denied medical treatments because of age
- Outliving your pension and savings
- Suffering from uncontrollable pain
- Spending all your money on long-term care
- Losing your memory
- Not being productive

Where other parts of this national survey documented that most Americans would be happy to live to age 75 (noted in Chapter 5), nonetheless they are substantially worried about losing their memory in old age: 65% say they are worried, with the next biggest worry being spending all your money on long-term care, at 57%. And while the level of worries about outliving your pension and spending your retirement money on long-term care are a bit different for older and younger, more wealthy and less wealthy people, all age and income groups show *memory loss* as their biggest future worry. (A statistical comparison of the long-term care and pension worries is shown in Table 10-2).

Thus, whatever the true rate of AD is in the United States, the fear and the worry are substantial and real. Knowing that the one predictor of the disease is age, and constantly hearing that life expectancy is increasing, it is no wonder that memory loss and AD have become widespread anxieties. It is also understandable that when financial advisor and client get together to talk about the future, issues of aging, family, health, and many other nonfinancial gerontological and geriatric care questions will also come up. In this Wealth Span context, the following may be useful.

How to Find a Geriatrician

- The American Medical Association web site is a good place to start (www.ama-assn.org) (alas, ama.org is the American Marketing Association). The AMA home page has a tab called "Doctor Finder," which takes you to a search engine called "AMA Physician Select." The data include virtually all 690,000 physicians in the United States whether they are AMA members or not. The web site states that medical school, residency training, and licensing information for each doctor have been verified for accuracy. The first page of Physician Select asks you to choose from a list of specialties, which includes geriatrics. The next page asks for a specific physician name or for a state. If the state-level search produces too many names, you are asked to specify a zip code or a city.
- A more broadly useful source is the web site of the American Geriatrics Society (AGS) (www.americangeriatrics.org) (alas, ags.org is the American Gem Society). While geriatrics has been a formal teaching and residence specialty in medical schools for only about 20 years, AGS was formed in 1942 to promote interest and education concerning health care for the aged among physicians. Although physicians began the organization, current membership is about 6,000 physicians, nurses, researchers and educators, social workers, and pharmacists. The AGS physician referral service is through the organization's home office and not through online search software. AGS can be contacted by phone at 1-800-247-4779, by e-mail at amger@americangeriatrics.org, or by clicking the "contact us" button on their home page.

Aside from helping to locate a geriatrician, the AGS website is a very valuable source of geriatric information. It is organized as a specialized megasite with links to dozens of health-oriented governmental, academic, and private web sites. Clicking on "Health Links" produces 10 pages of links to health web sites, some of which are megasites themselves. For example: www.healthfinder.gov is a gateway site that includes links to over a thousand federal, state, academic, and other nonprofit health web sites. www.nih.gov/health/ provides a single entrance to the consumer health information resources of the National Institutes of Health (NIH). Click on any health problem or disease from a very detailed alphabetic index, and you arrive at the web site home page of the appropriate NIH institute. MEDLINE (www.nlm.nih.gov/databases/freedmedl.html) is the most extensive collection of published medical reports in the world and has provided free public access since 1997.

- A medical specialty that is especially important in the context of AD and other aging-related cognitive problems is the geriatric psychiatrist. The web site of the American Association of Geriatric Psychiatrists (www.aagpgpa.org) focuses more on patient and consumer education than on its own professional activities. The web site includes user-friendly discussions of the expertise and role of the geriatric psychiatrist and a summary of the nature and trajectory of AD well written for consumers. Their referral service is by telephone: 1-301-654-7850 in Bethesda, Maryland.
- Given the Alzheimer's context of this discussion, we repeat two organizations that were mentioned in earlier discussions of health and long-term care. In addition to substantial information about the characteristics and costs of the disease, the national Alzheimer's Association, at www.alz.org, offers families a special kind of support: a nationwide network of local chapters and support groups. Members of the local chapters include both families of Alzheimer's patients and other caregivers and community health professionals. Most chapters also have their own specialized libraries, video collections, and other materials for families, advisors, and caregivers; some have their own web sites. alz.org offers a state-level search by means of a clickable map of the United States, which returns a list of all local chapters in the state. Alternatively, typing in a zip code will identify the closest local chapter.
- The Alzheimer's Disease Education and Referral Center (ADEAR) (www.alzheimers.org/adear) is a service of the National Institute on Aging (NIA), one of the U.S. National Institutes of Health. ADEAR organizes and offers a massive collection of consumer-oriented Alzheimer's information available to the public. The materials include discussions of the disease's symptoms, current information on treatments, an information and referral hotline (1-800-438-4380), how to contact any of the 30 academic Alzheimer's Research Centers funded by the NIA, and a special health and Alzheimer's set of links to other federal web sites.

CHAPTER 13

A Wealth Span Resource Guide

This Book Has No Appendices

When this book was being designed, one early idea was to include several working appendices. Some would direct you to key organizations involved in health and social services available to older people. Others would identify information resources relevant to private and public policy trends and issues in financial gerontology. Chapter 12, for example, describes how State Units on Aging coordinate local and statewide programs that provide services and referral information useful both to financial advisors and to older clients and their families. Because long-term care has become a crucial element of the human Wealth Span, financial professionals should be able to direct their clients to the nearest office of the federally mandated Long-Term Care Ombudsman Programs that now exist in every state.

Further, as noted in Chapter 1 and throughout these pages, the Wealth Span concept has its roots in issues of health and the human Health Span. Especially in times of changing health situations, clients and advisors should have efficient access to the most complete information and guidance about the variety of health issues that affect older persons. Toward that end, we began to compile an appendix of a few dozen of the most relevant national geriatric health and disease-specific organizations. All of these major national organizations have practical information–rich web sites, and many (e.g., the national Alzheimer's Association at `www.alz.org`) also include directories of local chapters and support groups.

The plan was changed for two reasons. First, a number of other retail guidebooks and library reference books already print several of these lists. For example, the 600-page Consumers Union's *Complete Guide to Health Services for Seniors* cited several times in these chapters includes about 300 pages of appendices, including lists of the state agencies mentioned above.

A much more important reason, however, is the rapid development over the past few years of Internet resources. More and more organizations are crafting useful, informative, interactive, and continuously updated web sites. At the same time, more and more consumers and professionals have Internet access to this body of information—at the office, in the home, and at the library.

While there are zillions of web sites out there, fortunately several large organizations and public agencies have established *megasites* that include literally thousands of links to other sites, editorially selected for their quality and relevance. In turn, these selected web sites virtually always include additional links to web sites that *they* have deemed valuable to their users. In financial gerontology as in other fields these days, the metaphor of a seamless web really does describe the current informational reality.

The question of bibliographies and reference lists can be answered in a similar way. From local libraries to Amazon.com to a dozen search engines, you can easily compile a long list of books and articles on aging topics. Instead of duplicating such an effort, I've put together an annotated (and somewhat opinionated) guide to a selective set of especially useful materials. These are books, authors, and organizations that in my financial gerontology teaching and research I've found to be of great value to professional Wealth Span advisors.

Following these published resources, this Resource Guide describes seven Internet megasites from different areas of aging that I've used in my work and find unusually valuable. Because these sites are truly comprehensive megaresources of concepts, issues, and facts about old age and aging, I believe them to be of unique practical value to Wealth Span professionals.

Printed Materials

Atchley, Robert C. *Social Forces and Aging: An Introduction to Social Gerontology.* 9th ed. Belmont, CA: Wadsworth, 2000. With this 9th edition of a first-class textbook Atchley's experience and expertise as a teacher–researcher truly stands out. I have used several editions of the book over the years. Because it is written in a way that is interesting and educational for both undergraduates and graduate students, it is a very valuable resource for the financial services professional. The logically ordered chapters cover the biology, psychology, and sociology of aging along with history and demographics. There are chapters on family, employment and retirement, recreation, religion and spirituality, widowhood and bereavement, housing, health care, ethnicity, and politics. For all these subjects and chapters, Atchley identifies and clearly explains basic concepts, yet also provides deeper analysis of issues along with plentiful graphs, tables, and illustrations. The citations throughout the book are fully documented in a comprehensive bibliography. A synopsis can be found in the publisher's online catalog, `www.wadsworth.com`, and a listing of the full table of contents is included on the Barnes and Noble web site, `www.bn.com`.

Bengtson, Vern L. Professor Vern Bengtson holds the AARP Endowed Chair in Gerontology and Sociology at the University of Southern California, and is Director of Research at USC's internationally respected Andrus Gerontology Center (`www.usc.edu/dept/gero/research/4gen`). He is the foremost scholar of family and aging issues in the United States. In the early 1970s, he started a longitudinal three-generation study of families and aging: His team interviewed one parent, one child, and one grandparent from the same family, for a sample of families in southern California. He has continued to interview the same people over three decades, as the children became parents, and the parents became grandparents. Now as a sample of four-generation families, Dr. Bengtson's longitudinal data provide a unique view of how aging affects family life and how family structure affects aging. Two review essays that summarize his prolific work are: Norella M. Putney and Vern L. Bengtson, "Families, Intergenerational Relationships, and Kinkeeping in Midlife," Margie E. Lachman, ed., *Handbook of Midlife Development* (New York: John Wiley, 2001); and Vern L. Bengtson, Carolyn Rosenthal, and Linda Burton, "Families and Aging: Diversity and Heterogeneity," Robert H. Binstock and Linda K. Gorge, eds., *Handbook of Aging and the Social Sciences,* 3rd ed. (New York: Academic Press, 1990).

Frontsin, Paul and Deborah Holmes, et al. *EBRI Databook on Employee Benefits,* 4th ed. Washington, DC: Employee Benefit Research Institute, 1997. If you want to have one volume on your bookshelf that has as much relevant and useful numerical information as any single book could possibly have, this is the one. A quarter of the book is devoted to retirement benefits, a quarter to health benefits, a quarter to other employee benefits (e.g., family leave, disability), and a quarter to general reference material on demographics, labor force trends, and macroeconomic indicators. A glossary of relevant economic and workforce terms is an especially valuable resource, as is a history of federal employee benefit, pension, and health legislation since 1921. Overall, this is primarily (but not only) an almanac of statistical tables focusing on the various employee benefit areas. Some of the tables describe just the most recent data, and others include trend data since the early 1970s. Each section includes a 2- to 5-page clearly written executive summary and highlights of the section's tables and charts (`www.ebri.org`).

Gregg, Davis W. "Human Wealth Span: The Financial Dimensions of Successful Aging". Neal E. Cutler, Davis W. Gregg, and M. Powell Lawton, eds. *Aging, Money, and Life Satisfaction: Aspects of Financial Gerontology.* New York: Springer Publishing, 1992. Dr. Davis Gregg is the grandfather of the Wealth Span concept. In the three decades of his leadership of The American College (of Life Underwriters) in Bryn Mawr, Pennsylvania, he recognized the need for professional training in financial services and so presided over the creation of the Chartered Financial Consultant (ChFC) designation, as an expansion of the college's life insurance–oriented Chartered Life Underwriter (CLU) designation. When he recruited me to Bryn Mawr from the University of Southern California to direct a new research institute, one of our first tasks was to formally conceptualize the Wealth Span concept, and to make it one of the pillars of the new Institute's mandate: to systematically bring gerontological knowledge to financial services professionals and to educate gerontologists about the importance of financial services. In addition to the article cited above, Dave Gregg's Wealth Span writings can be found in: "The Human Wealth Span and Financial Well-Being in Older Age," (with Neal E. Cutler) *Generations,* Winter 1991; and "The Human Wealth Span: A Life-Span View of Financial Well-Being," Annual Boettner Lecture, Boettner Institute of Financial Gerontology, University of Pennsylvania, 1992.

Kaye, Lenard W. and Jeffrey S. Applegate. *Men as Caregivers to the Elderly.* Lexington, MA: Lexington Books, 1990. The traditional image of people who provide personal care to elders is that of a middle-aged woman. Since the cultural role of the woman in traditional views of family and society is the care-providing mother, it seems only reasonable to assume that she also becomes the caregiver of elderly family members. Certainly, the recent metaphor of a "sandwich" generation (discussed in Chapter 4) is one of a mother providing care simultaneously to her teenage children and to her elderly mother and often her mother-in-law. Professors Kaye and Applegate of the Bryn Mawr College Graduate School of Social Work document that this is not necessarily so and will become less so in the future. The book reports their unique study of the facts, the attitudes, the burdens and frustrations, and responsibilities of men as caregivers. Their research is noted in Chapter 4, but its direct relevance to Wealth Span planning (and Well Span planners) is aptly summarized by their characterization of the future. After noting that for a variety of reasons there is likely to be in the future fewer women to take on the role of caregivers to their elderly relatives: "Standing in the shadows just beyond the spotlight are the husbands, sons, sons-in-law, brothers, and other men who take care of their frail elderly. Though still a minority, they constitute up to a third of primary caregivers in some settings; and as families continue to change and conceptions of gender roles broaden, their numbers are likely to grow."

Lachman, Margie E., ed. *Handbook of Midlife Development.* New York: John Wiley & Sons, 2001. "Middle age" or "midlife" is a relatively new stage in the human life span. As reviewed in Chapter 7, demographic trends (increasing longevity), sociocultural patterns (the empty nest phenomenon), and changes in the human Wealth Span (the invention of pension, retirement, and now early retirement) have all conspired to create middle age as a separate, identifiable stage of the life span. As Brandeis University Psychology Professor Margie Lachman says, because of this "newness" the emerging analysis of middle aging has not been well organized either conceptually or in terms of being available in specialized journals or handbooks. (By contrast, she notes, the fifth edition of the *Handbook of Aging and the Social Sciences* and the *Handbook of the Psychology of Aging* are about to be published.) Although the organizational themes of this new *Handbook* are the biomedical, psychological, and social aspects of midlife development, the articles themselves are substantially interdisciplinary in nature. An article in the biomedical section, for example, focuses on health and coping with stress. Wealth Span advisors will find the chapters (in the social factors section) on the role of work in midlife and on midlife preparation for retirement especially valuable. Note that these articles are state-of-the-art reviews of the literature written by specialists; they are not intended as introductory instructional materials for consumers. Rather, to learn more about the essential midlife processes that drive much of Wealth Span fears and hopes, the concepts, explanations, data, and substantial bibliographic references in this volume are immensely useful. Dr. Lachman is a member of the MacArthur Foundation Research Network on Successful Midlife Development whose research agenda reflects the work of Rowe and Kahn discussed in Chapter 8, and summarized later in this Guide.

Lieberman, Trudy and the Editors of *Consumer Reports*. *Complete Guide to Health Services for Seniors.* New York: Three Rivers Press, 2000. On several occasions in the second half of this book we have cited this Consumers Union guidebook. While no one book can really be a *complete* guide, this Consumers Union book is certainly comprehensive in the degree to which it identifies many of the issues and concerns that an older person, a family member, or a professional advisor is likely to have. Some of the material (such as the chapter on long-term care insurance) is reprinted from articles already published in *Consumer Reports*. But even this material becomes more valuable when included in the larger *Guide*. The continuing theme of the book is how to find appropriate health and long-term care services and how to finance the selected services. All of the chapters are written with the well-respected *Consumer Reports* kind of sometimes cynical but valuable buyer-beware consumer orientation. Many of the topics and chapters are supported by the immense Consumers Union product evaluation and consumer questionnaire data. Equally valuable are the books' appendices, almost half of its 600 pages. As noted at the beginning of this chapter, some of these are lists of State Units on Aging and State Long-Term Care Ombudsman Programs. Many of these are available on the Internet, but having them in a single volume on your shelf is also useful. Other appendices are more useful because they include Consumers Union ratings of specific companies and products, including long-term care insurance policies, medigap policies, and Medicare HMOs. What is missing from this section of the *Guide* are the references to web sites where updated information can be found, especially for those appendices that are based on publicly available data bases. This Resource Guide identifies several of these web sites.

Mace, Nancy L. and Peter V. Rabins. *The 36-Hour Day: A Family Guide to Caring for Persons with Alzheimer's Disease, Related Dementing Illnesses, and Memory Loss in Later Life,* 3rd ed. Baltimore, MD: Johns Hopkins University Press, 1999. This is the most widely used handbook for family members and others who are currently caring or anticipating having to care for an Alzheimer's patient. The authors are associated with the Department of Psychiatry at Johns Hopkins University. The focus of the book is on understanding the nature of the disease so that the family member can both provide the best care and also learn how to personally cope with the challenges of the situation. The title phrase, *36-Hour Day,* refers to the continuing burden on the caregivers. As such, a Wealth Span advisor whose clients begin to mention their parent's increasing forgetfulness in terms of possible dementia or Alzheimer's should become familiar with this book and be able to recommend it to the client. The appropriate web site to list here is the national Alzheimer's Association, previously known as ADRDA—the Alzheimer's and Related Disorders Association (`www.alz.org`). The Alzheimer's Association not only educates and advocates on the national level for Alzheimer's research and development of caregiving services, but has a national network of local chapters, primarily support groups for families of Alzheimer's patients. Our recent NCOA surveys on public understanding of Alzheimer's disease show that for many worried family members, the local Alzheimer's Association chapter is or will be the first place to call, sometimes even before a geriatric specialist is called in. (*Note:* www.alzheimers.org is the web site of the Alzheimer's Disease Educational and Referral [ADEAR] Center, a service of the National Institute on Aging. It too provides substantial user-oriented practical information about the medical aspects of the disease and where professionals and consumers can find additional information and local assistance.

Manton, Kenneth G. "Changes in the Prevalence of Chronic Disability in the United States Black and Nonblack Population Above Age 65 from 1982 to 1989" (with XiLiang Gu). *Proceedings of the National Academy of Sciences,* Vol. 98, May 2001. Professor Kenneth Manton is Director of the Center for Demographic Studies at Duke University. For over 20 years he has been the preeminent medical demographer in the United States, if not the world, known for the sophistication of his statistical modeling of population health patterns and trends. As described in Chapter 2, his work in directing and analyzing the National Long Term Care Surveys, 1982 to 1999, has documented dramatic and unexpected *declines* in the chronic disabilities of older persons in the United States. The Center for Demographic Studies web site (www.cds.duke,edu) includes detailed descriptions of the National Long-Term Care Surveys and of Manton's work with them.

Minois, Georges. *History of Old Age, from Antiquity to Renaissance.* Translated from the French by Sarah Hanbury Tenison. Chicago: University of Chicago Press, 1987. In the book's Foreword, a colleague of Minois's wondered if the book had been stimulated by France's coming aging boom, articulating the historian's mantra that to understand the present and the future we must first understand the past. To whatever extent this might be true (probably not, as this is a substantial book by an experienced medievalist historian), Minois does find interesting parallels between then and now. The story travels from biblical times through the Greek and Roman worlds, to the middle ages and through the sixteenth century. It should be emphasized that despite the meticulous scholarship—or maybe because of it—this is no dry historical recitation of the names of forgotten rivers or anonymous political underlings. The names are there but so is a remarkable inclusion of what could be called medieval actuarial science. Minois draws his conclusions about aging back then with data describing the age at death of popes and playwrights, the percentage of people in different age groups from township church records, as well as demographic estimates computed by other scholars interested in the period. (There's a temptation to offer some kind of quip about a middle-ager studying middle age in the Middle Ages, but the temptation shall be resisted.) But being a historian and not an actuary or a demographer, Minois also draws his conclusions about the activities of old people in society and how they are perceived from such other "data sources" as how old people are pictured in secular and religious paintings, in plays, and in poetry. As we mention in Chapter 2, Minois identifies some interesting parallels between aging back then and aging nowadays, primarily in terms of the *ambiguity* of the position of old people in society—honored but not necessarily valued, old age seen as both a curse and as a blessing. This is a fascinating book.

Moody, H. R. *Aging: Concepts and Controversies,* 3rd ed. [paperback] Thousand Oaks, CA: Pine Forge Press, 2000. This is a most different kind of introductory text. Where the Atchley textbook is a comprehensive text organized like a college course, Dr. Moody's book is as eclectic as the man himself. Harry "Rick" Moody is a doctor of philosophy who is in fact a philosopher, and who has written extensively on ethics and spirituality in aging, as well as the politics and economics of aging. He is also a gerontology practitioner, as the long-time president of the Elderhostel board of directors, and the former director of the Brookdale Center on Aging in New York City. The book begins with a comprehensive look at such basic concepts as the biology, epidemiology, and economics of aging. The rest of the book is organized around nine controversies, each of which has both a philosophical and a scientific dimension, for example, Does Old Age Have Meaning? Does Retirement Make Sense? Should Families Provide for Their Own? Should We Ration Health Care on Grounds of Age? The basics and the controversies each include Professor Moody's exposition, plus readings reprinted from the appropriate literature. In a single volume, it's like having a small (500-page) specialized library at your fingertips (`www.hrmoody.com`).

National Council on the Aging. *American Perceptions of Aging in the 21st Century* (2000). The National Council on the Aging (NCOA) is a nonprofit membership organization focusing on improving the lives of older people by supporting the organizations and the professionals who provide services and care to elders. By comparison, where AARP's membership is older men and women, NCOA is an organization of organizations that includes directors of senior centers, adult day centers, Area Agencies on Aging, employment services, health centers, and consumer organizations. One of these organizations of direct relevance to readers of this book is the National Institute on Financial Services for Elders (NIFSE). NIFSE is a membership association of about 300 financial planners, insurance counselors, geriatric care managers, elder law attorneys, market researchers, and a couple of wayward academics, all of whom share an interest in financial aspects of aging and middle aging. While all have their primary professional membership in a disciplinary society or organization, their mutual interests in finance and aging bring them to this interdisciplinary association. Information about NIFSE can be seen on the NCOA web site of `www.ncoa.org`.

As part of its research activities, NCOA organized, funded, and fielded a major national survey of the opinions and attitudes *of* older people and attitudes *toward* older people by people of all ages. Selected results of the study are described in several places throughout this book. *American Perceptions of Aging in the 21st Century* (APA21), supported by unrestricted grants from Oppenheimer Funds, Inc., and Pfizer Inc., is a representative sample of the adult U.S. population interviewed in January–March 2001 by Harris Interactive (formally known as the Harris Poll). Compared to usual public opinion studies, APA21 interviewed an unusually large number of respondents (3,000). This design was used in order to be able to examine patterns *within* older age groups—not only by gender, education, income, and marital status, but in terms of differences in health status, work and retirement status, and family characteristics. The oversampling of respondents aged 65 and older produced a subsample of 1,155 respondents age 65+, a number as large as many polls of the full adult population.

One of the major aims of the 2000 survey was to repeat the asking of key questions that were asked in the NCOA's *The Myth and Reality of Aging in America* study completed in 1974 (with interviewing also done by the Harris Poll). The set of repeated questions focuses on the kinds of problems that the public sees as being serious problems for most old people, including, for example, "not having enough money to live on." The survey then asks older respondents in the survey how they rate the seriousness of these same problems. The comparison of how the public views older people versus how older people view themselves is fascinating. The 1974-to-2000 trends show that (1) older (65+) people see these problems, including "not enough money," as being less serious now than a quarter century ago, but (2) younger people, both now and back then, perceive and judge the problems as being much more serious for old people than older people judge them. A large section of APA21 focuses on issues directly relevant to the Wealth Span, for example, older and middle-age fears about the costs of long-term care, the relationship between age and retirement, the factors that influence the decision to retire, and the fact that substantial numbers of people in their late fifties and sixties call themselves retired, but also work full time or part time. Financial results of the survey have been published recently in the *Journal of Financial Service Professionals* by this writer, who also served as

NCOA's Director of Survey Research during the years APA21 was developed and completed.

Regnier, Victor A. *Assisted Living Housing for the Elderly: Design Innovations from the United States and Europe.* New York: Van Nostrand Reinhold, 1994. Compared to nursing homes, assisted living is a relatively new form of long-term care. It is very different from nursing homes in that it provides assistance and living accommodations for elderly persons who for personal, health, or family reasons can no longer live totally on their own, but who do not need the medically intensive health services of a nursing home. But where can we find out about the definition, meaning, and experience of this new form of long-term care? Professor Victor A. Regnier of the University of Southern California decided to search for answers by comparing facilities in the United States with similar facilities in northern Europe. In particular, he wanted to study how the design of facilities interacted with the health and psychological needs of elderly residents. He won a Fulbright Fellowship and in 1990 spent his sabbatical roaming around Scandinavia and the Netherlands with his camera, his sketch pad, and a keen eye for gerontological detail.

The product is a most amazing analysis and assessment of assisted living. With photographs, floor plans, and sketches he illustrates his detailed analysis of how internal room design, social community spaces, and internal and external landscaping can work together to facilitate the health and well-being of the residents. Mr. Regnier is exceptionally qualified to write and illustrate such a book. He holds a unique joint appointment as a USC Professor of Architecture (where he also served as dean) and Professor of Gerontology at USC's prestigious Andrus Gerontology Center. He is a Fellow of the Gerontological Society of America and a Fellow of the American Institute of Architects, perhaps the only fellow in the country to have this dual distinction. Professor Regnier's academic work is informed by substantial hands-on practitioner experience, as he consults on the architectural, interior and landscape designs of all the Sunrise Corporation assisted living projects in the United States and Europe. *Caution:* This book is not a narrow, how-to-do-it consumer guide for choosing an assisted living facility for your client or your client's mother (several of these are noted at the end of Chapter 10). It is, rather, an ultimate source of guidance for evaluating the facilities where mother might stay, to be able to assess and compare them through the analytic screen of a truly elegant piece of research, writing, and illustration. Professor Regnier's new book is *Design for Assisted Living: Guidelines for Housing the Physically and Mentally Frail* (New York: John Wiley & Sons, 2002).

Rowe, John W. and Robert L. Kahn. *Successful Aging.* New York: Pantheon Books, 1998. (See also Rowe and Kahn, "Human Aging: Usual and

Successful," *Science* 237 (1987):143–149). As discussed in Chapter 8, Rowe is a geriatric physician, former president of Mt. Sinai Hospital in New York, and recently named CEO of Aetna. Kahn is an internationally renowned Professor of Psychology and Public Health at the University of Michigan. Their 1987 article argued that what has often been identified as "usual" aging—decline, illness, frailty—is not normal. By contrast, "successful aging" builds on interventions that people can make in their life, with improvements in both mental and physical functioning being possible even when these changes in behavior, lifestyle, and environment are made later in life. The article marked the beginning of a decade-long series of national and international studies funded by the MacArthur Foundation. Their book is a nontechnical but seriously informative summary of the social, psychological, physiological, and medical research projects that comprise the MacArthur Foundation Study of Aging. Now available in paperback as well as a large-print edition, there is a good chance that the information in this book can literally add years to your and your client's life. The continuing, fascinating work of the MacArthur aging studies can be found at `midmac.med.harvard.edu` (no www).

Schaie, K. Warner and Sherry L. Willis. *Adult Development and Aging,* 5th ed. New York: Prentice Hall, 2001. Schaie and Willis have written what is perhaps the most complete and relevant text on psychology and aging that is available today. Although both Schaie's and Willis's own research has focused on the older end of the life cycle, the book is about the aging process from young adulthood through old age. The focus is not just on individual psychology, however. Separate chapters on gender differences, families, and on basic personality and psychological processes make this a most comprehensive text. Of special value is thc chapter on middle aging, which has direct relevance to Wealth Span issues. This is a comprehensive text that can be used as a reference handbook, as well as a textbook. Its 60-page listing of references (all cited in the text) is probably the most complete and comprehensive bibliography on the subject in the English language. The continuing research of Schaie and Willis is reported by the Gerontology Center at Penn State University, `geron.psu.edu` (no www).

Scholen, Ken. *Your New Retirement Nest Egg: A Consumer Guide to the New Reverse Mortgages,* 2nd ed. Apple Valley, MN: NCHEC Press, 1996. Scholen is the founder–director of the National Center for Home Equity Conversion and a principal advocate for using reverse mortgages to finance long-term care and other older-age expenses. His book is really two books in one. It is a consumer-oriented public education guide that introduces the idea of the reverse mortgage to consumers who know little about it. The opening sections are presented in a folksy, fairly easy-to-read style. It is also a detailed manual for Wealth Span planners who want to become familiar with the financial and technical aspects of reverse mortgages. There are chapters on each of several different reverse mortgage programs, including the better-known HUD and Fannie Mae plans and a half-dozen lesser-known commercial programs. Scholen now works in partnership with AARP to educate the public about reverse mortgages. His web site (`www.reverse.org`) includes the following instruction: "If this is your first time here at `reverse.org` (or if you haven't been here since this site was completely revised), we strongly encourage you to first review AARP's materials. (*Note:* These are described in Chapter 11 of this book.) Beginning at `www.aarp.org/revmort/` you will find 30 pages of independent consumer information provided in a recommended order. By clicking 'Next Page' at the bottom of each page you can work your way through a basic primer on reverse mortgages. After completing this comprehensive tutorial, you may return back here to `reverse.org` if you want additional details, background information, or supplementary materials."

Schulz, James H. *The Economics of Aging,* 7th ed. Dover, MA: Auburn House, 2000. Brandeis University Economics Professor Schulz has written one of the most readable expositions of the many facets of the economics of aging available. Although presented as a textbook, it is not a technical economics or econometric volume, but rather a well-written introduction to many of the issues that are part of the Wealth Span. In addition, as discussed in Chapter 3, his study of interconnections between economics and population aging is a rare example of a cross-national study that is rich in systematic quantitative data and simultaneously presents qualitative information that effectively communicates the texture of the three cultures being analyzed: James H. Schulz, Allan Borowski, and William H. Crown, *Economics of Population Aging: The "Graying" of Australia, Japan, and the United States* (New York: Auburn House, 1991).

Uhlenberg, Peter. "Mortality Decline in the Twentieth Century and Supply of Kin Over the Life Course." *The Gerontologist,* 1996, 682–685. Dr. Uhlenberg, a Professor of Sociology at the University of North Carolina, and Fellow of the university's Carolina Population Center, has done some especially imaginative work in the field of historical demography. Using historical census data and other relevant vital statistics, he integrates birth rates, average age of marriage and childbearing, and death rates for males and females of various ages for each decade of the twentieth century. His analysis then identifies, as discussed in Chapter 4 (Family Aging), trends over the twentieth century in, for example, how many middle-agers were and are likely to have surviving older parents. His earlier article is equally fascinating in estimating such historical family patterns as the probability that a child would become orphaned by the age of 15 and the likelihood that a teenager would have three or four living grandparents: Uhlenberg, Peter, "Death and the Family," *Journal of Family History,* 1980, 313–320.

U.S. Bureau of the Census. *65+ in the United States.* Washington, DC: U.S. Government Printing Office, 1996. One of the most useful single sources of statistical information about aging, this book serves two related functions. First, it has a very comprehensive set of uncomplicated census tables on health, income, longevity, and related aspects of the American older population, but less data than the *EBRI Databook* mentioned earlier. Second, half the book is text, interpretation, and explanation. Consequently, the smaller set of data tables plus the interpretations and educational guidance make it an especially valuable collection of reference materials. Along with a web site full of Census 2000 national and local data, the full text (with tables and figures) of *65+ in the United States* is available on the Census Bureau web site (`www.census.gov`). Click on "A" on the alphabetic index, then "Aging/ Elderly Population Data," and finally "Elderly (65+)."

Vitt, Lois A. and Jurg K. Siegenthaler, eds. *Encyclopedia of Financial Gerontology.* Westport, CT: Greenwood Press, 1996. Dr. Vitt, director of the Institute for Socio-Financial Studies, and Dr. Siegenthaler, Professor Emeritus of Sociology at the American University in Washington, D.C., have assembled a one-volume handbook of brief articles relating to finance and aging that is truly encyclopedic in breadth. In addition to articles on standard topics such as Medicare and long-term care costs, you'll find solid introductory articles on such topics as ethics, veterans' benefits, hospice care and funerals, marketing to elders, pharmacists, guardianships and elder abuse, and even an article on the Wealth Span. Perhaps the most unusual article is an analysis of the "King Lear Syndrome," reviewing the King's estate planning errors as he relied on the advice of his children and their expressions of love, rather than his court advisors (and Wealth Span advisors?) for the disposition of his estate (`www.isfs.org`).

Weisheit, Eldon. *Aging Parents: When Mom & Dad Can't Live Alone Anymore.* Elgin, IL: Lion Publishing, 1994. Reverend Weisheit has both substantial experience counseling families who are facing long-term care choices and a gift for writing. This is an excellent practical book that financial planners should have on a bookshelf for clients to use. It serves as a highly readable introductory guide to dealing with the difficult task of guiding a parent into some form of long-term care, including nursing homes and assisted living. For example, Weisheit makes the point that after all the abstract discussions about kinds and cost of care, "your parents need a zip code," suggesting that eventually, specific locations have to be identified and evaluated. Practical stuff.

Cutler, Neal E. My earlier Wealth Span writing, co-authored with Davis

Gregg, is cited above. Additional work connecting the Wealth Span to issues of financial literacy and changing family demographics is included in *Financial Dimensions of Aging,* the Summer 1997 Special Issue of *Generations,* which I edited for the American Society on Aging. Beyond my Editor's Introduction and a somewhat tongue-in-cheek book review of *Personal Finance for Dummies,* a bit more substance appears in "The False Alarms and Blazing Sirens of Financial Literacy: Middle-Agers' Knowledge of Retirement Income, Health Finance, and Long-Term Care." Much of my work in financial literacy is from *Financial Literacy 2000,* carried out with the support of Dean Ira Schwartz of the University of Pennsylvania School of Social Work. A national sample of 1,010 adults was interviewed by the Opinion Research Corporation in February 1996. The research recognizes that "financial literacy" includes both a cognitive dimension—knowledge about various financial topics—but also a social–psychological dimension—personal feelings that one has the confidence to use that knowledge in making sound or wise financial choices. My new analysis of changes in the American pension system was published in the December 2001 issue of the *Journal of Applied Gerontology:* "Divine Benefit vs. Divine Contribution Pensions: Approaches to Monitoring Improvements in American Retirement Income Security Over the Next Decade."

There are a lot more connections among the Wealth Span and these topics discussed in the bimonthly "Financial Gerontology" column I wrote in the *Journal of American Society of CLU & ChFC* from 1990 to 1997. I restarted contributing to that column in 2001 in the renamed *Journal of Financial Service Professionals,* of which I am an associate editor. I am co-author of *Can You Afford to Retire?* (Chicago: Probus Publishing Co., 1992) with Bob Doyle, Kenn Tacchino, Ted Kurlowicz, and Jeff Schnepper. While some of the regulatory facts are now outdated, the book is still conceptually and strategically on target with respect to Wealth Span planning. My earlier work on public understanding of and worries about Alzheimer's disease is reported in: "Someone I Know Has Alzheimer's: A Statistical Portrait from the First National Opinion Survey of Alzheimer's Disease," *American Journal of Alzheimer's Care and Related Disorders & Research,* November/December 1987; and "The Alzheimer's Quiz," *Psychology Today,* May 1987.

Internet Megasites in Aging and Finance

www.aoa.gov Of the several Internet resources suggested in this Resource Guide, the web site developed by the Administration on Aging is at the top of the list for two essential content-oriented reasons, preceded by a very important "process reason"—its ease of navigation and multiplicity of search tools.

For example, the home page includes a traditional search function, a "what's new" button, and of special value to nonspecialists a "quick index" button. This button leads to a one-screen matrix with 25 selections, including such choices as Retirement & Finance, a Resource Directory for Older People, an Alzheimer's Resource Room, the Eldercare Locator, Consumer Fact Sheets, Statistics about Older People, and Aging Related Web Sites. The web master has clearly made the extra effort to include practical materials on aging that users who are not aging specialists will consider useful and easy to find. For these kinds of reasons `aoa.gov` is an especially valuable resource for Wealth Span advisors who want to learn about aging resources and be able to direct their clients to valuable information.

The first content reason for this web site's top rating is the comprehensiveness with which it provides information about the agency's own structure and program responsibilities. Information and resources are "packaged" for older persons and their families, for practitioners and professionals, for aging network officials and staff, and for researchers and students. The site also provides current news about aging issues, policies, and people, and notices of new publications and reports from a variety of public agencies—including, for example, Health Alerts for older people from the Centers for Disease Control and Prevention.

The second content reason is the breadth of the web site's links to other web sites that offer valuable aging-related information. In this sense, `aoa.gov` is truly an exceptional megasite. Examples include the "Resource Directory for Older People" `(www.aoa.gov/aoa/resource.html)`, which presents a list of literally hundreds of private and public organizations and agencies concerned with aging. It can be scanned by content category or by alphabetically listed name. It is largely health oriented and includes dozens of disease-specific associations, as well as societies of medical specialists that are of interest to older people and the professionals and caregivers who work with them. Each organizational name appears in bright blue, indicating that it is an active hyperlink to a one-page summary description of the organization prepared by `aoa.gov`. In turn, that summary includes, among the other contact information, the organization's web site address.

A second example of the megasite value of `aoa.gov` is the box on the quick index labeled "Statistics about Older People." It first includes a list of dozens of studies and reports from the Census Bureau, from the National Institute on Aging, and from the AoA itself. Most of these are reports plus data tables in either standard text or Acrobat.pdf files. However, a button modestly labeled "Online Statistical Data on the Aging" opens to a table of contents that offers hyperlinks to sections on demographics, health, long-term care, and income and employment. The income–employment link then opens up to reports from the Census Bureau, Bureau of Labor Statistics, Social Security Administration, and others. The printed numerical tables in many of the reports include an additional attractive feature: a pair of buttons labeled "Excel" and "Lotus."

www.aarp.org The organization formerly known as the American Association of Retired Persons maintains a web site that is especially valuable to Wealth Span planners and advisors because it is designed to communicate directly to clients and consumers. AARP's experience with literally millions of older members establishes a broad basis for identifying the concerns and aspirations of older people, and then developing educational materials in response. The `aarp.org` home page has the look and feel of a magazine. Alongside major sections about health and money are buttons for leisure and fun, life transitions, computers, and legislative issues. The magazine style is seen in several other ways as well. The pages use illustration and color to emphasize topics and direct the user to various next steps. The magazine style is also apparent as AARP uses the same styles, fonts, instructions, and other visual cues in all of the thousands of topics, documents, and exhibits throughout the web site. But the most notable characteristic is in the writing. The topics are clearly explained so that consumers can be both educated generally and acquire practical instructions. Major topics, such as retirement and financial planning, have multiple sections. Other topics may be the subject of individual articles.

Several of the topics discussed in this book are presented with substantial consumer-oriented how-to-do-it detail, including Medicare, medigap insurance, reverse mortgages, and long-term care insurance. Knowing the kind of information clients can acquire before they work with professional advisors can help to better guide the Wealth Span interaction. Also in keeping with the focus of this book, the AARP web site does not exclusively focus on "old" or "retired" people. For example, in a section titled "Health Insurance Options for Midlife Adults," the web site describes the conditions under which COBRA can be used to retain a family's health insurance.

We've labeled `aarp.org` as a megasite even though most of its links are to topics and pages within the same site. The range of these other topics is substantial enough to justify the megasite label. In addition, however, most topics also include hyperlinks to other sites, often government agencies, to provide more detailed information.

www.elderweb.com In several chapters throughout this book, we have referred to the immense value of `elderweb.com.` It integrates the best features of the previous two web sites in the following way. Like the AoA's "Resource Directory for Older People," `elderweb.com`'s purpose is to be a megasite referral mechanism to aging-related sites. But like aarp.org, it uses a more traditional magazine style format to "talk to" the users. Elderweb.com began and is still the nonprofit activity of a single interested citizen; there are no advertising banners or boxes on the site. The introductory "About ElderWeb" article says that the site was created eight years ago by Karen Stevenson Brown, a CPA with interests in long-term care, finance, and technology. It started out because of a professional desire to find and then share information on long-term care. This was a time, in 1994, when the browser of choice was Mosaic and most of the information was in the form of phone numbers to call for the "real" information.

Elderweb.com now includes over 6,000 reviewed links. In addition, however, the site's home pages also include the *ElderWeb Newsletter* as well as an archive of previous *Newsletter* articles. The site offers the user an initial menu of five topics: news, finance and law, living arrangements, body and soul, and the Eldercare Locator. (The last one, mentioned briefly in Chapter 10, is a toll free 800 telephone service administered by the Administration on Aging.) Each of the main topics or buttons moves the user to the broad array of ElderWeb-authored articles, and then links to hundreds of articles published elsewhere on the web, information sources, and organizations.

Elderweb.com can be of value to the Wealth Span advisor because it is purposely designed to provide information to both professionals and family members who work with older people on issues of finance and long-term care. The site recognizes that many users are not gerontology specialists, and thus has glossaries and other explanations to assist in using the material.

www.medicare.gov and **www.ssa.gov** Two megasites representing older and traditional aspects of Wealth Span planning, Medicare and Social Security, are represented by two very useful and multifeatured web sites. Citizens whose images of these large federal bureaueracies have been shaped by confusing telephone menus, abrupt telephone behavior, uncaring form letters, or less-than-elegant local offices will be surprised by the user friendliness of these web sites. Medicare.gov was described in some detail in Chapter 11. The two major professional and client resources mentioned there are (1) the availability of a large number of comprehensive and understandable documents, including the annually updated *Medicare and You;* and (2) the three interactive "compare" web site utilities: Nursing Home Compare, Medigap Compare, and Medicare Health Plan Compare.

The Social Security Administration web site also serves professionals as well as clients. The opening pages are brightly colored news and general information pages, not unlike the AARP web pages. The uniquely valuable material, however, are the client-oriented descriptions of the range of Social Security benefits, and of the procedures and age deadlines for application. `ssa.gov` mostly stays away from advising people about retirement planning, but rather apprises citizens about recent and pending changes in laws, regulations, and rulings—including the rising full benefits age from 65 to 67 from 2003 to 2027. As another user-friendly service, `ssa.gov` provides most of the forms needed to apply for benefits, to change benefit status, and even to request a hearing to challenge benefit decisions; all forms are presented as Acrobat.pdf files. Finally, we should note that in true megasite form, the site includes links to several other agency web sites, limited to federal government agencies and web sites. The range is fairly broad, including the U.S. Senate and House of Representatives, the Department of Veterans Affairs, the IRS, the official White House web site, the new U.S. Consumer Gateway (the first Internet site to offer one-stop access to federal consumer information), and the U.S. Postal Service Zip Code Directory.

www.FAAR.org We come full circle with the *FAAR* web site—an acronym for *Financial Aspects of Aging Research.* FAAR is a joint project of the AARP Andrus Foundation and Brandeis University. Several years ago, AARP's Andrus Foundation recognized that while the linkages between aging and finance were becoming increasingly important to practitioners in both finance and gerontology, the multidisciplinary nature of the emerging field of financial gerontology means that key studies are spread across a broad range of professional and academic journals. The response to this dilemma was the establishment of `FAAR.org` as an online archive of the key studies in the area.

FAAR is not simply another database of academic articles and data sets. Rather, its contents are the concise abstracts of both published and unpublished reports and articles, each of which is presented in a format that is both readable and retrievable. The focus is on studies of financial attitudes and public policy in the context of retirement and financial planning. The abstracts are classified into three general subject areas: economic security, retirement income, and consumer expenditures. The web site can be searched by content word, author name, or organizational name. The web site also includes a useful set of links to a fairly broad range of organizations that do policy research in the area of aging and finance. The most useful characteristic of `FAAR.org` is that many of the one-page abstracts also include a hyperlink to an Internet location where the full text of the article or report is available. The abstracts of articles in the *Social Security Bulletin,* for example, become much more valuable when the full text is a few clicks away. The main limitation of the web site is that, as a relatively new resource, it includes as of this writing fewer than 300 abstracts. When the archive includes a few thousand abstracts, it will be a truly valuable tool for Wealth Span practitioners.

Index

T

U

V

W

Y